D1095089

Cooking for Family
& Friends

Philippa Davenport

Cooking for Family & Friends

Drawings by Dorothy Ann Harrison

JILL NORMAN & HOBHOUSE

FOR
Michael, without whom this book might never have been begun and certainly never would have been finished.

Jill Norman & Hobhouse Ltd
90 Great Russell Street
London WC1B 3PY

First published 1982
Copyright © Philippa Davenport, 1982

British Library Cataloguing in Publication Data
Davenport, Philippa
  Cooking for family and friends.
  1. Cookery
  I. Title
  641.5   TX717

  ISBN 0-906908-32-9

Designed by Wendy Bann
Typeset by Inforum Ltd, Portsmouth
Printed and bound in Great Britain by
Mackays of Chatham

Contents

Cold Starters & Pâtés

Winter & Summer Vegetables

Making a Meal of Vegetables

Rice & Pasta

Joints, Poultry & Game

Pieces of Meat

Fish & Shellfish

Fresh & Dried Fruits

Proper Puddings

Custards & Creams

Weights & Measures

Measurements throughout this book are given in both imperial and metric units. It is important to use either all imperial or all metric measurements in a recipe, never a mixture of the two.

All spoon measurements are level unless otherwise indicated. The metric equivalents to British standard measuring spoons are:

2.5 ml	½ teaspoon
5 ml	1 teaspoon
15 ml	1 tablespoon

Introduction

All the dishes in this book are suitable for serving to guests and for serving to the family. I do not subscribe to the school of thought which has one style of cookery for entertaining and another for family cooking. The implication that guests should be regarded as VIPs and the family treated, in effect, as second-class citizens seems to me unnatural and wrong.

If we can eat well always, albeit modestly, is there anything to be gained by altering the style of cookery just because friends are coming to share a meal with us?

With this thought in mind, I have concentrated for some years on one style of cookery which, although not grand, aims at achieving consistent excellence across a wide range of dishes. In essence, the idea is to make the standards of family cooking high enough that "upgrading" for entertaining becomes unnecessary, and to do so by exploiting the fact that it is the care taken in preparing a dish which makes it excellent, not the cost of the ingredients.

I have found that this approach makes cooking more rewarding, it enables the family to enjoy every day the same standard of fare as we serve to our friends when they visit us, and it makes entertaining a natural and easy extension of everyday cooking. We eat better on a daily basis, and entertain more often and more enjoyably than before - simply and well, without undue formality and fuss.

There are, of course, some differences between my family meals and entertaining, but these are tactical not qualitative differences. For example, when friends are present the cook naturally wants to minimise her absence from the table, to choose dishes which are practicable to cook for large numbers, and so on. Some of the recipes and recipe variations in this book are, of course, more expensive and celebratory than others, but I see no good reason to reserve "special" dishes for guests. My decision as to when to cook a particular dish depends not so much on who will eat it, but on such practicalities as the state of the housekeeping budget, how much time is available and what foods are in season. When the standard of cooking is always high, no dish need be regarded as suitable for entertaining only, and none as exclusively for family occasions.

I love good food and enjoy cooking and entertaining friends, but I fight shy of holding "dinner parties". Somehow the words no longer suggest relaxed and happy social occasions, but over-blown menus and disproportionate effort and expense. Ritual conspiracies of tradition, at odds with late 20th century living.

There seems to be a tendency for mere mention of the words "dinner party" to create havoc in the kitchen. Not only is an extra course or two added to the menu, but often the whole character of the cooking is radically changed — the good taste of the food is stifled with lashings of cream and alcohol, and one rich and elaborate dish is followed by another.

Why aim to stuff and impress? Why feel obliged to put on a show? Coping with a kitchen marathon single-handed is exhausting. Darting crimson-flushed between guests and stove is not conducive to a convivial party atmosphere. "Dinner party dishes" which are cooked relatively infrequently are prone to misfire. The unaccustomed richness and quantity of the fare can suffocate the appetite, but who dares decline any of it when the hostess has so clearly gone to so much trouble.

The main aim of giving a party is to create a relaxed and enjoyable occasion. Food is just one of the elements involved: a warm welcome, good talk and generous drinks with agreeable company are every bit as important. This is not to deny that good food will not greatly add to everyone's pleasure, but there is little sense in straining to produce culinary fireworks when setting oneself more modest culinary targets, and achieving them with shining perfection, will better please the guests and cause the cook less anxiety.

A high standard of home cooking is within the grasp of any cook who actively seeks it. It is not a gift of the gods bestowed capriciously on a lucky few; it is, like any other craft, acquired by careful application.

The "secret" of good food lies in the scrupulous observance of three principles: good eating begins with good shopping; simple menus and simple cooking methods skilfully executed are best, and handsome presentation plays an important part in our enjoyment of food.

Faithfully practise these principles at every meal and you will eat well always. You discover that it does not matter whether you can afford humble or exotic ingredients: if they are the freshest and best of their kind, and if they are sensitively handled, they will always make a dish which can be brought to the table with pride.

On the other hand, a thoughtless, hurried approach, skimping on attention to detail, invariably produces undistinguished results. I am sure it is the regular churning out of such mediocrity for family consumption which leads to the confusion of simple dishes with dull dishes, and creates the need to resort to a separate, more elaborate style of cooking for entertaining.

Experience of just how excellent careful and unpretentious cooking can be makes one realise that fear of "letting the side down" by serving simple dishes to guests is totally unfounded. When good home cooking is practised with love and skill, the results are good enough for *every* day of the year.

Turning from the principles to the tactics — what to cook when — I have found two ways of giving the cook plenty of flexibility of choice. One is to build variations on successful recipes, and the other is to be willing to vary the menu pattern.

Dealing first with variations on a theme, tactical options are given throughout this book whereby many of the recipes can be adapted by minor adjustments and with minimum fuss. These enable the cook to add variety, to extend the repertoire and to have a choice to suit the circumstances. These variations are ways of capitalising on foods in season, and varying the amount of time required for preparation or the expense.

For example, I suggest using courgettes in a ragôut when broad beans are no longer as young and tender as they should be; cooking beef one way and serving it with different sauces which alter simply but radically the character of the finished dishes; substituting more expensive ingredients, such as pheasant for chicken, on special occasions — whether family or social; presenting identical or almost identical ingredients in different guises, such as traditional summer pudding versus lazy summer pudding, to meet different time schedules without altering the cost.

Where the variations and options require only very brief notes, they are given at the end of the main recipe. Where more detailed explanation seemed sensible, the variation is presented as a separate recipe. The recipes are grouped so that those using similar cooking methods, and those linked by ingredient, are close together.

As to menu patterns, many people seem to regard it as *de rigueur* to serve at least three courses when entertaining. The traditional menu of soup or starter, a main-course meat or fish dish with accompanying vegetables, then pudding (and very often a cheeseboard and bowl of fresh fruits are offered as well) can, without doubt, provide a delicious and beautifully balanced meal. But it is a great pity to regard it as an obligatory routine, when there are so many other good ways of composing a menu.

In practice I find the three-course routine is often the least successful solution for a party because you want to be there with your friends, not disappearing and reappearing from excursions to the stove, and because most vegetables and other hot dishes are only worth serving when freshly cooked. This pattern can work very well indeed if the first and third courses are cold, and if the hot main dish does not require much last-minute work or is good tempered enough to be kept in the oven. But even then, unless the dishes are judiciously chosen and light, three courses often seem to me to be simply too much food.

Appetites seem to be smaller now than they were when the three-course menu was first introduced, and we are all becoming increasingly conscious that to overeat is not good for us. Today most people dining *en famille* normally eat, and are well satisfied by, one or two simple dishes, followed perhaps by cheese and/or fresh fruit, and it is noticeable that few people order both first course and pudding when eating in restaurants. There is no reason to suppose that anyone expects or wants more when dining in other people's houses. What they will appreciate is good food, thoughtfully chosen and skilfully cooked.

Why not start the meal with a dish which cannot be kept waiting once cooked? Most grilled and fried meat and fish dishes are not only delicious but very quickly prepared, as are most pasta dishes, and it is perfectly normal for the cook to be out of the room for 20 minutes or so immediately before serving the meal. This hot dish can then be followed by salad and cheese and/or a cook-ahead pudding so that, once at table, the cook can remain with the party.

Other ways I have found successful in breaking away from the rigidity of the three-course menu include combining the functions of the traditional first and main course in one substantial hot dish, as illustrated by the English fish soup on page 25. This dish is, in effect, a fish soup and a delicious fish stew rolled into one. Another tactic is to serve a hot vegetable dish as the first course. Yet another is to serve tempting savoury appetisers, such as dukka and poor man's caviar, not at the dining table, but with pre-dinner drinks.

Freedom from the three-course routine will stimulate originality, allow the cook to spend more time with her guests, and at the same time provide meals which please and satisfy the appetite without terrorising it.

Abandoning those distinctions between family fare and dishes for entertaining has not been to the detriment of either my friends or my family. Rather the reverse is true, because a beautifully prepared steak and kidney pudding or daube is a great delight to all, whereas an indifferently prepared beef Wellington is a ghastly disappointment and a terrible waste of money. Good home cooking is not intended to be grand but, when it is practised with love and skill, both family and friends will recognise and appreciate its excellence.

Soups

GAZPACHO

Good soup is quickly and easily made. It is inexpensive and it can be truly excellent. It has to be said, however, that we are fickle about soup and soup-making. In times of plenty we tend to ignore soup in favour of more exotic hors d'oeuvre. In times of hardship soup comes to the fore — but when times are very thin, the soup itself is inclined to be thin, a make-do concoction inspired by desperation and founded on the tradition of the "beneficent broths" once served in the workhouse and other charitable institutions.

In this century, for example, during the Second World War when all ingredients were scarce, the soup pan was continually at work in almost every kitchen. It was treated as a form of recycling dustbin into which leftovers were indiscriminately thrown in the hope that a square meal would emerge. In the rich 1960s the memory of those dreary soups, and the soup pans themselves, were thankfully hidden away at the back of the kitchen cupboard. Foods such as avocados and prosciutto crudo, tasted on holiday abroad, became readily available here. Our allegiance to the starter, as distinct from soup, became firmly established, and so it has remained until quite recently.

The economic troubles of the late 1970s have brought with them the beginnings of a revival of interest in soup — a renaissance I find very heartening since it coincides with rediscovered pride in the vegetable plot, and the re-emergence of proper respect for simple, skilful home cooking.

The fact that soup is inexpensive is increasingly regarded as a virtue, rather than a cause to despise it. Soup is quick and easy to prepare which makes it a highly practical choice for today's cook-hostesses whose duties often include those of mother, career woman and chief bottle-washer as well. That many soups can be made in advance is better news still. It makes soup a natural candidate for entertaining, so much so that every cook would do well to invest in a handsome soup tureen.

Some people still remain wary of soup, suspicious that it will be mediocre at best, and rate it (albeit subconsciously) as second-class food, fit for feeding the family perhaps, but not quite good enough for guests. And it is noticeable that soups still figure relatively rarely on "better" restaurant menus. Bad connotations, it seems, die hard.

But prejudice dwindles daily as more people discover the

pleasures and blessings of good home-made soup, "the well-beloved of the stomach" as Carême so comfortingly put it. Not the most sophisticated of fare perhaps, but in many ways the perfect sustenance — an admirable combination of food and drink which soothes and revives. I'd certainly choose good soup if obliged to settle for just one "desert island" food.

Soup can be the introduction to a meal, or a meal in itself. It can be delicate or robust; it can be steaming and fragrant or icy cool; it can be translucently clear, or as smooth and as rich as thick cream, or so chunky that it is more like a stew than a soup. The scope is huge and this makes soup an ideal choice for all sorts of occasions and all sorts of weathers.

A soothing delicate broth is a great restorative. Other light soups make a lovely preface to dinner. Creamy vegetable purées make perfect lunchtime food with perhaps a salad or pâté or an egg dish to follow. The more substantial soups are almost a meal in a bowl: spinach soup with green lentils, for example, makes a very satisfying Sunday supper round the fireside, as can English fish soup with aioli. Both also provide a delicious basis for a supper party; served with a large green salad and a slab of creamy ripe Brie, and rounded off with elegant little sorbets.

Although, in practice, good soup-making does not demand much money, time or effort, first-class results depend on devoting as much care to its making as to the preparation of any other dish. Choosing fresh, high quality ingredients is important. So too is taking care not to overcook them — vegetable soups in particular are easily robbed of their freshness by prolonged stewing.

As for cooking liquid, water is all that is needed for a vegetable soup with good natural vegetable flavour, although many people prefer the extra dimension of stock. Stock cubes are acceptable for vegetable soups when home-made stock is not available, but dilute them well to get rid of the predominant "manufactured" taste. Soups such as stracchiatella and tarragon chicken soup, however, are not worth making unless you use well-flavoured home-made stock.

The presentation of soup warrants more thought than it sometimes gets. Soup cups, bowls or plates, as well as the tureen, must be hot if the soup is to be served hot. If the soup is a cold one, chill the dishes briefly in the fridge and resist the temptation to serve the chilled soup with a flotilla of ice cubes on top — melting ice dilutes flavour and can curdle the texture.

Flotillas of other sorts, however, can be pleasing first to the eye then to the taste buds. Crisp buttery fried croûtons are always eaten up greedily, but, like marbled swirls of cream, they have become something of a garnishing cliché. Serving anything too frequently cheapens its currency, but the little excitements caused by fresh and appropriate finishing touches can stimulate the appetite wonderfully — for example, a few marigold petals strewn over a pale cream of vegetable soup, wafers of raw button mushrooms added to a dark green spinach soup, and papery slices of scallop floating across a fish soup.

Courgette Soup

It is the hint of basil and Parmesan cheese that gives this soup its distinction. A splendid recipe for making inroads into a glut of courgettes. Save the smallest and best courgettes to eat as vegetables, and use the oversized ones for this soup. Serves 4.

375 g [generous ¾ lb] courgettes, trimmed weight
1 medium-sized onion
65 g [2½ oz] butter
30 ml [2 tablespoons] plain flour
850 ml [1½ pt] light chicken stock or water
30 ml [2 tablespoons] fresh chopped basil
40 ml [generous 2 tablespoons] freshly grated Parmesan cheese
salt and freshly ground black pepper

Chop the onion finely and slice the courgettes. Soften both vegetables in a saucepan for about 12 minutes in 40 g [1½ oz] butter, just stirring occasionally as they cook over low heat, and increasing the heat a little at the end to colour the vegetables slightly. Reduce the contents of the pan to a purée with a little of the stock — a brief blending in a liquidiser or food processor gives a good flecked texture.

Make a roux in the saucepan with the remaining butter and the flour. Blend in the rest of the hot stock and bring to the boil stirring, then blend in the purée. Check seasoning. Put the freshly chopped basil and Parmesan cheese into a warmed soup tureen and pour on the soup, whisking with a balloon whisk as you do so.

Almond & Artichoke Soup

The amount of almonds used here may at first seem over-generous, but plenty of crunch makes a particularly pleasing foil for a smooth vegetable purée which is unthickened by flour. Serves 4–6.

750 g [generous 1½ lb] Jerusalem artichokes
50 g [2 oz] split and well-toasted almonds
4 rashers streaky bacon
1 small onion, finely chopped
3 celery stalks
40 g [1½ oz] butter
850 ml [1½ pt] light chicken stock or water
150 ml [¼ pt] single cream
salt and freshly ground black pepper

Remove the rind from the bacon and cut into matchstick strips. Cook gently in a saucepan until the fat runs, then drain and reserve. Add the butter to the pan and soften the finely chopped onion for a few minutes. Add the artichokes, peeled and cut into chunks, and the celery cut into thin crescents. When the fat is absorbed, pour on the stock and season with a good grinding of pepper and some salt. Bring to the boil, cover and simmer gently until the vegetables are tender.

Blend to a purée in a liquidiser or food processor, or pass the soup through the fine blade of a vegetable mill. Return the soup to the pan, reheat gently, stir in the bacon and cream and check seasoning. Sprinkle with toasted almonds just before serving.

Artichoke Soup with Prawns: Make the soup exactly as described above but replace the chicken stock with canned tomatoes mashed into their juices, and garnish with prawns (generously sprinkled with lemon juice, salt and pepper) instead of almonds.

Cream of Parsnip Soup

Based on a cheap root vegetable, this soup tastes much more luxurious than the ingredients suggest. Flavour is difficult to define: spicy and warm but it certainly doesn't, or shouldn't, taste "curried". Serves 6.

500 g [1 lb] parsnips, peeled and diced weight
250 g [½ lb] onions
1 fat garlic clove
125 g [¼ lb] butter or melted bacon fat
about 7 ml [1½ teaspoons] cumin seeds
about 7 ml [1½ teaspoons] curry powder or paste
20 ml [1½ tablespoons] plain flour
700 ml [1¼ pt] light chicken stock or water
600 ml [1 pt] milk
150 ml [¼ pt] single cream
salt and freshly ground black pepper

Buy a good quantity of parsnips to allow for peeling and discarding any woody cores. Finely chop the vegetables and garlic and turn them in melted fat, cover the pan and sweat for 10 minutes. Crush the cumin seeds with mortar and pestle, add them to the saucepan together with the curry powder (or paste) and flour and stir for a minute or so. Blend in the stock (or water) and milk and bring to the boil stirring. Cover the pan and simmer gently for 10 minutes or so until the vegetables are quite tender.

Reduce the soup to a purée in a liquidiser and reheat it gently, blending in the cream and adding a good seasoning of salt and a little more curry or cumin to taste. Garnish with a little raw grated parsnip for nutty sweetness, or matchsticks of fried bacon for salty crispness.

Smoky Celeriac Soup

Another unexpectedly flavoured root vegetable soup, made in exactly the same way as the previous recipe. Serves 5–6.

1 celeriac root large enough to give a trimmed weight of about 500 g [1 lb]
1 onion
4 or 5 dried fennel stalks or fennel or dill seeds
75 g [3 oz] butter
50 g [2 oz] plain flour
850 ml [1½ pt] light chicken stock or water
150 ml [¼ pt] milk
150 ml [¼ pt] single cream
dried dillweed
salt and freshly ground black pepper

Chop the onion finely. Peel the celeriac and cut into small dice. Put the vegetables into a saucepan with the butter, cover and sweat for about 10 minutes, or until most of the butter has been absorbed. Shake the pan occasionally to prevent sticking. Sprinkle on and stir in the flour. Pour on the stock (or water) and add the fennel stalks or fennel or dill seeds loosely tied in butter muslin. Bring to boiling point, stirring, cover and simmer for about 20 minutes, then let the covered pan stand on one side for 15 minutes or so.

Discard the butter muslin and reduce the soup to a purée in a liquidiser. Reheat gently with the milk and cream, seasoning to taste with salt and pepper and a good sprinkling of dillweed.

Celery Soup with Stilton

I confess I rate celery as celeriac's poor relation, and I first made this soup merely to use up Christmas leftovers. It is less distinguished than the previous soup, but so agreeably colourful and piquant that I now make it regularly for its own sake. Serves 4–5.

1 head of celery
2 onions
75 g [3 oz] Stilton, Dolcelatte or Gorgonzola cheese
75 g [3 oz] melted bacon fat or butter
700 ml [1¼ pt] light chicken or turkey stock
1 × 400 g [14 oz] can of tomatoes
45 ml [3 tablespoons] plain flour
celery salt
salt and freshly ground black pepper

Break the celery into stalks and reserve a few of the leaves for garnish. Clean the stalks, scraping them to remove any stringy threads, and chop into thin crescents. Peel and chop the onions fairly finely. Turn both vegetables in melted fat or butter until well coated, cover the pan and sweat the contents gently for 10 minutes.

Sprinkle on and stir in the flour, add a good pinch of celery salt and a generous grinding of pepper. Pour on the stock and the canned tomatoes mashed into their juices, and bring to simmering point, stirring all the while. Cover and simmer gently for about 20 minutes.

Meanwhile mash the cheese in a soup plate until creamy, add a few spoonfuls of the hot soup and continue mashing to make a thin paste. Tip the contents of the soup plate into the pan, draw the pan aside from the heat and whisk for a minute to distribute and melt the cheese. Check seasoning and serve the soup with a scattering of chopped celery leaves over the top.

Crème Vichyssoise

By the time the weather is warm enough to want to serve iced soups, leeks are too large and woody to make a tender purée, so this is a soup I make early in the season and freeze for summer eating. Serves 4.

approx. 1 kg [2 lb] leeks
350 g [¾ lb] potatoes
700 ml [1¼ pt] light chicken stock or water
5 ml [1 teaspoon] dried tarragon
150 ml [¼ pt] milk
300 ml [½ pt] double cream
150 ml [¼ pt] single or soured cream
a bunch of chives
salt and freshly ground black pepper

Trim, thickly slice and thoroughly wash the leeks including delicate green parts as well as white. 500 g [1 lb] prepared weight of leeks is needed for this recipe.

Crème Vichyssoise

Peel the potatoes and cut into small dice. Bring the stock to the boil. Add the vegetables, tarragon and a good seasoning of salt and pepper. Cover the pan and simmer gently for 10 minutes or so until the vegetables are tender. Reduce the contents of the pan to a thick purée in a liquidiser and, when it is cold, freeze it.

On the day you plan to serve the soup, defrost the purée and reheat it very gently. Then blend it again in a liquidiser or food processor. Scald the milk and double cream and add to the blender with the machine still on. This very thorough blending is important to ensure that the final soup has a velvety smooth texture. Cool the soup, stir in half the finely chopped chives, cover and chill for several hours.

Just before serving, stir in the single or soured cream to give a marbled look, garnish with remaining chopped chives and serve in chilled bowls.

Leek & Potato Soup: For a warming winter version of Vichyssoise, cook the vegetables and seasonings in stock and reduce to a purée as described, then blend in 150 ml [¼ pt] each hot milk and single cream. Reheat gently and scatter with crumbled grilled bacon or crisply fried crôutons.

Irish Potato Soup

Much less often served but even quicker to make than leek and potato soup, this nourishing and comforting soup is particularly good if made using bacon fat. Serves 5–6.

450 g [1 lb] potatoes
250 g [generous ½ lb] onions, peeled weight
12 rashers streaky bacon
75 g [3 oz] melted bacon fat or butter
1 litre [2 pt] milk, or more
half a chicken stock cube (optional)
salt and freshly ground black pepper

Remove rind from the bacon and cut it into matchstick strips. Cook it in a large saucepan over low heat until the fat runs, then increase the heat and fry the bacon until crisp. Remove the bacon with a slotted spoon and keep hot.

Add the bacon fat or butter to the saucepan. Finely chop the onions and fry them gently for 8–10 minutes until golden and tender.

Peel and grate the potatoes, add them to the pan and stir briefly to coat with fat. Pour on the milk. Increase the heat and cook, stirring continuously and scraping the base of the pan well, until the liquid is thickened with the potato starch and simmering point is reached. Season the soup well with salt and pepper, add the crumbled stock cube if you wish. Reduce the heat as low as possible, half cover the pan with a lid and let it simmer very gently for 8 minutes or so, just stirring occasionally, until the vegetables are quite tender.

Thin the soup with extra milk if it is too thick and creamy. Check seasoning and stir in the bacon pieces. Scatter a few chopped watercress leaves over the soup if available and/or a few crisply fried croûtons of bread.

Fennel Vichyssoise

Substituting Florentine fennel for leeks and potatoes makes an intriguing variation on classic Vichyssoise. Fennel imported from Italy is much more aromatic than that grown in Britain, so use the larger quantity of British if that is the only type available. Serves 4.

350–575 g [¾–1¼ lb] Florentine fennel
400 ml [¾ pt] light chicken stock or water
salt and freshly ground black pepper
300 ml [½ pt] double cream

Chop off and reserve the feathery fronds of fennel for garnish. Scrub the bulb and dice it. There is no need to scrape away any fibrous strings as they will be extracted after cooking. Put the fennel dice into a saucepan, add the stock or water, cover and simmer gently until the fennel is quite tender.

Pass the contents of the pan through the fine blade of a vegetable mill to reduce them to a smooth purée and to extract any coarse vegetable fibres. Season generously and stir in the cream. Cover and chill the soup for several hours. Before serving check for seasoning and thin with a little milk if necessary. Garnish with the reserved fennel fronds just before serving.

Green Pepper Soup

Peppers can be used to make a Vichyssoise-type soup, with a subtle flavour. A little flour is needed to give extra "body" to this lighter textured vegetable. Serves 4–6.

3 large green peppers, total weight about 450 g [1 lb]
a bunch of parsley
50 g [2 oz] butter
40 g [1½ oz] plain flour
275 ml [½ pt] light chicken stock or water
275 ml [½ pt] milk
275 ml [½ pt] double cream
Hungarian paprika
salt and freshly ground black pepper

Remove the stalks from the peppers with a small sharp knife, pulling out the cores with them, and shake out the seeds. Put the whole peppers under a very hot grill and turn frequently until the skins are blistered and black all over and the flesh is tender. Wrap the peppers in a clean cloth until cool enough to handle, then peel away the papery black skins and chop the flesh roughly.

Make a golden roux with the butter and flour. Blend in the milk and stock and let the béchamel simmer gently for a few minutes. Pour a little of the sauce into a liquidiser or food processor, add the chopped green peppers and parsley, and reduce to a thick green purée. Return this mixture to the pan, blend it carefully with the sauce, add the cream, seasoning with salt and pepper, and simmer for a few minutes. Chill the soup for several hours. Thin it as necessary with extra cold creamy milk just before serving, and top with a shake of paprika.

Gazpacho

Plenty and very varied garnishes are an essential part of the pleasure of eating gazpacho. Tradition has it that when stirred into the thin puréed soup these garnishes should so thicken it that a spoon can be stood upright in the bowl. Serves 4–6.

For the soup:
600 g [1¼ lb] tomatoes
1 large red pepper
1 large cucumber
3 spring onions
2 garlic cloves
a slice of brown bread reduced to crumbs
575 ml [1 pt] canned tomato juice
15 ml [1 tablespoon] wine vinegar
45 ml [3 tablespoons] olive oil
5 ml [1 teaspoon] fresh chopped basil

For the garnishes:
1 green pepper
1 Spanish onion
50–75 g [2–3 oz] black olives
cold garlic-flavoured croûtons

Remove the seeds and chop half the red pepper, reserving the rest for garnish. Peel and seed a quarter of the cucumber, and save the rest for garnish. Skin, seed and chop the tomatoes. Trim the spring onions and crush the garlic with some salt.

Put the breadcrumbs into a liquidiser together with the garlic, spring onions, olive oil and vinegar, and blend to a smooth purée. Add a little of the tomato juice if necessary to prevent the blades sticking. Gradually add the remaining vegetables and the rest of the tomato juice and reduce the mixture to a smooth purée. To achieve a creamy texture, it is well worth blending the ingredients in small batches and putting everything through the liquidiser at least twice. When the soup is perfectly smooth, thin it to the consistency of pouring cream by stirring in some ice cold water. Season with salt, pepper and a little more vinegar if you wish. Liquidise once more then cover and chill for several hours.

Pit the olives, chop them if large, and put them into a small bowl. Quarter the Spanish onion, slice it very thinly and put it into a separate small bowl. Chop the cucumber and the red and green peppers. Put them and the croûtons each into a separate bowl. The garnishes, like the soup, should be very cold when served.

Instant Iced Tomato Soup

A useful and admirable alternative to gazpacho, this soup is marvellously quick to prepare. If fresh basil is not available use a little mint instead. Thick home-made yoghurt can be used instead of soured cream, but I find commercial yoghurt too sharp and acid-tasting. Serves 4.

2 × 400 g [14 oz] cans of tomatoes
1 small garlic clove
a few fresh basil leaves
10 ml [2 teaspoons] lemon juice
5 ml [1 teaspoon] caster sugar
300 ml [½ pt] soured cream or thick home-made yoghurt
salt and freshly ground black pepper

Crush the garlic clove with some salt. Put it into a liquidiser together with most of the basil. Add the sugar, lemon juice, a generous grinding of pepper and about half the contents of one can of tomatoes. Blend until reduced to a smooth purée. Add the rest of the tomatoes and their juices and blend again (if your liquidiser is small, it may be necessary to do this in batches), then blend in the soured cream or yoghurt. When the mixture is a perfectly smooth, pale rosy cream, try it and adjust seasoning to taste. Cover and chill for several hours before serving.

This soup keeps well for several days, but the garlic flavour becomes more pronounced as time passes so use half a garlic clove only if preparing well ahead. Garnish with extra chopped basil and/or a few wafer-thin slices of cucumber just before serving.

Iced Avocado Soup

Another cool creamy soup which involves no cooking, this one should always be eaten on the day it is made or the delicate green colouring will give way to an undistinguished shade of khaki. Over-ripe and slightly bruised avocado pears, which conscientious greengrocers sell off cheaply, are ideal for this soup. Serves 6.

2 large very ripe avocado pears
2 spring onions
30 ml [2 tablespoons] fresh chopped chives
30 ml [2 tablespoons] fresh chopped parsley
25 ml [1½ tablespoons] lemon juice
about 600 ml [1 pt] chilled chicken stock
275 ml [½ pt] soured cream or thick home-made yoghurt
Hungarian paprika
salt and freshly ground black pepper

Put the cleaned and chopped spring onions (green parts as well as white) into a liquidiser with the chives, parsley, lemon juice and a spoonful or two of the chicken stock (which should be ice cold). Blend until reduced to a thin green purée.

Add the roughly chopped avocado flesh, taking care to scrape the insides of the avocado skins very thoroughly with a teaspoon. (The flesh that clings to the skin is well flavoured and its beautiful colour enhances the soup.) Add most of the soured cream and a little more stock. Blend again to make a perfectly smooth purée.

Turn the mixture into a chilled bowl or soup tureen. Stir in as much chicken stock as required to give the soup the consistency of pouring cream. Season to taste with salt and pepper. Cover the soup and chill it for 3–4 hours.

Shortly before serving, swirl the remaining soured cream over the surface of the soup to create a marbled effect, and sprinkle a little paprika over the top.

Yoghurt Soup with Green Herbs

Possibly the quickest of all soups to prepare, very healthy and much appreciated by lovers of yoghurt and fresh herbs. If you use commercial yoghurt I suggest adding a few extra almonds. Serves 4.

600 ml [generous 1 pt] yoghurt
2 garlic cloves
50 g [2 oz] blanched almonds
45 ml [3 tablespoons] sunflower oil
mixed fresh herbs — such as parsley, chives, tarrigon, dill, marjoram, mint and
    lovage
salt and freshly ground black pepper
squeeze of lemon juice (optional)

Crush the garlic with some salt. Put it into a liquidiser or food processor with the almonds, oil, a few sprigs of herbs and a spoonful or two of yoghurt. Process until the almonds are reduced to a perfectly smooth purée. Beat in the rest of the yoghurt and season to taste with pepper, perhaps more salt and/or a squeeze of lemon juice. Cover and chill for at least 1 hour or overnight.

Give the soup a good stir just before serving, and scatter the surface generously with more chopped fresh herbs. Little bites of greenery go well with the smooth tangy taste of almond and yoghurt cream.

Yoghurt Soup with Grapes: Omit herbs and season the soup with a little wine vinegar or lemon juice. Just before serving add 120 g [¼ lb] grapes. Either black or green grapes can be used, but they must be peeled, halved and seeded. This creates the impression of something very special for 10 minutes' work. If plump sweet grapes are not available or are prohibitively expensive, use melon scooped into tiny balls instead.

Stracchiatella

Few soups are as quickly and easily made as this delicate broth. It is the perfect antidote to overeating, a breath of fresh air to revive the system after the Christmas blow-out for example. Serves 2–3.

600 ml [1 pt] well-flavoured chicken or turkey stock
a squeeze of lemon juice
1 egg
25 ml [1 slightly heaped tablespoon] fine semolina
20 ml [1 tablespoon] freshly grated Parmesan cheese
salt and freshly ground black pepper

Break the egg into a cup, add the semolina, cheese and a few spoonfuls of cold stock and beat to a creamy consistency with a fork. Bring the rest of the stock to boiling point and season it with lemon juice, salt and a good grinding of pepper. Reduce the heat to very low and add the egg mixture to the pan, pouring it in slowly and whisking vigorously with the fork all the time. Continue whisking for 5 minutes or so while the soup barely simmers, the semolina thickens and the egg sets into threads. Serve immediately.

Tarragon Chicken Soup

A soothing and restoring broth, infused with tarragon and lightly enriched with an egg and cream liaison. Serves 4.

700 ml [1¼ pt] well-flavoured chicken stock
4–5 sprigs fresh tarragon
a long spiral of lemon peel
3–4 teaspoons lemon juice
2 egg yolks
150 ml [¼ pt] double cream
salt and freshly ground black pepper

Measure the stock into a saucepan, add the lemon peel and 2 or 3 sprigs of tarragon, cover the pan and simmer very gently for 20 minutes or so to infuse the broth. Remove and discard the tarragon and lemon peel and blend in the lemon juice. Beat the egg yolks and cream and 5–10 ml [1–2 teaspoons] fresh chopped tarragon in a cup. Carefully blend in a few spoonfuls of the hot broth, then blend the contents of the cup into the soup pan. Stir over a very gentle heat until the soup is delicately thickened.

Spinach Soup with Parmesan

A light vegetable soup which is very quickly made using frozen spinach. Choose whole leaf spinach for preference. Coarsely chopped frozen spinach makes a good alternative but avoid puréed spinach which is usually so finely chopped that it is dusty and tasteless. Serves 6.

500 g [1 lb] frozen spinach — whole leaf or coarsely chopped
600 ml [1 pt] hot chicken stock
600 ml [1 pt] creamy milk
50 g [2 oz] butter
salt, pepper and freshly ground nutmeg
3–4 tablespoons freshly grated Parmesan cheese

Unwrap the spinach and turn it into a saucepan. Pour on a little hot stock and bring quickly to simmering point. Break up the spinach with a fork to encourage it to thaw quickly. Chop the spinach if whole leaf is used.

After 5 minutes or so, when the spinach is quite tender, add the remaining hot stock and the butter. Season with a little nutmeg and salt, and plenty of freshly ground black pepper. Pour on most of the milk and stir continuously until the soup returns to simmering point. Thin the soup with the remaining milk, as required, and check seasoning.

Put the grated Parmesan into a warmed soup tureen. Slowly

pour on and stir in the spinach soup. Serve immediately, perhaps garnishing the soup with a few wafer-thin slices of raw mushroom or snippets of grilled bacon.

Chilled Spinach Soup: For a cool, summery soup, omit the butter and use only 300 ml [½ pt] milk. Let the soup become cold, then cover and chill for a few hours. Stir in 150–300 ml [¼–½ pt] home-made yoghurt just before serving.

Spinach Soup with Green Lentils

This is a much more substantial spinach soup, which makes a healthy and nutritious lunch or supper dish for 6 people or more. Slices of Frankfurter or other boiling sausage (or scraps from a bacon or gammon joint, or tiny grilled mincemeat balls) can be added to the soup pan at the same time as the spinach.

250 g [½ lb] frozen spinach — whole leaf or coarsely chopped
2 onions
50 g [2 oz] butter
350 g [¾ lb] whole green lentils
125 g [¼ lb] brown rice
2 fat garlic cloves
1 teaspoon cumin seeds
1 teaspoon coriander seeds
1 teaspoon turmeric
2 litres [3½ pt] water or light stock
salt and freshly ground black pepper

Unwrap the spinach and leave it to defrost in a covered saucepan for several hours or overnight. Chop the spinach if whole leaf is used.

Chop the onions. Melt the butter in a large soup pan, turn the onions in the fat and leave them to cook gently while you prepare the other ingredients.

Carefully pick over and rinse the lentils, and drain them well. Pound the cumin and coriander seeds with pestle and mortar and mix them with the turmeric. Crush the garlic cloves.

Add the garlic and spices to the soup pan, stirring gently to warm and coat the spices with fat. Add the rinsed lentils and the rice and stir for a minute or so before adding the water or light stock. Bring the mixture to simmering point, stirring all the time. Cover the pan with a well-fitting lid and leave the soup to cook over very low heat for 45–60 minutes, until the ingredients are tender.

Add the defrosted spinach to the pan, and let the soup simmer for a further 5–10 minutes. Check seasoning and serve the soup piping hot in warmed bowls, adding a generous spoonful of chilled yoghurt, fromage blanc or soured cream to each bowl.

Mussel Soup with Saffron

Fragrant and creamy, this soup makes a happy alternative to the ever popular moules à la marinière. Serves 6 as a starter or 3 as a light main course.

3½ litres [6 lb] mussels
3 small leeks
4 celery stalks
25 g [1 oz] butter
a few strands of saffron pounded with mortar and pestle and soaked in 150 ml
    [¼ pt] boiling water
150 ml [¼ pt] dry white wine
150 ml [¼ pt] double cream
2 egg yolks
salt and freshly ground black pepper
hot garlic-flavoured croûtons

mussel soup
with saffron

Thoroughly scrub the mussels and wash them in several changes of cold salted water. Discard any mussels that are damaged or refuse to shut tightly when tapped sharply.

Bring the wine to the boil, add the drained mussels, cover and cook until the mussels are opened. Strain the mussel liquor through butter muslin and measure it. Discard any mussels that have not opened and remove empty half shells from the rest.

Sweat the thinly sliced leeks and celery in the butter for a few minutes. Pour on the strained mussel liquor, the saffron liquid plus extra water if needed; the total liquid content should be 600 ml [1 pt] or just over. Cover and simmer until the vegetables are just tender.

Add the mussels to the pan and season well. Beat egg yolks and cream together in a cup, blend in a little of the soup liquid, then stir the contents of the cup into the pan. Let it heat through and thicken without boiling, garnish with croûtons and serve.

Breton Mussel Soup

This is a much more substantial soup, so generously afloat with mussels and other good things that it is more like a stew than a soup. It is definitely a main course dish. Serves 4–6.

4½ litres [8 lb] mussels
450 g [1 lb] onions
2 fat garlic cloves
60 ml [4 tablespoons] olive oil
175 g [6 oz] long-grain rice
2 ×400 g [14 oz] cans of tomatoes
a few saffron strands pounded with mortar and pestle and soaked in 250 ml [½ pt] boiling water
250 ml [½ pt] dry white wine
salt and freshly ground black pepper

Thoroughly scrub the mussels and wash them in several changes of cold salted water. Discard any mussels that are damaged or refuse to shut tightly when tapped sharply.

Warm the oil in a saucepan, add the onions, peeled, finely sliced and pushed into rings, and the chopped garlic. Soften gently for a few minutes. Add the rice and stir for 2 or 3 minutes until the grains are transparent. Pour on the saffron liquid, the roughly chopped tomatoes and their liquid and bring to the boil, stirring. Cover the pan and simmer over a low heat for 15–20 minutes until the rice is tender and has absorbed most of the liquid.

Meanwhile, cook the mussels. Unless you have a really large pan it is best to cook them in two batches. Bring the wine to simmering point, add the mussels, cover and cook over fierce heat for a minute or two to steam the shells open. Shake the pan occasionally so that the steam circulates easily. Then reduce the heat and simmer for a further 2–3 minutes.

Turn the contents of the mussel pan into a colander placed over a large bowl. Throw away any mussels that have not opened. Remove empty half shells and place the cooked mussels in a warmed soup tureen. Strain the mussel liquor into the rice pan, passing it through a muslin-lined sieve to extract any grit. Bring gently back to simmering point. Season, pour the soup over the mussels and serve.

English Fish Soup

Another fish dish that neatly combines first and main course in one, this could be described as a very English version of bouillabaisse. Serves 4.

2 large fresh mackerel, filleted
225 g [½ lb] fillets of whiting or haddock
450 g [1 lb] leeks
450 g [1 lb] potatoes
4–5 celery stalks
1 fat garlic clove
1× 400 g [14 oz] can of tomatoes
150 ml [¼ pt] dry white wine
butter
thyme
marjoram
1 bay leaf
parsley
salt and freshly ground black pepper

Ask the fishmonger to bone and fillet the fish, and get a generous supply of extra bones to make a really well-flavoured stock. Try to include a turbot head or sole bones if possible. To make the stock, simply cover the fish bones and trimmings with water, add peppercorns and fresh herbs and simmer for 20 minutes.

Strain, reduce to 600 ml [1 pt] by fast boiling, season well with salt and pepper and stir in the wine.

Thoroughly clean and slice the leeks (green parts as well as white), cut the celery stalks into thick crescents and peel and cut the potatoes into cubes. Cook the three vegetables gently, together with the crushed garlic clove, in a little butter until the fat is absorbed. Then add the canned tomatoes, their liquid and 150 ml [¼ pt] water, a generous grinding of black pepper, plenty of salt and the herbs. Cover and simmer until barely tender. Pour the fish stock into the vegetable pan, cover it and set aside. Cut the fish fillets into thick slices, cover and leave in a cool place until shortly before serving.

To finish the soup, bring it slowly back to boiling point and taste for seasoning. Add the prepared fish, cover the pan and simmer gently for 10 minutes or so until the fish is cooked. Serve piping hot with a large bowl of chilled aioli. Diners should help themselves to dollops of the rich garlicky sauce, stirring it into the soup to enrich and flavour it to taste.

Aioli

2 egg yolks
3–6 fat garlic cloves
275 ml [½ pt] oil
squeeze of lemon juice
mustard powder
salt and freshly ground black pepper

Beat the egg yolks with a pinch of mustard powder and a grinding of pepper. Crush the garlic with salt and blend it into the egg yolks — how much garlic you use is a matter of taste, three cloves are probably quite enough if you have never eaten aioli before. Blend in the oil drop by drop at first as though making mayonnaise; when the mixture is thick, add the oil in a slow trickle. Finally stir in the lemon juice.

Hot Starters & Savouries

Anchovy Twists.

Most cook-hostesses instinctively seem to show more interest in recipes for cold starters than for hot ones — no doubt for the eminently practical reason that a hot main course, preceded and followed by cold cook-ahead dishes, makes a very manageable workload. However, I have a special affection and enthusiasm for little hot dishes of the sort that are given in this chapter, not only because they are so good to eat, but also because I find them so useful.

Although appropriate and attractive throughout the year, these starters really come into their own in summer, when optimism inclines us towards serving cold, rather than hot, main courses. It is one thing to serve a lunch menu composed entirely of cold dishes, but in a climate as mild as ours it is rarely advisable to plan a dinner along these lines. A hot appetiser is the natural prelude to a cold main course and is always welcome; if the evening proves decidedly cool a hot appetiser will be especially appreciated.

The major advantage of little hot savoury dishes, however, is their great suitability for serving in a multitude of contexts other than as starters. They are excellent examples of "convenient" foods — (as opposed to what are called "convenience" foods) quick and easy dishes to turn to at any time.

"Un oeuf is as good as a feast" as Hilaire Belloc pointed out with schoolboyish glee, and most of the dishes given here are sufficient for a lunchtime meal by themselves. Smoked haddock soufflé and salady meat dishes, such as fresh-tasting polpette al limone and bacon and chicken liver salad, are virtually self-contained light meals, needing only the simple accompaniment of good bread to make delectable little feasts. Egg dishes which include cheese, such as creamy pots de fromage and farmhouse eggs, are equally convenient and nutritious — but, because they are richer, they are best followed by a clean-tasting green salad or fresh fruit. Precede any of these dishes with soup then follow up with salad or fruit, and you have a simple and very pleasing supper, which is neither expensive nor time-consuming to prepare.

Many of these recipes are a boon when a satisfying but elegant snack is called for rather than a full-scale meal. I find, for example, that crostini di fegatini and herring roes with wine or lemon make perfect pre-threatre bonnes bouches, substantial enough to prevent tummy-rumbling during the third act, but not so heavy as to send you to sleep or discourage the appetite from enjoying a post-theatre supper. Similarly tempting foods, such as mozarella in carozza, that most delicious and sophisticated of all toasted sandwiches, greatly appeal to teenage children and are a blessing on those potentially problematic pit-stop occasions when children dash into the house for 15 minutes *en route* from school to evening class!

Parmesan straws, anchovy twists and mouthwatering smoked oysters with bacon are among the lightest and slightest of the recipes given here, but none the less useful for that. Because they can be eaten in the fingers, they are perfect with pre-dinner drinks, which makes them tactically excellent appetisers for occasions when the main course is a fried or grilled dish that needs last-minute cooking and must, therefore, be served as soon as you sit down at table.

I like best of all, however, to serve these three very English savouries in the traditional English manner — after pudding or in lieu of it. Whilst most savouries are regrettably rather impracticable for today's cook-hostess, these three present no problems. They can safely be prepared ahead, be put into the oven to heat through while you eat the main course, and be served to great delight in their "rightful" place at the end of the meal.

Crostini di Fegatini

An elegant and quickly prepared bonne bouche which can be served as a first course or a pre-theatre snack for 4 people, or, with a crisp green salad on the side, as a light lunch dish for 2.

250 g [½ lb] chicken livers
50 g [2 oz] Parma ham (or bacon)
30 ml [2 tablespoons] well-flavoured chicken stock
10 ml [2 teaspoons] lemon juice
a little well-seasoned flour
unsalted butter
olive oil
4 thick rounds of bread
fresh chopped parsley

Rinse the livers, cut away any yellowish-green bile and any white stringy threads, and pat dry carefully. Cut the livers into fairly small pieces and dust them lightly, but thoroughly, with well-seasoned flour. Cut the ham or bacon into snippets.

Warm a sauté pan over medium–low heat and melt 40 g [1½ oz] butter in it. When the butter foam subsides add the livers and cook gently until lightly coloured all over. Add the ham or bacon, stock and lemon juice and stir until the liquid bubbles up. Reduce heat as low as possible and cover the pan. Cook, shaking the pan occasionally, for about 10 minutes until the livers are cooked and the sauce is syrupy. Meanwhile fry the rounds of bread in a mixture of butter and olive oil until golden and crisp on the outside, but the crumb remains tender within.

Stir the parsley into the sauce and check seasoning. Pile the liver mixture onto the rounds of well-drained, piping hot fried bread and serve immediately.

Chicken Livers with Grapes

During the grape season, this makes an attractive variation on the previous recipe, but it takes a little longer to prepare because the grapes have to be peeled and seeded. Serves 2–4.

250 g [½ lb] chicken livers
125 g [¼ lb] white grapes
a little well-seasoned flour
unsalted butter
olive oil
4 thick rounds of bread
half a glass of dry white wine
salt and freshly ground black pepper

Rinse and dry the livers carefully cutting away bile and any white threads. Peel and pip the grapes, dropping them into boiling water to loosen the skins if they do not come away easily. Fry the rounds of bread in a mixture of oil and butter until golden. Drain well and keep hot.

Wipe out the pan. Return it to medium-high heat and add a generous nugget of fresh butter. Quickly dust the chicken livers with well-seasoned flour. Add them to the pan as soon as the butter foam dies down, and sauté until browned and sealed on the outside but still juicy and pink within. Lift them out with a slotted spoon and pile onto the rounds of fried bread. Pour the wine into the pan, stir to scrape meaty sediment from the pan base and let the liquid bubble with the butter until reduced to a syrupy sauce. Add the grapes, season lightly and cook very gently until the grapes are hot. Pour over the livers and serve immediately.

Bacon & Chicken Liver Salad

This is a rather more substantial chicken liver dish, one of those useful and flexible recipes which can be conjured up quickly and varied to suit the occasion. Use whatever greenery is in season; increase quantities and/or alter proportions of meat to salad ingredients depending on whether you want to serve the dish as a first course or as a main course salad. Quantities given here make a good lunch dish for 3 people or, if salad ingredients are increased to 700 g [1½ lb], a first course for 6–8.

400 g [¾ lb] prepared weight crisp shredded lettuce and watercress sprigs (or spinach or chicory)
250 g [½ lb] chicken livers
6–8 rashers streaky bacon
15 ml [1 tablespoon] olive oil
30 ml [2 tablespoons] mustardy vinaigrette dressing
a dash of wine vinegar
salt and freshly ground black pepper

Shred the salad greens into a salad bowl and grind a little salt (depending on the saltiness of the bacon) and pepper over them. Clean the chicken livers, cut them into small pieces and check that they are thoroughly dry. If they were frozen it is a good idea to dust them lightly with flour. Cut the bacon into snippets and cook over very low heat until the fat runs, then increase the heat and crisp the bacon. Remove with a slotted spoon and add to the salad bowl.

Add the olive oil to the pan and heat it. Sauté the chicken livers until browned and sealed on the outside, but still juicy and pink within, then transfer them to the salad bowl. Add the vinegar and vinaigrette dressing to the frying pan, quickly stir in any meaty sediment from the pan base, shake the pan gently to mingle the sauce and pour it over the salad. Toss lightly and serve with warmed bread.

Polpette al Limone

Another dish along similar lines to bacon and chicken liver salad,
deliciously fresh-tasting, and a good choice for slimmers. Quantities given are sufficient for a lunch dish for 4 or, with extra
lettuce, a first course for 8. To make a more filling dish, the herb
and lemon-scented meatballs can be served on a bed of garlic-
buttered tagliatelle (see page 135) with salad on the side.

500g [1 lb] shoulder of veal or pie veal, boned weight
1 large Cos or Webbs lettuce, shredded
1–2 garlic cloves
1 handful of fresh chopped parsley
5 ml [1 teaspoon] fresh lemon thyme leaves
10 ml [2 teaspoons] fresh chopped marjoram
1 lemon, juice and grated zest
50 g [2 oz] fresh white breadcrumbs
45 ml [3 tablespoons] freshly grated Parmesan cheese
1 egg
butter and olive oil
a little flour
3–4 tablespoons dry Martini (optional)
salt and freshly ground black pepper

If you have a food processor, the preparations of this summery
dish take only a few minutes. Reduce the bread to fine crumbs
and mix in the herbs, Parmesan cheese and very finely grated
lemon zest. Mince the veal finely and mix it with the beaten egg,
crushed garlic, the juice of half the lemon, plenty of pepper and a
little salt, then knead and mix in the dry ingredients. Using
well-floured hands shape the mixture into about 36 small balls.

Choose a frying pan large enough to take all the meatballs in a
single layer or cook them in separate batches in a smaller pan.
Heat it well, add 15 ml [1 tablespoon] olive oil and 50 g [scant 2
oz] butter and reduce heat to medium. When the butter begins to
stop foaming add the meatballs and fry for about 8 minutes,
shaking the pan occasionally to turn the meatballs, until they are
browned all over. Lift the meatballs out of the pan into a salad
bowl containing the shredded lettuce and perhaps a few snipped
chives or spring onions. Increase pan heat to high, pour on the
Martini (or the juice of the remaining half lemon plus 15 g [½ oz]
butter) and stir for a minute or so to scrape up the meaty sediment. Pour the bubbling hot sauce — there is little of it but it is
richly flavoured — onto the salad and toss to mix everything well.

Smoked Haddock Soufflé

A well-flavoured substantial fish soufflé which will serve 6 people as a first course or 3–4 as a lunch dish. In the latter case, the soufflé is delicious served with baked tomatoes (which can be cooked in the oven at the same time) and a green salad.

350 g [¾ lb] smoked haddock, filleted weight
275 ml [½ pt] milk
65 g [2½ oz] butter
40 g [1½ oz] plain flour
45 ml [3 tablespoons] freshly grated Parmesan cheese
4 eggs, separated
45 ml [3 tablespoons] fresh chopped parsley
15 ml [1 tablespoon] snipped chives
1 bay leaf
salt, paprika and black pepper

Preheat the oven to 200°C [400°F], gas mark 6, placing a baking sheet on an upper shelf. Butter a soufflé dish and dust it with one-third of the Parmesan cheese. Choose a small pan into which the cut up fillets will fit snugly. Put the fish into it, add the bay leaf and the milk. Bring slowly to the boil, cover and set the pan aside for 6–8 minutes.

Make a sauce with the butter, flour and strained fishy milk. Away from the heat stir in the remaining Parmesan cheese and a good grinding of black pepper. Skin and flake the fish, mash it slightly with a fork and stir it into the sauce. Beat in the egg yolks, one at a time, stir in the herbs, and season to taste with salt. Turn the mixture into a large mixing bowl. Whisk the egg whites until stiff but not dry, fold them in and turn the soufflé mixture into the prepared dish. Dust with paprika and bake for 35–40 minutes.

Fisherman's Eggs

Eggs baked en cocotte with a little cream are deliciously easy and always popular. This simple variation includes smoked haddock, and all the preparations can be done well ahead if you wish. Serves 4.

4 eggs
150 g [generous ¼ lb] smoked haddock, filleted weight
60 ml [4 tablespoons] double cream
45 ml [3 tablespoons] fresh chopped parsley
butter
salt and freshly ground black pepper

Put the fish into a pan and pour on boiling water to cover. Cook over gentle heat for 3–4 minutes. Then drain the fish and, as soon as it is cool enough to handle, skin and break the flesh into large flakes. Divide the fish between 4 very generously buttered cocotte or individual soufflé dishes, sprinkling the fresh chopped parsley plus a good grinding of black pepper and just a dribble of cream between layers. Break an egg into each dish, pour on the remaining cream and add a pinch of salt and another grinding of black pepper. Cover each dish with a foil "lid" and stand the dishes in a roasting pan.

To cook, pour sufficient boiling water into the pan to come halfway up the sides of the dishes, and bake in an oven preheated to 200°C [400°F], gas mark 6, for about 10 minutes or until the egg whites are set but the yolks are still creamy.

Farmhouse Eggs

Like fisherman's eggs, this is another variation on baked eggs and is quick and easy to prepare. Although the soured cream and fresh herbs nicely temper the richness of the cheese, it is a fairly filling dish. Suitable as a first course for 4 people only if the main course is a very light one; best as a lunch or supper dish for 2, served with wholemeal bread and a crisp green salad.

4 eggs
175 g [6 oz] mature Cheddar cheese (or a mixture of Cheddar and Gruyère)
60 ml [4 tablespoons] fresh chopped parsley
60 ml [4 tablespoons] fresh snipped chives
150 ml [¼ pt] soured cream
butter
salt and freshly ground black pepper

Lightly butter the base and sides of a gratin dish or 4 individual dishes. Sprinkle half the grated cheese over the base and scatter the herbs over the cheese. Make rough hollows in the cheese with the back of a spoon and break an egg into each hollow. Season lightly with salt and generously with pepper. Cover the eggs with the remaining cheese and dribble the soured cream over the top.

To cook, preheat the oven to 190°C [375°F], gas mark 5, placing a baking sheet on the top shelf of the oven. Place the egg dish(es) on the hot baking sheet and bake for 12–15 minutes until the egg yolks are beginning to set and the cheese is melted and bubbling.

Petits Pots de Fromage

Eggs and cheese again, this time combined to make savoury custards — quiche-like but without the pastry. They are no trouble to make but they are rich and therefore best served before a light, simple main course. Serves 6.

3 large eggs
90 g [3 oz] Gruyère cheese
30 g [1 oz] Parmesan cheese
150 ml [¼ pt] double cream
275 ml [½ pt] milk
freshly ground black pepper

Preheat the oven to 160°C [325°F], gas mark 3, and bring a kettle to the boil.

Beat the eggs with a fork in a large mixing bowl. Beat in the finely grated cheeses and a good seasoning of pepper. Then beat in the cold milk and cream. Ladle the mixture into 6 greased cocotte dishes, making sure each one gets its share of the cheese. Cover with foil lids and stand in a roasting pan. Pour in enough freshly boiled water to come halfway up the sides of the dishes and bake in the oven until set to a creamy consistency — about 35–40 minutes.

Cheddar Custards: For a cheaper, less rich version use mature Cheddar in place of Gruyère and Parmesan. Add a grating of nutmeg and a little salt. These are best topped with a little crisp bacon. A couple of rashers is plenty. Cut them into matchstick strips and spread out on a baking tray placed on the floor of the oven 15 minutes before the custards complete cooking. Sprinkle the bacon over the custards just before serving.

Mozzarella in Carozza

This is probably too substantial to serve as a first course, but is a favourite for a quick snack lunch, pre-theatre bite or midnight feast. Serve with an undressed watercress salad to temper the richness of the cheesy fried bread. Serves 2.

200 g [6 oz] Mozzarella cheese
4 slices white or brown bread
1 large egg
salt and freshly ground black pepper
olive oil for frying

For really delicious results slice the bread thinly and remove the crusts. Thickly slice the cheese. Lay the slices of cheese on 2 slices of the bread, taking care not to put them too close to the edge of the bread or the filling will ooze out during cooking. Season well with salt and pepper, and cover with the remaining slices of bread. Beat the egg in a soup plate with some salt and pepper. Soak the 2 sandwiches in the beaten egg for about 15 minutes, turning them occasionally, so that they absorb all the egg and are well moistened. Pinch the cut edges of bread with your fingers to seal the filling inside the sandwiches.

Heat a good quantity of olive oil (it can be strained through butter muslin afterwards and re-used for frying other things), and fry the sandwiches quite quickly so that the eggy bread is golden and the cheese hot and just melted. Drain well and serve immediately.

Four Cheese Gougère

This is a dip which goes well with a glass of wine when relaxing with friends round the fireside in winter.

For the choux pastry:
75 g [3 oz] butter
225 ml [8 fl oz] water
115 g [¼ lb] plain flour
a pinch of cayenne pepper and mustard powder
salt and freshly ground black pepper
3 large eggs
50 g [2 oz] Gruyère cheese
50 g [2 oz] Parmesan cheese

For the filling:
115 g [¼ lb] curd cheese
115 g [¼ lb] cottage cheese
150 ml [¼ pt] soured cream or thick home-made yoghurt
1 garlic clove
120 ml [8 tablespoons] chopped fresh herbs, preferably parsley and basil
salt and freshly ground black pepper

To make the filling, sieve the cheeses, pour on the soured cream or thick yoghurt, add the garlic clove crushed with some salt and beat with an electric whisk until perfectly smooth and well blended. Stir in the herbs and a good grinding of black pepper. Cover and chill very thoroughly.

Place a baking sheet on the top shelf of the oven and preheat the oven to 220°C [425°F], gas mark 7. Butter a really large gratin dish and grate the Gruyère and Parmesan. Sift the flour, cayenne and mustard powder into a bowl. Measure the diced butter and water into a small pan. Add salt and a good grinding of pepper and bring to a rapid boil. Away from the heat, immediately tip the flour into the saucepan and beat with a wooden spoon until the mixture is smooth and leaves the sides of the pan clean. Turn the contents of the pan into a mixing bowl, and beat in the lightly beaten eggs a spoonful or so at a time. When the dough is very smooth and glossy, beat in the grated cheeses. Dollop the mixture in upright spoonfuls all round the edge of the gratin dish. Bake for 45–50 minutes until the cheese pastry is puffed up and set to a crisp golden brown. Quickly spoon the very cold cream cheese mixture into the centre of the dish and serve.

Parmesan Straws

Most savouries have to be eaten within minutes of making, which means it is impractical to serve them at the end of a meal. Parmesan straws, however, can be made whenever it is convenient and stored in an airtight tin; reheat and crisp them in the oven while you eat the main course.

180 g [6 oz] plain flour
120 g [¼ lb] butter
60 g [2 oz] Gruyère cheese
60 g [2 oz] Parmesan cheese
1 egg yolk
salt and cayenne pepper

Parmesan
Straws

Sift the flour, a little salt and cayenne pepper into a mixing bowl. Using a palette knife stir in the grated cheeses. Add the butter at room temperature, cut it up into tiny pieces with the palette knife then rub it in with your fingertips. Make a well in the centre of the dry ingredients. Beat the egg yolk with a scant teaspoon of cold water. Pour it into the well. Using the palette knife gradually draw the dry and liquid ingredients together to make a rich crumbly dough. Draw the dough into a ball with your hands and knead it very briefly and lightly to ensure that everything is well blended. Wrap the pastry in clingfilm and chill for at least 30 minutes. This is very important with such a rich pastry.

Towards the end of the chilling time, preheat the oven to 200°C [400°F], gas mark 6. Roll out the pastry to a rectangle 6 mm [¼ inch] thick, and cut into narrow strips about 7 cm [3 inches] long. Lay the cheese straws on a baking sheet and chill again for 10 minutes before baking. Bake on a shelf just above the centre of the oven for about 20 minutes, until the straws are golden and crisp.

Nutty Cheese Straws: If your budget won't run to using Gruyère and Parmesan, replace both cheeses with mature Cheddar cheese. The trick which makes these cheaper cheese biscuits successful is to replace half the white flour with wholewheat flour.

Cheese Crisps

A change from cheese straws and a useful recipe for using up leftover egg whites, these crunchy savoury mouthfuls are good to float in soups and to nibble with pre-dinner drinks.

2 egg whites
20 g [¾ oz] Parmesan cheese
a little oil

Preheat the oven to 150°C [300°F], gas mark 2, and lightly oil a baking sheet. Whisk the egg whites until they stand in glossy peaks. Finely grate and fold in the Parmesan cheese. Drop tiny coffeespoon blobs of the mixture onto the prepared baking sheet and cook until dried out and crisp — about 35–40 minutes.

Stored in an airtight tin as soon as the crisps are cold, they will keep well for a couple of days. If stored for longer, reheat briefly before eating.

Anchovy Twists

A recipe for anchovy addicts, these biscuits can be served as a savoury, with pre-dinner drinks or with a fish soup. Makes about 48.

1 × 225 g [½ lb] packet puff pastry
2–3 × 50 g [2 oz] cans of anchovy fillets
beaten egg for glazing

Drain the anchovies and cut each fillet into 2 or 3 long narrow strips — depending on the size of the anchovies and on how piquant you want the biscuits to be. Roll out the pastry a little less thinly than usual and cut into fingers slightly longer than the anchovy strips and about 3 times their width. Lay an anchovy strip on each piece of pastry. Fold and pinch the ends of the pastry over the anchovy, then twist with both hands so the pastry spirals around and encloses the anchovy.

Space the twists out on a lightly floured baking tray and refrigerate for 15 minutes before glazing carefully with beaten egg. Bake at the top of the oven at 200°C [400°F], gas mark 6, for 12–15 minutes until puffed up and golden.

Baked Mussels with Almonds

More original than mussels with garlic butter, this is every bit as good. All the preparations can be done well ahead of meal time. Serves 6.

3 litres [6 lb] fresh mussels
200 g [6 oz] softened butter
100 g [3½ oz] flaked almonds
90 ml [6 tablespoons] fresh chopped parsley
10 ml [2 teaspoons] fresh chopped tarragon
1 small garlic clove
salt and freshly ground black pepper
a Vienna loaf

Mash the butter until it is creamy and beat in the chopped herbs, the garlic crushed with some salt and a good seasoning of pepper. Using wet hands, wrap the butter in damp greaseproof paper and chill it while you prepare the mussels.

Scrub the mussels very thoroughly and wash them in several changes of cold salted water. Discard any with damaged shells or which refuse to shut when tapped sharply. Cook the drained mussels in a closed pan over fierce heat for 3 minutes, or until opened – there is no need to add any liquid to the pan, but shake it occasionally to encourage even circulation of steam. Discard any mussels that have not opened and remove empty half shells of those that have opened. Smear the base and sides of a large gratin or shallow baking dish with butter, and cover the base with thin slices of bread. Arrange the mussels in their half shells on the bread (2 mussels to 1 half shell makes economic use of space). Top each with a nugget of the flavoured butter. Crush the almonds lightly and sprinkle them over the top.

Shortly before serving preheat the oven to 230°C [450°F], gas mark 8. Bake the dish of mussels for about 10 minutes until bubbling hot and the almonds are lightly browned.

Baked Mussels with Mushroom Butter: For an alternative savoury butter to use in autumn, chop 50 g [2 oz] mushrooms very finely, mix with a few crushed coriander seeds, some snipped chives and salt and pepper, and mash into 125 g [¼ lb] softened butter. Replace almond topping with 15 ml [1 tablespoon] grated Parmesan cheese mixed with dried crumbs made from 3 slices of bread.

Herring Roes with Lemon

On the (unhappily rare) occasions when I see fresh soft herring roes for sale, I snap them up for this excellent and very British dish. Very good as a first course for dinner, as a light lunch dish, pre-theatre bonne bouche or midnight snack. Serves 3–6.

500–700 g [1–1½ lb] soft herring roes
a little plain flour
about 150 g [5 oz] butter
2 lemons
watercress
rounds of lightly toasted and buttered bread
salt and freshly ground black pepper

Dust the herring roes with a little very well-seasoned flour and shake off excess. Melt a little of the butter in a large frying pan and, when foaming ceases, add the roes. Cook, turning as necessary, until the roes stiffen and curl and are lightly coloured. Pile the roes onto the hot toast. Add the remaining butter and the juice of half a lemon to the pan. Cook over low heat until syrupy, season with salt, pepper and extra lemon juice to taste, and pour over the roes. Garnish with wedges of lemon and sprigs of watercress.

Herring Roes with White Wine: Half a glass of dry white wine makes a fine alternative to lemon juice. Let it bubble up with the butter and reduce for a few minutes before pouring over the roes, then sprinkle with a dash of cayenne pepper.

Smoked Mussels with Bacon

Smoked mussels taste so different from fresh mussels that they are really a delicacy in their own right. Smoked mussels are an invaluable store-cupboard item, and their preparation involves blissfully little work for the cook. Serves 6.

3 × 100 g [3½ oz] cans of smoked mussels
500–700 g [1–1½ lb] streaky bacon rashers
6 large rounds of toasted and lightly buttered bread
cayenne pepper and watercress to garnish

Preheat the oven to 180°C [350°F], gas mark 4. Drain the oil from the mussels in the cans and use some of it to grease lightly a large baking tray. Remove the rind from the bacon, cut each rasher in half, flatten and stretch it with the back of a knife. Roll each piece of bacon round 1 large or 2 small mussels. Place the rolls, seam side down, on the baking tray and cook for about 25 minutes until the bacon is slightly crisp and the mussels thoroughly heated through. Pile onto hot toast, dust with cayenne pepper and surround with watercress sprigs. Alternatively (and more practical if the mussels are to be served with pre-dinner drinks) spear the rolls with cocktail sticks and pile them onto a hot dish.

Angels on Horseback: Replace smoked mussels with fresh oysters, sprinkling them with a little lemon juice and dusting them with cayenne pepper. Chicken livers can also be used.

Devils on Horseback: Almond-stuffed prunes make a cheap and very good stuffing for bacon rolls. Plump the prunes in hot tea, drain, dry and stone them. Replace the stones with whole blanched almonds which have been fried until golden and rolled in salt and cayenne pepper.

Poor Man's Blinis

It is the contrast of chilled filling and piping hot pancakes that makes this such an acceptable substitute for real blinis with Beluga caviar. Serves 6–8.

For the kipper salad:
300 g [10 oz] kipper fillets
10 ml [2 teaspoons] Dijon mustard
15 ml [1 tablespoon] lemon juice
60 ml [4 tablespoons] olive oil
5–10 ml [1–2 teaspoons] dillweed
1 shallot or pickling onion
300–400 ml [½–¾ pt] soured cream
salt and freshly ground black pepper

For the pancake batter:
50 g [2 oz] buckwheat flour
50 g [2 oz] plain white flour
2 eggs
150 ml [¼ pt] milk
150 ml [¼ pt] water
30 ml [2 tablespoons] melted butter
salt

First, skin the raw kippers and cut the flesh into matchstick strips. Beat the mustard, lemon, oil and dillweed together. Pour the sauce over the kippers. Add the onion cut into wafer-thin slices. Toss gently, cover and leave in a cold place for 24–48 hours, turning the mixture occasionally during this time.

To make the pancakes, beat the eggs, milk and water together and blend them gradually into the flours and salt to make a creamy, perfectly smooth batter. Stir in the cool melted butter. Use the batter to make 20 very thin pancakes, each 15 cm [6 inches] in diameter. Cook them over medium-low heat for about 30–45 seconds on one side and for less than 30 seconds on the other side. Stir the batter vigorously between making each pancake or all the buckwheat flour will sink to the bottom of the mixture.

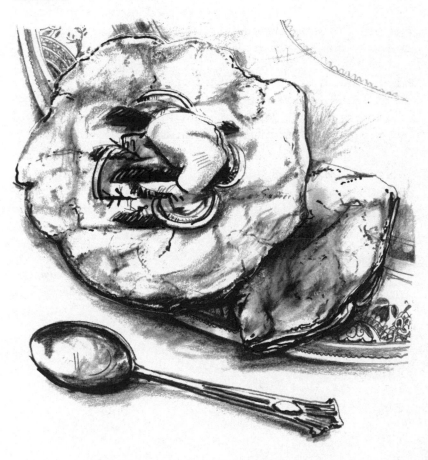

Pancakes can be made up to 5 days before serving if you wish. Cool them on a cake rack — this allows steam to escape which prevents them from becoming rubbery. Stack when cold, interleaving them with circles of greaseproof paper, wrap the stack in foil and refrigerate. Reheat by placing the foil-wrapped parcel in an oven preheated to 190°C [375°F], gas mark 5, for 20–30 minutes.

Serve the pancakes piping hot, folded into triangles. Serve the kipper salad (drained of the liquid) and the chilled soured cream (seasoned with a little salt and plenty of black pepper) in separate bowls so that everyone can help themselves.

Smoked Salmon or Tuna Pancakes: Smoked salmon or Kenyan smoked tuna fish, lightly moistened with olive oil, lemon juice and black pepper, can be used instead of marinated kippers. This is a delicious way to share a small quantity of expensive smoked fish among several people.

Kipper Salad: If time is short, forget the pancakes and serve the marinated kippers and chilled soured cream with thick slices of a granary cob loaf. Put the loaf into the oven until very hot and crusty before cutting it into thick wedges.

Cold Starters & Pâtés

GREEK ISLAND SALAD

All the recipes given in this chapter make attractive first-course dishes for dinner but, like the recipes in the previous chapter, most of them are admirably suited to other occasions as well.

In fact avocados with watercress purée and piquant savoury pears are the only two recipes in this chapter that I never serve other than as first courses. Both have a freshness and lightness which seem to me intrinsically right for awakening appetites at the outset of a meal, and they are perhaps a little too light to be very useful in other ways. These qualities are the special characteristics of fresh vegetables and fruit, and I find them so very appealing that I tend increasingly to draw away from the traditionally organised British sequence of serving dishes. More often than not I serve vegetable dishes as first courses, preferring to reserve many dishes officially designated as cold starters for other occasions.

Pâtés, for example, are wonderfully versatile foods, so good for lunch with baked potatoes and a salad, or as the basis for picnics and cold buffet suppers, that it seems a pity to restrict them to first-course eating. Moreover, they are so rich in protein that it seems extravagant to regard them merely as appetisers. Pâtés are easy to make and rewardingly handsome. Meat pâtés in particular keep well for several weeks providing they are sealed with a layer of clarified butter and stored in a cold place, and the flavour is greatly improved if a few days' maturation is allowed between making and eating. I always feel reassured by the sight of a good pâté in the larder, and confident that I can cope with any number of people dropping in.

It is too much to hope, however, that friends will develop the knack of turning up unexpectedly only when you happen to have a fine pâté at the ready. With this practical thought in mind, I include a tangy lemon and tuna pâté, and a richer-tasting Portuguese pâté, which have proved reliable allies on emergency occasions. Both are based on store-cupboard items, take only 5 minutes or so to make and, unlike most pâtés, can be served immediately. In fact, neither keeps very well for long: I recommend that they always be eaten with 24 hours of making.

Mousses, like pâtés, also make excellent lunch dishes, simply served with good bread and a salad, and those given here are very little trouble to prepare. They look most attractive for first courses if individually made, but for lunch the use of one large soufflé dish or bowl seems more appropriate. I never unmould mousses for serving: they look just as inviting served in the dishes in which they are set, and this spares you the time and worry of unmoulding them neatly. Much more important, though, is the fact that relatively little gelatine need be used, so allowing the true flavours of the mousse to show themselves off to best advantage, whilst keeping the texture creamy and light. If you want to unmould any mousse (whether sweet or savoury) for which I have given a recipe, use more gelatine than I have specified to ensure the mixture is sufficiently firm to unmould without danger of splitting or collapse.

The summer lunches that linger most agreeably in my memory have no formal menu structure, but consist of numerous small dishes, like the mezze of Mediterranean countries — nutty hummus, gleaming black olives, a dish of hard-boiled eggs lavishly sprinkled with fresh chopped herbs, creamy taramasalata, fresh salty prawns, poor man's caviar, slices of salami with curls of sweet butter, and dolomades — piled onto the table with plenty of good bread and wine. There is something especially sympathetic about the breaking of bread, the shared dipping and sipping, that such good natured occasions bring. Just the thing for a leisurely and langorous afternoon . . .

Any of these mezze-type dishes can also be served alone, of course, and it is in this role that they are invaluable for combating "seven o'clock shadow" — when working wife and husband arrive home as late and as tired as each other.

If an inviting dish — and the drinks, of course — are ready and waiting to greet your homecoming, the cookhouse call becomes much less urgent; the cook can relax and revive from a numbing working day before cooking the evening meal.

Taramasalata, hummus, dolmades and dukka are all excellent dishes to nibble with drinks. All can be made in advance in quantity (say, over the weekend when more time is available) and stored in the fridge ready to delve into and enjoy during the week. Delicatessen foods, such as smoked fish, ham and salamis, are also ideal for this purpose and, although more expensive, involve no preparation at all.

Crudités can also be superbly reviving, with a bowl of, say, soft cheese mixed with herbs or mayonnaise into which to dip a variety of raw vegetables. This, incidentally, is a dish particularly worth remembering when no one type of vegetable in the garden is ready to harvest in sufficient quantity to make a dish on its own.

Avocados with Watercress Purée

The green hues of avocado and watercress look lovely and the smooth texture of the one and the peppery taste of the other go very well together. Serves 4.

2 large ripe avocado pears
watercress
75 ml [5 tablespoons] olive oil
10–15 ml [2–3 teaspoons] wine vinegar
50 g [1 oz] split and well-toasted almonds (optional)
lemon juice
salt

Strip the leaves from half a bunch of watercress. Put them into a liquidiser with the olive oil, vinegar and some salt and reduce to a perfectly smooth green purée.

If the avocados are really ripe they should be easy to peel. Skin, halve and stone them and cut into slices. Brush with a little lemon juice to prevent discolouration and arrange on plates with a few small watercress sprigs. Serve the purée in a small jug so everyone can help themselves.

Alternatively simply halve and stone the avocados. Fill the hollows with watercress purée and well-toasted almonds.

Savoury Pears

Dessert pears, like avocados, make an easy and inviting appetiser. The contrast of sweet juicy fruit and piquant blue cheese is exceedingly good. Serves 4.

2 large ripe dessert pears
a little lemon juice
a small bunch of watercress
175–225 g [6–8 oz] Dolcelatte or Bresse Bleu

Thinly pare the skins from the pears with a potato peeler. Halve and core them, cut into thick slices and brush with a little lemon juice to prevent discolouration. Arrange the slices on small plates with a few dark green watercress sprigs and a small wedge of blue cheese, and serve with oatcakes or water biscuits that have been warmed through in a low oven.

Iced Parmesan Creams

A very soft-textured mousse that includes no gelatine, is extremely quick to prepare, and extremely rich. Serves 6–8.

3 large eggs
50 g [2 oz] freshly grated Parmesan cheese
50 g [2 oz] finely grated Gruyère or Cheddar cheese
Dijon mustard and cayenne pepper
150 ml [¼ pt] double cream
150 ml [¼ pt] soured cream or fromage blanc
watercress

Separate the egg yolks from the whites. Cream the yolks with a very generous shake of cayenne pepper and about 5 ml [1 tea-spoon] Dijon mustard. Grate the cheeses and beat them into the seasoned yolks to make a thick paste. Whip the creams together and beat a few tablespoonfuls into the cheese mixture to slacken it a little. Then fold the two mixtures together using light movements to keep it well aerated.

Whisk the egg whites until stiff but not dry. Gently but thoroughly fold in the cheese cream and check seasoning — salt is usually unnecessary. Spoon into 6–8 ramekins. Cover and chill for at least 3 hours.

To offset the richness of the dish, scatter generously with coarsely chopped watercress just before serving. Oatcakes or water biscuits that have been heated through in the oven go well with this dish.

Fresh Tomato Ice

This captures the real taste of fresh tomatoes. It is a quick and easy ice to prepare, good as a first course or a refresher after a spicy dish. Serve it as it is, or topped with a few prawns or chopped basil, with oatcakes on the side. Serves 6.

225 g [½ lb] tomatoes
15 ml [1 tablespoon] tomato purée
5 ml [1 teaspoon] caster sugar
4 ml [scant 1 teaspoon] Worcester sauce
2.5 ml [½ teaspoon] salt
200 ml [7½ fl oz] soured cream

Skin and roughly chop the tomatoes. Put them into a liquidiser and reduce to a smooth purée, breaking up the pips as much as possible. Add the remaining ingredients and blend again to mix everything very thoroughly.

Pour the mixture into a chilled loaf tin, cover with foil and freeze for about 45 minutes until solid around the edges. Turn the ice out into a bowl and beat with an electric whisk for a minute or so. Cover and freeze again until completely solid.

Let the ice mature in the main part of the fridge for 45–60 minutes before scooping it into small ramekins for serving. The texture of this ice is rather crystalline — more like water-ice than ice-cream.

Smoked Haddock Mousse

An inexpensive fish mousse of good "meaty" texture which will serve 8 as a first course. Alternatively, with the addition of a cucumber salad, it makes an attractive summer lunch dish for 4.

450 g [1 lb] smoked haddock, filleted weight
425 ml [¾ pt] milk
40 g [1½ oz] butter
40 g [1½ oz] plain flour
a slice of Florentine fennel (or a few dried fennel stalks or seeds)
1 small carrot
1 small onion (or 6–7 spring onions)
15 ml [3 teaspoons] gelatine powder
5 ml [1 teaspoon] dillweed
a squeeze of lemon juice
75 ml [5 tablespoons] soured cream
2 egg whites
salt and freshly ground black pepper

Chop the vegetables very finely. Put them into a pan with the milk and bring to scalding point as slowly as possible to infuse the milk well. Add the fish, pushing it well down into the liquid, and bring back to simmering point. Switch off the heat, cover the pan and leave for 10 minutes.

Drain the fish, reserving the liquid and discarding the vegetables. When cool enough to handle, skin the fish and break it into chunks. Meanwhile, cook the butter and flour to a pale straw-coloured paste, and blend in the fishy milk to make a rich sauce. Add the fish to the pan and simmer, without a lid, over very low heat for 5–10 minutes, stirring occasionally.

Sprinkle the gelatine into a spoonful or so of cold water with a squeeze of lemon juice in a cup and dissolve over a pan of hot water. Thoroughly stir it into the fish pan. Away from the heat, stir in the soured cream and dillweed and season with plenty of pepper and salt to taste. Turn the mixture into a bowl and set aside until cold and beginning to thicken.

Whisk the egg whites, fold them into the mousse mixture, turn into ramekins or a soufflé dish, cover and refrigerate for about 4 hours to set.

Note: For slightly richer results, omit lemon juice and dillweed, dissolve the gelatine in sherry, replace soured cream with fresh cream and season with a dash of cayenne.

Smoked Salmon Mousse

When time is more important than cost, I make this instead of smoked haddock mousse. Rich-tasting, prettily coloured, very quick and straightforward to make. Serves 6–8.

200 g [6 oz] smoked salmon — end pieces or frozen will do perfectly well
5 ml [1 teaspoon] Dijon mustard
5 ml [1 teaspoon] dillweed
20 ml [4 teaspoons] lemon juice
30 ml [2 tablespoons] olive oil
7 ml [1 slightly heaped teaspoon] gelatine powder
30 ml [2 tablespoons] cold water
150 ml [¼ pt] double cream
2 egg whites
salt and freshly ground black pepper

Cut off and reserve a few slivers of smoked salmon for garnish. Roughly chop the rest and put it into a food processor or liquidiser. Add the mustard, dillweed, lemon and oil and reduce to a smooth pink purée. Soak the gelatine in the water, dissolve over low heat and allow to cool for a minute or two before beating into the fish purée.

Whip the cream softly. Fold it into the fish purée. Check seasoning, adding extra lemon, salt and pepper to taste. Whisk the egg whites to soft peaks and fold them into the fish purée. Divide between 6–8 ramekins, cover and chill for a couple of hours.

Jellied Eggs with Green Herbs

If you grow herbs, this is a useful store-cupboard cheat of a recipe to remember when you feel too lazy to spend much time in the kitchen. Serves 4.

4 eggs
1 × 415 ml [14 fl oz] can of consommé
1 × 50 g [2 oz] can of anchovy fillets
a good squeeze of lemon juice
fresh chopped parsley, chives and tarragon

Unless you are an anchovy addict you won't need the whole can for this dish. Mash any leftovers into some butter and use it in fish pies or scrambled eggs.

Turn half the consommé into a small pan, add a squeeze of

lemon juice and place over a low heat until barely melted. Divide the softened jelly between 4 ramekins, each lined with a few chopped anchovies and a generous teaspoon of mixed fresh herbs (mostly parsley and chives with just a hint of tarragon). Chill the ramekins and refrigerate the consommé remaining in the can until set.

Soft boil the eggs for 5 minutes. Cool them quickly by plunging them in cold water for 5 minutes or so. Shell carefully and place 1 egg in each dish. Surround and top the eggs with the remaining jelly, chopped, alternating spoonfuls with a further scattering of anchovies and another teaspoon or so of herbs for each dish. Cover and chill for at least 1 hour.

Jellied Eggs with Pâté: Omit anchovies and line each ramekin with a round of a creamy textured pâté and a slice of skinned tomato.

Mansion House Eggs: A ritzy version of this dish can be made without increasing your workload by substituting lumpfish caviar for the anchovies. Be slightly mean with the herbs, top each egg with a spoonful of soured cream and crown it with a generous heap of the lumpfish caviar. Serve with wedges of lemon.

Caesar Salad

An American recipe, despite the Roman implications of the name, this makes a substantial first course for 6. A favourite of mine, with omelettes to follow, for an easy and attractive summer lunch.

2 Cos lettuces
4–5 thick slices of slightly stale bread
a little butter and oil
1 large egg
105–120 ml [7–8 tablespoons] olive oil
1 fat garlic clove
15 ml [1 tablespoon] lemon juice
45 ml [3 tablespoons] freshly grated Parmesan cheese
salt and freshly ground black pepper

Remove the crusts from the bread, cut the crumb into large dice and fry in a mixture of butter and oil until golden. Drain well on crumpled kitchen paper and allow to become quite cold.

Wash and dry the lettuces — a salad spinner is a blessing here as it is quick, efficient and minimises the chances of bruising leaves. Lightly beat the raw egg with a fork. Add the olive oil and beat again: as the two ingredients amalgamate the mixture will thicken a little. Add the garlic, crushed with some salt, the lemon juice and a good grinding of pepper. Mix together well and add more lemon and/or pepper to taste. Pour the sauce over the lettuces. Sprinkle with freshly grated Parmesan cheese, and toss lightly but thoroughly. Scatter the cold croûtons over the salad and serve it immediately (the croûtons will become soggy if the salad is left to stand for more than a minute or two).

Greek Island Salad

Warmly scented, this cheese salad makes a first course for 4–6, or a lunch dish for 2–3. Fetta cheese can be bought from Greek and Cypriot shops; if difficult to find use white Stilton instead.

600 g [1¼ lb] tomatoes
half a large cucumber
half a Spanish onion
200 g [6–8 oz] Fetta cheese
5 ml [1 teaspoon] coriander seeds
a little fresh thyme and marjoram
a small handful of black olives
olive oil
salt and freshly ground black pepper

Slice the tomatoes thickly; dice the cucumber without peeling it. Quarter the onion, slice very thinly indeed and push into rings. Cut the cheese into matchstick strips. Crush the coriander seeds in a mortar or with the back of a spoon. Put these ingredients into a salad bowl and mix lightly together, sprinkling in the herbs. Strew with a little coarse salt and add a good grinding of black pepper. Pour on a few tablespoons of olive oil, preferably one with a fruity flavour, and set aside for a few minutes before adding the olives and tossing lightly.

Mozzarella & Tomato Salad: Even quicker to prepare, this cheese salad serves 4 as an appetiser. Slice 6–8 firm and well-flavoured tomatoes. Arrange on a plate, interleaving with slices of mozzarella cheese. Sprinkle lavishly with fresh coarsely chopped basil and a little coarse salt and drizzle with a good, fruity olive oil. Leave for just a few minutes for salt, basil and oil flavourings to impregnate the tomatoes and cheese.

Dukka

I first ate dukka with friends in Cairo: they told me that every Egyptian family makes its own version, altering the proportions of ingredients to taste. I rate dukka as the best of all nibbles to serve with drinks. It is also very good sprinkled over boiled rice and soups.

100 g [¼ lb] whole hazelnuts or peanuts, shelled weight (salted or dry roasted nuts are not suitable)
50 g [2 oz] sesame seeds
25 g [1 oz] coriander seeds
30 ml [2 tablespoons] cumin seeds
salt and freshly ground black pepper

Warm a frying pan over medium heat (without any fat). Add the nuts to the pan and cook, stirring and turning them until the skins begin to blacken and peel away. Empty the pan and reduce heat to low. Lightly toast the sesame seeds until pale golden, then warm the coriander and cumin seeds together until lightly crisped and exuding a delicious aroma.

Mix all 4 ingredients together with some coarse salt and a good grinding of black pepper. Crush them coarsely by passing them through the largest blade of a meat mincer. Don't attempt to use a liquidiser — it may be quicker, but it will reduce at least some of the ingredients to a fine powder. Check seasoning and, if not for immediate use, store in an airtight jar. Dukka keeps for several weeks but is best when toasty and crisp. If it has been made some time ago, spread it on a baking tray and heat in a moderate oven for a few minutes before serving.

Serve dukka with warm French or pitta bread and a small bowl of good olive oil. To eat, break off a small piece of bread. Holding it by the crust, dip the crumb into the oil to moisten it well, then press it into the spiced nutty mixture.

Green Dukka: A delicious herb version of dukka can be made in summer by simply chopping a mugful of fresh mixed herbs sprinkled with salt. I always use parsley as the main herb and add a few of the following, depending on mood and availability: basil, coriander, chives, chervil, tarragon, marjoram, lovage, fennel, dill, mints and thymes — especially lemon thyme. Green dukka must be eaten straight away.

Poor Man's Caviar

The secret of success for this dish lies in using an oil that is very light in texture and flavour, and only the tiniest garlic clove, so that the delicate flavour of the aubergines is enhanced, not overpowered. Serves 4–6.

2–3 aubergines weighing a total of about 450 g [1 lb]
1 very small garlic clove
15 ml [1 tablespoon] lemon juice
30–45 ml [2–3 tablespoons] safflower or sunflower oil
fresh chopped parsley
salt and freshly ground black pepper

Heat the grill until very hot. Wipe the aubergine skins and prick them in 2 or 3 places to prevent exploding during cooking. Cook the whole aubergines under the grill, turning them as necessary, until the skins are blackened and blistering — about 10–15 minutes.

As soon as the cooked aubergines are cool enough to handle, strip away the skins. Cut each aubergine into 3 or 4 pieces, put them into a sieve and press with a wooden spoon to extract the juices. Turn the flesh into a liquidiser. Add the garlic, crushed with some salt, the lemon juice and 30 ml [2 tablespoons] of the oil. Reduce to a smooth purée and season with a little pepper. Stir in a spoonful or so of chopped parsley. Add a little more oil if the mixture seems too stiff, and salt and pepper to taste. Turn the vegetable pâté into a pretty pot, cover and keep in a cool place until ready to serve — it should be eaten within 24 hours. Garnish with extra chopped parsley just before serving: serve with plenty of warm pitta bread, no butter.

Hummus bi Tahini

Another famous vegetable pâté, which can be excellent if made with top quality tahini paste (health food shops usually stock the best) and generous quantities of lemon, garlic, parsley and cumin. Serves 6.

125 g [¼ lb] chick-peas
150 ml [¼ pt] tahini paste
2 large juicy lemons
2 fat garlic cloves
10 ml [2 tablespoons] oil
salt
fresh chopped parsley
cumin seeds

Soak the chick-peas overnight. Drain, rinse well under a tap, put into a saucepan and cover with plenty of fresh cold water. Do not add any salt — it will toughen the skins. Bring slowly to boiling point then cover and cook until the chick-peas are quite tender. This takes 2 hours on average, but it is almost impossible to overcook chick-peas. Drain, and reserve the cooking liquor separately from the peas.

Put the garlic, crushed with plenty of salt, most of the lemon juice, the chick-peas and 75 ml [5 tablespoons] of their liquor into a liquidiser. Reduce the mixture to a smooth purée.

Scrape the purée out into a mixing bowl and gradually beat in the tahini paste. Add some salt and dilute the mixture to a very thick cream with extra cooking liquor and/or lemon juice — 90 ml [6 tablespoons] is about right. Beat in the oil and add more garlic and/or salt to taste. Cover, chill and eat within 5 days. Garnish the pâté with chopped parsley and a few crushed cumin seeds. Serve with plenty of pitta bread and/or sticks of raw carrot, cucumber and other vegetables to dip into the pâté.

Soured Cream Herrings

Pickling herrings at home is child's play. These fish taste very much better (and work out considerably cheaper) than shop-bought rollmops. But the latter can, of course, be used when speed is of the essence. Serves 6 as a light lunch dish or 12 as an appetiser.

8 fat fresh herrings, boned and filleted
700–800 g [1½–2 lb] Cox or Granny Smith apples
1 small Spanish onion
3–4 bunches watercress
75 g [3 oz] walnut pieces
600 ml [1 pt] soured cream
10 ml [2 teaspoons] Dijon mustard, or more to taste
Hungarian paprika

For the pickle:
200 g [6 oz] coarse salt
1¾ litres [3 pt] cold water
1¾ litres [3 pt] cider vinegar
50 g [2 oz] soft brown sugar
60 ml [4 tablespoons] pickling spice
10 ml [2 teaspoons] black peppercorns
10 ml [2 teaspoons] coriander seeds
1 large bay leaf
1 onion

To make the pickle, dissolve the salt in the cold water in a large bowl. Add the herring fillets and leave them submerged in the brine for 3 hours. Meanwhile, bring to the boil all the rest of the pickle ingredients (except the onion). Draw the pan away from the heat, cover and leave until completely cold before straining off the liquid.

Drain and thoroughly dry the herrings. Lay them skin side down and put a few wafer-thin onion rings on each. Roll up each fillet from neck to tail end, and secure with a cocktail stick. Pack the fish into scrupulously clean glass jars and pour on enough pickling liquid to immerse them completely. Cover with airtight and vinegar-proof lids and refrigerate for a minimum of 3 days before using. (Pickled herrings will keep for up to 3 weeks, but are at their best 3–4 days after pickling.)

To serve, drain and unroll the herrings. Discard the pickling onion, chop the fish into bite-size chunks and put them into a bowl. Add the cored but unpeeled apples, cut into chunks, and the Spanish onion cut into paper-thin slivers. Stir gently to mix the ingredients. Pour on the soured cream, flavoured with mustard and stirred until creamy. Toss gently and pile the fish salad onto a generous bed of watercress. Sprinkle with walnuts and dust with paprika.

Terrine of Fish with Spinach

Serve this on its own, cut into thick slices. It is not a pâté to spread on toast, although slices can be wrapped in crisp lettuce leaves to make not-so-fattening sandwiches for picnics. Serves 8 or more.

225 g [½ lb] smoked haddock, filleted weight
500 g [1¼ lb] whiting or coley, filleted weight
225 g [½ lb] frozen whole leaf spinach
75 g [3 oz] fresh white breadcrumbs
50 g [2 oz] melted butter
the juice and zest of 1 lemon
1 garlic clove
a good pinch of mace
2 eggs
salt and freshly ground black pepper

Defrost the spinach overnight. Squeeze it as dry as possible with your hands and chop it roughly. Cut the smoked haddock into matchstick strips, sprinkle it with plenty of pepper, pour on half the lemon juice and set aside in a cool place.

Make sure that the white fish is quite dry and cut it up roughly. Put it into a liquidiser or food processor together with the eggs, crushed garlic, mace, remaining lemon juice and the zest, and reduce to a smooth purée. Soak the crumbs in the melted butter until swollen, and beat them into the purée together with the juices drained from the smoked haddock. Beat in the well-squeezed and chopped spinach and, finally, the strips of smoked haddock.

Pack the mixture into a lightly buttered loaf tin and cover with a buttered foil lid. Make a couple of steam holes in the lid. Stand the dish in a roasting pan containing enough freshly boiled water to come halfway up the sides of the dish. Cook in the centre of an oven preheated to 160°C [325°F], gas mark 3, for 1½ hours.

Chill overnight and serve the pâté next day: wipe round the rim of the dish (the fish may have exuded juices), loosen the pâté with a palette knife, turn out, cut into slices and garnish with lemon.

Terrine of Haddock and Prawns

Made in the same way as the previous recipe, this is my favourite
fish pâté — very pretty with nuggets of pink prawns embedded
in the pale gold haddock mixture, and with a fresh, delicate
lemony taste. Serves 8 or more.

225 g [½ lb] peeled prawns
700 g [1½ lb] smoked haddock, filleted weight
115 g [¼ lb] each, butter and fresh white breadcrumbs
the juice and zest of 1½ lemons
2 eggs
a bunch of parsley
salt and freshly ground black pepper

If the prawns are very large, chop them a little. Squeeze the juice
of half a lemon over them. Add salt and pepper, toss lightly and
set aside.

Put the remaining lemon juice and the zest into a food processor or liquidiser. Add the skinned and boned smoked haddock
cut into chunks and reduce to a fine smooth purée. Soak the
breadcrumbs in warm melted butter and stir the beaten eggs into
them. Beat this mixture into the pounded fish. Add the juices
drained from the prawns, a generous seasoning of pepper and a
little salt. When the mixture is smooth and well blended, stir in
the prawns and the coarsely chopped parsley.

Pack the mixture into a lightly buttered loaf tin and cover it
with a buttered foil lid. Make a couple of steam holes in the lid.
Stand the dish in a roasting pan containing enough freshly boiled
water to come halfway up the sides of the dish. Cook in the
centre of an oven preheated to 160°C [325°F], gas mark 3, for 1½
hours.

Chill overnight and serve next day, bringing the pâté back to
room temperature before serving — allow 1 hour for this. Serve
cut into thick slices, garnished with wedges of lemon and parsley
or watercress.

Lemon & Tuna Pâté

Fresh–tasting and quick to prepare, this pâté looks most attractive if served in lemon "shells", but it can equally well be served in tiny ramekins or a pâté dish. Serves 4–6.

2 × 200 g [7 oz] cans of tuna fish in oil
150 g [5 oz] cream cheese or softened butter
10 ml [2 teaspoons] Dijon mustard
10 ml [2 teaspoons] fresh chopped dill or 5 ml [1 teaspoon] dried dillweed
60 ml [4 tablespoons] lemon juice
salt and freshly ground black pepper
parsley sprigs or bay leaves

If you want to serve the pâté in lemon "shells", cut 3 really large lemons in half, carefully scoop out all the pulp and membrane and press this in a sieve placed over a bowl to extract the juice. There will be much more juice than is needed for the pâté: save the leftovers to use in other dishes or drinks. Cut a small slice off the point of each lemon half so the "shell" will stand upright like a cup.

Drain the fish well. Put it into a food processor or liquidiser together with all the other pâté ingredients except the parsley (or bay leaves) and reduce to a smooth firm purée. Alternatively, mash the ingredients very thoroughly in a large soup plate with a fork. Pile the pâté into the lemon shells or a pot, having checked seasoning. Chill the pâté for an hour or so before serving to allow flavours to blend. Decorate with parsley or bay leaves and serve with fingers of brown toast.

Portuguese Pâté

Another pâté made with canned fish, this is ideal for emergencies as all the ingredients are likely to be in your store-cupboard and preparation takes only 5 minutes.

2 × 120 g [¼ lb] cans of sardines
5–10 ml [1–2 teaspoons] Dijon mustard
5 ml [1 teaspoon] lemon juice
a few spoonfuls of soured cream, thickened yoghurt or curd cheese
salt and freshly ground black pepper

Drain the sardines, turn them into a soup plate and mash well with a fork. Add mustard, lemon juice, salt and pepper and a few spoonfuls of soured cream, thick yoghurt or curd cheese (sieve the cheese first). Mash and beat again until the mixture is well blended and smooth. Check seasoning and adjust to taste. Press the pâté into a pretty pot or small bowl and, to make it look special, decorate with a slice of lemon and 2 bay leaves.

Taramasalata

In the 1960s this pâté was served at every other dinner party; today it seems almost extinct on the domestic scene. But it remains a favourite in restaurants, which suggests that many of us still enjoy eating it. It is naturally cheaper to eat at home, and much cheaper if you skin the roe yourself rather than buy it in a jar. Serves 4–6.

175 g [6 oz] smoked cod's roe
175–200 ml [6–7 fl oz] olive, groundnut or sunflower oil
50–65 g [2–2½ oz] fresh brown breadcrumbs
1 very fat garlic clove
about 30 ml [2 tablespoons] lemon juice
freshly ground black pepper

Put the cod's roe into a small bowl. Pour on boiling water to cover and leave for 3–4 minutes. Drain well and pat dry. Use a sharp knife to make a small nick in the skin, ease out a tiny piece of the roe and taste it. If it seems excessively salty, return the whole roe to the bowl of water and leave to soak for a while. Pour on fresh boiling water just before peeling to loosen the skin. Pull back the skin from the original incision, then peel all of it away. Break the sticky roe into pieces, put it into a soup plate, add a few spoonfuls of the oil and mash with a fork until reduced to a smooth purée.

Reduce the bread to crumbs. Put them into a separate soup bowl and mix to a paste with 60 ml [4 tablespoons] cold water. Add the crushed garlic clove and a few spoonfuls of the oil, and mix together well. Then add the prepared cod's roe, a spoonful or so at a time and mash and beat with a fork until the mixture is very well blended and smooth. Beat in the lemon juice, then as much as you need of the olive oil — add just a tablespoonful at a time and check that it is absorbed before adding the next spoon-

ful. The pâté is ready when it has the consistency of thick cream.
Check seasoning and adjust to taste. Cover, chill and eat within 2
days. Black olives, quartered lemons and unleavened bread make
ideal accompaniments.

Cod's Roe Dip: This is made without oil and breadcrumbs.
The result is less oily than taramasalata and of a consistency that
is good for dunking small biscuits and crudités without spills.
Pound the cod's roe with 10–15 ml [2–3 teaspoons] lemon juice
and crushed garlic until smooth. Season with pepper and gradually beat in up to 150 ml [¼ pt] soured cream.

Chicken & Walnut Pâté

This Turkish combination of chicken and walnuts is exceedingly
good. Take care, however, to avoid using old nuts. Shelled
walnut kernels become more oily with age, easily turn rancid and
will spoil the dish. Fresh walnuts are best but their skins are very
bitter and must be peeled off: drop the shelled nuts into a bowl of
boiling water to loosen the skins, drain and rub off the skins.
Serves 8.

1½–1¾ kg [3½–4 lb] chicken
250 g [½ lb] walnut kernels
1 onion
a few sprigs of parsley and thyme and some peppercorns
a bunch of chives
30 ml [2 tablespoons] thick yoghurt, soured cream or curd or cream cheese
salt, Hungarian paprika and freshly ground black pepper

First poach the chicken. Put it into a pan into which it fits snugly,
tuck the giblets, sliced onion, sprigs of herbs and some peppercorns round it. Pour on hot but not boiling water to cover the
thighs of the bird, and bring to boiling point. Skim, cover with a
lid and simmer gently for 1 hour. Set the covered pan aside in a
cold place until the poached chicken is cold.

When cold scrape the solidified fat off the surface of the liquid
and lift out the chicken. Fast boil the liquid until reduced to
425 ml [¾ pt] well-flavoured stock. Strain and season generously
with salt, then allow to cool.

Pour two-thirds of the cold stock into a liquidiser. Add the walnuts, thick yoghurt, soured cream or curd or cream cheese, and a generous seasoning each of paprika and black pepper. Blend until the mixture is reduced to a very smooth, thick sauce.

Skin and bone the chicken and cut the flesh into slivers. Gently stir the chicken into the walnut sauce together with some snipped chives. Season to taste and thin the mixture with some or all of the remaining stock as necessary. Press the pâté into a dish and level the top. Cover and chill until about 1½ hours before serving. Garnish with more chives and paprika, and serve with plenty of good bread.

Country Pork Pâté with Thyme

A homely and economic pâté, which goes very well with baked potatoes and a salad. Serves 4–6.

350 g [¾ lb] belly of pork — boned and de-rinded weight
225 g [½ lb] pig's liver
115 g [¼ lb] streaky bacon
7–10 ml [1½–2 teaspoons] dried thyme
1 fat garlic clove, crushed with salt
the zest of a lemon
15–30 ml [1–2 tablespoons] lemon juice or sherry
a bay leaf
salt and freshly ground black pepper

Mince the belly of pork and pig's liver. Cut the bacon into tiny pieces. Thoroughly mix in the remaining ingredients, cover and refrigerate for several hours to allow flavours to blend.

Pack the mixture into a small loaf tin. Press the bay leaf on top and cover with a foil lid. Stand the container in a roasting pan and pour in enough boiling water to come halfway up the sides of the pâté dish. Bake at 160°C [325°F], gas mark 3, for 1¾ hours, removing the foil lid for the last half hour. Cool, cover and chill the pâté until 45 minutes or so before serving.

Italian Veal Pâté: For a lighter meat pâté make up the meatball mixture as described in polpette al limone (page 32), but omit breadcrumbs and add 250 g [a generous ½ lb] belly of pork. Mince both meats fairly coarsely. Let the mixture stand in a cold place for a few hours then pack it into a dish and cook as for country pork pâté with thyme.

Winter & Summer Vegetables

potato

peas

leek

onion

garlic

artichoke

carrot

mushrooms

Fresh vegetables are a pleasure both to cook and to eat. Many look beautiful, most are inexpensive, and few require much time or effort to prepare. Choose them carefully, treat them delicately, serve them prettily and without delay, and you are likely to gain the reputation of being rather a good cook.

Pleasing though this compliment may be, it is in itself a sad reflection on the ill-treatment to which vegetables have been subjected by British cooks in the past, and are still by many today.

Inedibly waterlogged vegetables have long been a hallmark of British cookery. In 1748 Hannah Glasse was advising that "all things green should have a little crispness, for if they are over-boiled they neither have any sweetness or beauty". Yet, only in the past few years has this message begun to be heeded and has it become more usual to serve vegetables "al dente". Although we are no longer so guilty of killing vegetables by drowning (indeed some cooks have gone to the opposite extreme, confusing al dente with semi-raw), vegetable cookery remains our Achilles heel. Even cooks who devote great care to other dishes are inclined to pay only lip service to vegetables, rating them as mere accompaniments rather than as a principal part of the meal.

In truth vegetables warrant far greater respect. We should regard them as a worthy dish in their own right, not just as an adjunct to meat, and treat them accordingly. In this way, both meat course and vegetables become more enjoyable. In the words of Elizabeth David, "both must, when required to stand on their own, be more carefully bought and more meticulously cooked". Now that meat is so costly, and the choice of vegetables so splendid, the incentives to take vegetable cookery seriously are stronger than ever.

To treat vegetables with proper respect does not necessarily entail serving them as a separate course, but it does mean always devoting as much care and attention to vegetables as to any other dish, and that involves three "musts": to choose beautifully fresh ingredients, to cook them impeccably, and to serve them without delay. If vegetables are interestingly as well as carefully cooked, so much the better.

As to choosing fresh vegetables, gardeners will always have the edge over shoppers. Moreover, gardeners will make a point of growing the varieties with the best flavour, and will take care to harvest them when young and sweet. However, on the whole, shopping for vegetables is an increasing pleasure as the quality as well as the range of greengrocers' offerings is steadily improving. There are plenty of squeaky fresh leafy vegetables from which to choose. Many root vegetables are now sensibly sold with earth still clinging to them and foliage attached (which helps maintain moisture and freshness longer); and the peak condition of many imported vegetables, such as glossy aubergines, makes them wonderfully inviting. It is true that in some shops, vegetables are still to be found stripped naked, stale and sweating in plastic bags. But if we refuse to buy them, these unappetising offerings may one day disappear. Shoppers' demands for better vegetables are eventually heeded if we ask loudly and for long enough: for example, in some areas it is now possible to buy Marmande tomatoes and Kipfler potatoes.

As to the cooking, it is a pity that many cooks rarely consider doing anything with vegetables other than boiling and annointing them ritually with knobs of butter. (Cauliflower, broad beans and leeks seem the only vegetables allowed to break rank from this buttered routine: they are often subjected to a uniform blanket of cheese sauce instead!) Delicately boiled and buttered vegetables can be delicious, but to restrict oneself exclusively to this one method of presenting vegetables is to deny oneself the many and varied pleasures of vegetable cookery, some of which I hope are conveyed in the recipes that follow.

In addition to gratins, roasted, braised, fried, baked, stewed, grilled and stir-fried vegetable dishes, I have included a number of recipes in which boiled or steamed vegetables are finished with hot or cold salad dressings, flavoured butters or light coating sauces. These are good and easy ways to make boiled vegetables look and taste just that little bit different.

Although I have used the word "boiled" as a general term, in practice I nearly always steam vegetables rather than boil them. This takes slightly longer but it is a much kinder process. If you think about it, it is tempting providence to plunge into water any vegetable that has a high moisture content, or a delicate structure, or both. Water cannot help but increase the natural moisture of the vegetables, while the agitation of bubbling water is liable to damage delicate fibres. In steaming, vegetables are placed just above, rather than in boiling water, so they cook gently in the heat of the rising steam: there is much less danger of disintegration, and the chances of the vegetables absorbing much water are greatly reduced. I use a small, modern type of steamer, usually referred to as a "petal steamer", that is inexpensive and easily stored.

The third "must" of good vegetable cookery can be summed up in the maxim "vegetables should be eaten as soon as cooked". No matter how carefully vegetables are chosen and cooked, they will lose all their charm if left to keep hot in the oven between cooking and serving.

It is this aspect of vegetable cookery that can be rather daunting, particularly when the menu to be served follows the traditional pattern of soup or appetiser, followed by fish or meat with vegetables, then cheese and pudding (or pudding and cheese to be strictly British).

Many cooks turn a blind eye to the problem, cook vegetables ahead, leave them to stew in the oven and hope that the meat and other courses will prove good enough to distract attention from tasteless and textureless vegetables. Other cooks tackle the problem head-on, resolutely leaving the table between courses to cook vegetables, which certainly results in freshly cooked offerings, but greatly spoils the shared relaxation of those gathered round the table. Neither tactic is wholly satisfactory, but here are three suggested ways to enjoy both the company of your fellow diners and freshly cooked vegetables:

The first approach involves serving vegetables as a separate course, before the meat. I like this idea very much and use it more and more often. This is partly because many meat dishes seem positively better if served without the competing flavours and textures of vegetables; the blander background of a plain accompaniment (good bread, boiled rice, potato or lentil purée) is all that is needed, with perhaps a simple green salad on the side. Also vegetable dishes make a lovely fresh-tasting start to a meal, the ideal enticement to the appetite.

All the recipes given in this chapter (except for the roasts, purées and cabbage dishes) feature regularly as first courses on my menus. This may surprise those whose repertoire of vegetable appetisers is limited to asparagus and globe artichokes. But the reason why these two vegetables are so highly esteemed may be precisely because they are served alone and, therefore, considerable attention is paid to choosing and cooking them. Devote equal care to other vegetables and it becomes clear that they too can make delectable dishes in their own right. The Jerusalem artichoke becomes a treat, for example, if delicately steamed and served with Hollandaise sauce in the manner usually reserved for globe artichokes. Radishes grown by the children will make a dish to set before a king if the radishes are young, crisp and freshly picked, and served with a bowl of good creamy butter and a sprinkling of sea salt.

The second approach — and this is the solution when you want to serve meat and vegetables together, preceded by soup or an appetiser — is to choose a vegetable cooking method which enables you to do all the work before the meal begins and to time the cooking to finish just as you are ready to serve. Baking vegetables in foil parcels is an excellent answer. Braising is another: a few basic preparations, then a long slow stint in the oven, and the finished vegetables can be served in the dish in which they have cooked. The other great advantage of slow oven methods is that, contrary to the strict general rules of good vegetable cookery, perfect timing and temperature control are not crucial to success; if for any reason you are running behind schedule, you can safely reduce oven temperature a little and leave the vegetables to cook a bit longer without fear of spoiling.

The third approach is to start the meal with a main course of meat and vegetables served together, then follow this with pudding and/or cheese. These are the only occasions on which it is practicable to serve grilled and pan-fried meat and fish dishes which the cook must tend while they cook. It seems a great shame not to share these delectable dishes with friends, and it is no problem to cook vegetables by quick top-of-the-stove methods at the same time as cooking the meat or fish.

Three courses may be traditional for serving to guests, but I do not feel that an appetiser is an essential. Your guests are unlikely to feel deprived by its absence, and may do better justice to the pudding!

Young Carrots in a Parcel

The joy of this recipe is its ease of preparation. You simply make a parcel of raw vegetables with butter and flavourings, and put it into the oven to cook. Baking is timed so that the vegetables complete cooking as and when you are ready to serve them.

All root and fleshy vegetables (*not* leafy green or podded vegetables) are excellent cooked this way. Flavourings can be varied to taste, but basically 50–75 g [2–3 oz] fat plus seasonings and an optional 1–2 tablespoonfuls of liquid are needed for every 450 g [1 lb] vegetables to be cooked (the larger quantities for very hard, unjuicy vegetables).

How long each parcel will take to cook depends on the type and size of vegetable used. If very hard vegetables are cut into smallish pieces and baked near the top of the oven, and softer vegetables are cut into larger chunks and baked near the bottom of the oven, they take an average 1¼ hours at 160°C [325°F], gas mark 3. The size of the chunks and temperature and timing, however, can be altered to meet the requirements of the meat or fish dish to be cooked in the oven at the same time. Serves 4.

450 g [1 lb] finger carrots
75 g [3 oz] butter
6–8 spring onions
a pinch of sugar
a squeeze of lemon juice
salt and freshly ground black pepper
a handful of fresh chopped parsley

Preheat the oven to 160°C [325°F], gas mark 3. Take a very large, extra-wide piece of kitchen foil and fold it in half, closing the dull rather than the shiny sides together. Don't skimp on the quantity of foil you use (you can always wash it afterwards and re-use it).

Rub the central area of one side of the shiny foil with plenty of butter. Scrub the carrots, top and tail them and cut them in half lengthways (or quarter them if large). Lay the carrots on the buttered foil, sprinkle with salt, pepper and chopped spring onions and add knobs of butter between layers. Sprinkle with sugar and squeeze the lemon juice over and top with any remaining butter cut into flakes. Draw the sides and ends of the foil up and crimp them together to make a baggy parcel that is securely sealed yet roomy inside (if the vegetables are too tightly packed together, they won't cook evenly).

Lay the parcel on a baking tray (if unsupported the parcel may sag between the bars of the oven shelf and the bag may split and spill during cooking). Place the tray in the oven and cook for 1–1½ hours, until the vegetables are tender and butter, carrot juices and seasonings have mingled to make a delicious sauce. Scatter the vegetables with parsley just before serving.

To cook a double quantity, make 2 foil parcels: packets containing more than 450 g [1 lb] vegetables tend to cook unevenly.

Old Carrots in a Parcel: Slice, then quarter or halve the bigger rounds to make each piece approximately the same size. Mix with 2 very finely chopped onions, a pinch of sugar, salt, pepper, a tablespoon or so of well-flavoured chicken stock, plenty of butter, and a little dried dillweed or crushed rosemary.

Celeriac in a Parcel: 350 g [¾ lb] celeriac, peeled weight, cut into chunks the same size as meat for a stew. Sprinkle with a little lemon juice and 1 skinned and roughly chopped tomato. Season with salt and pepper and dot with generous knobs of butter.

Kohlrabi in a Parcel: Prepare exactly as for celeriac.

Jerusalem Artichokes in a Parcel: Prepare exactly as for celeriac.

Leeks in a Parcel: Slice 350 g [¾ lb] leeks (cleaned weight) and mix with 4–5 rashers streaky bacon cut into snippets. Add a dash of Worcestershire sauce and a sprinkling of Parmesan cheese. Smear foil and dot leeks with bacon fat.

Cauliflower in a Parcel: Break into sprigs and anoint with garlic butter, pepper, chopped parsley and a tablespoonful of tomato juice. Or use beef dripping mixed with a little curry paste.

Parsnips in a Parcel: Use 350 g [¾ lb] thickly sliced parsnips, and halve or quarter the bigger slices to make each piece approximately the same size. Smear generously with 50–75 g [2–3 oz] softened butter into which you have mashed 1–2 teaspoons French mustard and some ground cumin seeds.

Fennel in a Parcel: Cut into chunks after scrubbing and paring away any stringy threads with a potato peeler. Rub with lemon juice. Anoint very generously with butter, salt and pepper, and add a dash of dry vermouth. Scatter with toasted split almonds just before serving.

New Potatoes in a Parcel: 450 g [1 lb] small scrubbed new potatoes with plenty of butter, salt, pepper, a small crushed garlic clove and a sprig or two of bruised mint, or other herb. Remove sprigs before serving and add fresh chopped herbs.

Carrots with Olives

This recipe involves a little more preparation, but it makes a wonderful cold dish to serve as a first course. Serves 6–8.

1 kg [2 lb] carrots
300 g [10 oz] shallots or pickling onions
125 g [¼ lb] black olives, preferably tiny Provençal olives
100 ml [6 tablespoons] fruity flavoured olive oil
20 ml [1½ tablespoons] white wine vinegar
salt and freshly ground black pepper

Scrape the carrots and slice them into medium-thick rounds. Or, for a particularly attractive dish, cut them into matchstick shapes about 6 mm [¼ inch] thick and 40 mm [1½ inches] long. Warm the olive oil in a heavy-based pan or flameproof casserole. Add the whole peeled onions and brown them slightly all over. Then add the carrots, the vinegar and a good seasoning of salt and pepper. Stir the ingredients thoroughly to distribute the flavourings and to coat all the carrots with a thin film of fat. Reduce heat to very low, cover and cook very gently for 30 minutes, stirring the mixture very occasionally.

Meanwhile, if the olives were packed in brine, blanch them in fast-boiling water for a few minutes to rid them of briny bitterness, then drain well. Add the olives to the carrot pan and continue steam-simmering very gently for a further 30 minutes or so. The vegetables are ready when the onions are perfectly tender and the carrots are still slightly crunchy. Turn vegetables and juices into a china bowl, cover and chill. They will keep for 2–3 days.

Bring to room temperature, stir in a little more olive oil and add extra seasoning to taste an hour or so before serving. Sprinkle with a little coarsely chopped parsley and serve with warm crusty bread.

Mediterranean Red Peppers

A sunny ratatouille type of dish, this is equally good to eat hot or cold, as a first course or as a vegetable accompaniment to grilled fish or roast meats. If there are any leftovers, I use them as a filling for omelettes. Serves 4–6.

450 g [1 lb] onions
900 g [2 lb] tomatoes
700 g [1½ lb] red peppers
3 garlic cloves
75 g [3 oz] black olives
90 ml [6 tablespoons] olive oil
a squeeze of lemon juice
15 ml [1 tablespoon] coriander seeds
30–45 ml [2–3 tablespoons] fresh chopped basil
salt and freshly ground black pepper
5 ml [1 teaspoon] caster sugar

Choose a flameproof casserole with a large surface area so the vegetable juices will evaporate fairly quickly during cooking. Warm the olive oil in the casserole. Add the chopped onions and garlic and cook until lightly coloured and slightly softened. Meanwhile, skin and roughly chop the tomatoes.

Add the tomatoes to the casserole together with a teaspoon or so of caster sugar and a good squeeze of lemon juice. Simmer uncovered, stirring the mixture from time to time, for about 20 minutes until the tomatoes disintegrate and begin to pulp down.

Seed the peppers, cut them into thick strips and add to the casserole. Cook for a further 30–40 minutes, again stirring occasionally, until most of the moisture has been driven off and you are left with a rich red stew. Stir in the basil, the lightly crushed coriander seeds, some salt and pepper and the olives. Simmer for a minute or two longer and check seasoning before serving.

Garlic Baked Mushrooms

A very easy recipe. I relish it in autumn when shaggy field

mushrooms can be gathered, but it is surprisingly good using large commercial mushrooms. The savoury butter used is the one usually associated with snails and mussels. But, unlike baked snails and mussels, this is not a very oily rich dish. Mushrooms have a very high moisture content and the vegetable juices mingle with the butter during cooking to give a lighter effect. Enough for 4 as a first course or accompaniment to grilled meat, or a greedy supper dish for 2 with salad and cheese or fresh fruit to follow.

500 g [1 lb] large flat mushrooms
200 g [6 oz] butter
2 garlic cloves
30 ml [2 tablespoons] chopped fresh parsley
salt and freshly ground black pepper

Preheat the oven to 220°C [425°F], gas mark 7. Trim the mushroom stalks level with the caps. Chop the stalks and mash them into the softened butter. Add the crushed garlic and parsley and a good seasoning of salt and pepper, and continue mixing with a fork until the flavourings are evenly blended with the butter.

Lay the mushrooms, gill side up, in a single layer on baking trays — not baking sheets or the juices will run off during cooking. Dot the mushrooms with nuggets of the butter and bake near the top of the oven for 15 minutes. Serve sizzling hot with crusty bread (wrap the loaf in foil and heat it on the bottom shelf of the oven while cooking the mushrooms).

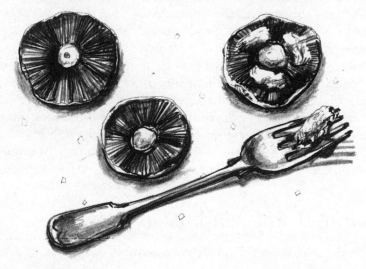

Garlic Baked Tomatoes: Even the dreaded Moneymaker is improved by garlic butter, although, for my money, well-flavoured tomatoes as large and knobbly as clenched fists are the only sort really worth baking. Halve them and lay them cut side up in gratin dishes. Lightly score the cut surface, dot with garlic butter and bake as described — allow 15–25 minutes depending on variety and size. I toast a tray of fresh breadcrumbs on the floor of the oven for the last 10 minutes of baking time; scatter these and a little fresh chopped basil or a grating of Parmesan cheese over the tomatoes just before serving.

Mushrooms with Cacik

Another delicious recipe for large flat mushrooms. Here they are crisply fried and served with a chilled garlic cream sauce. Serves 4 as a first course or as a side-dish with grills.

350 g [¾ lb] flat mushrooms
a few spoonfuls of vinaigrette dressing

For the batter:
125 g [¼ lb] plain flour
a pinch of salt
30 ml [2 tablespoons] sunflower oil
150 ml [¼ pt] tepid water
2 small egg whites

For the sauce:
150 ml [¼ pt] soured cream
75 ml [3 fl oz] thick yoghurt
1 garlic clove
30–45 ml [2–3 tablespoons] fresh chopped mint (optional)
salt and freshly ground black pepper

First make the sauce. Beat the soured cream and yoghurt together with the garlic, crushed with some salt and a grinding of pepper. Stir in some mint, if you like, cover and chill for an hour or so — it is the contrast of cold creamy sauce and piping hot, crisp vegetables that is so good.

Trim mushroom stalks level with caps, brush each mushroom with a very little vinaigrette and set aside, gill side down, for half an hour.

To make the batter, sift flour and salt into a bowl, gradually incorporate the oil and water and beat with a balloon whisk until smooth. If very thick (but bear in mind that the egg whites will lighten it later), beat in a little more water.

Immediately before cooking the mushrooms, whisk the egg whites and fold them into the batter. Coat the mushrooms lightly with batter, shake off excess and deep-fry in hot oil, a few at a time, until golden and crisply coated but still juicy within. Drain well before serving.

Aubergines with Cacik: Aubergines are superb served with cacik, but are best if shallow rather than deep-fried. Cut 700 g [1½ lb] unpeeled aubergine into 5 mm [¼ inch] slices. Layer with salt in a colander, put a soup plate on top, weight it down and leave to drain for 1 hour. Rinse and thoroughly dry the slices, dust lightly with flour and shallow-fry in batches until golden and crisp. Olive oil is best; use moderate heat or the surface of the aubergines may burn before the centres are cooked.

Courgettes with Cacik: Courgettes are another suitable candidate. Salt 700 g [1½ lb] sliced, but unpeeled, courgettes as described for aubergines, coat with batter and deep-fry as for mushrooms.

Vegetable Fritto Misto with Skordalia: For a richer and more pungent sauce to serve with fried mushrooms, aubergines or courgettes, crush 4 or more garlic cloves to a paste with mortar and pestle. Soak 40 g [1½ oz] fresh white breadcrumbs in water and squeeze out excess liquid. Gradually beat the breadcrumbs into the garlic paste, then beat in an equal quantity of ground almonds. Season with salt, carefully blend in enough olive oil (add it drop by drop at first) to give the sauce the consistency of mayonnaise, and sharpen it with a little lemon juice.

Runner Beans with Lemon Butter

I make no apology for including this exceptionally simple recipe. It is worthy of mention if only because anointing boiled or steamed vegetables with knobs of butter has become the stereotype way to serve vegetables in Britain, and good though this undoubtedly can be, it can become very monotonous. Adding a dash of extra flavouring and finishing the vegetables in the butter takes no time at all and accents the freshness of the dish. Serves 4–6.

1 kg [2 lb] runner beans
75 g [2 oz] clarified or unsalted butter
a pinch of finely grated lemon zest
10 ml [1½ teaspoons] lemon juice
salt and freshly ground black pepper

Runner beans have gained a rather poor reputation, partly because they are so prolific that it is difficult for the cook to keep pace with the crop as it matures. Coarse, gargantuan beans should be avoided at all costs, so should those whose green is tinged with yellow: they are over-mature and will make dull fibrous eating. But young freshly cropped runner beans are a juicy treat: you can recognise them by their vibrant green colour and the crisp snap when broken in half.

Top and tail the beans and, if stringy, pull away the threads from the side-seams. Cut the beans into manageable lengths, about 10 cm [4 inches] long. Shredding is not a good idea — so many cut surfaces encourage waterlogging, which reduces flavour as well as vitamin content.

To cook, either drop the beans into fresh boiling salted water and simmer until just tender — about 8 minutes — or, preferably, steam them. Drain well after boiling. Pat dry with kitchen paper towels after steaming to mop up beads of moisture.

Rinse the vegetable pan. Dice the butter and melt it gently in the pan. When hot stir in the lemon juice and zest, and a seasoning of salt and pepper. Add the drained vegetables to the pan and toss gently over very low heat for a minute or so to coat each bean with the flavoured butter.

Runner Beans with Garlic Butter: Omit lemon juice and warm the butter with a small clove of crushed garlic instead. Add salt and pepper and toss the cooked and drained vegetables in the buttery pan for a minute or two.

Note: All sorts of other vegetables lend themselves well to the lemon and garlic butter treatments. Lemon butter goes particularly well with *asparagus, globe artichokes, leeks, new potatoes,* *mangetout peas, French and broad beans.* Garlic butter is lovely with *beans, new potatoes* and *leeks* too, and it goes well with *courgettes, broccoli, curly kale* and *spinach*. Spinach will happily absorb nearly double the quantity of butter given in the main recipe.

Polish Cauliflower

Taking the flavoured butter theme a step further, in this recipe the vegetables are additionally garnished with fried breadcrumbs and chopped hard-boiled egg. Parboiled chicory or thick slices of fennel, steamed baby leeks or French beans or broccoli can also be served this way. An inexpensive and elegant dish, which deserves to be served alone as a first course. Serves 4–6.

1 large cauliflower
125 g [¼ lb] unsalted butter
a squeeze of lemon juice or a dash of anchovy essence
2 hard-boiled eggs
40 g [1½ oz] breadcrumbs
a few spoonfuls of fresh chopped parsley
salt and freshly ground black pepper

Break the cauliflower into sprigs and steam for about 10 minutes until just tender. Meanwhile, crumble the eggs with a fork and mix them into the parsley; fry the breadcrumbs in 40 g [1½ oz] butter, drain well and keep them hot.

Using kitchen paper towels mop up beads of moisture clinging to the steamed cauliflower. Then fry the florets gently in the remaining butter until they are streaked with pale gold. Draw the pan to one side, lift the sprigs out and arrange them, stalks down, on a warmed serving dish. Sprinkle first the egg and parsley, and then the fried breadcrumbs over the centre top. Add a dash of lemon or anchovy essence to the melted butter remaining in the frying pan. Stir it in with salt and pepper to taste and reheat until sizzling before pouring it over the cauliflower.

Insalata di Cavolfiore

This is another simple and pretty way to serve cauliflower as a dish in its own right. I often omit the anchovies and instead surround the cauliflower with generous slices of salami and halved hard-boiled eggs topped with black olives, to transform it from an appetiser into a lunch dish. Serves 4–6.

1 large cauliflower
vinaigrette dressing
a small bunch of parsley
a few spoonfuls of fresh snipped chives
45 ml [3 tablespoons] capers
6 anchovy fillets

Cut off the thickest part of the cauliflower stalk to make the base of the stem level with the lower rim of curds. Make a cross-shaped cut in the base so steam can penetrate easily. Sit the cauliflower in a steamer basket and cook over boiling water until tender.

Let the cooked cauliflower stand in the steamer basket on a draining board for a few minutes whilst steam evaporates, or mop up beads of moisture with kitchen paper towels. Gently turn the cauliflower, head down, into a mixing bowl. Pour on a generous quantity of vinaigrette dressing and leave for 10–15 minutes, basting the vegetable with the sauce from time to time.

Carefully lift the cauliflower out of the marinade, letting most of the vinaigrette drip back into the bowl, and sit it, right way up, in the centre of a serving dish (which, for most attractive results, should be lined with blanched cabbage leaves). Scatter the top of the cauliflower with the parsley, anchovies, chives and capers, all coarsely chopped and mixed together, and serve while still warm. Serve the cauliflower with plenty of good bread, and hand round a small jug of the vinaigrette dressing so that everyone can help themselves.

Provençale Leeks

Early season leeks, tender green and ivory, with slender stems, find a natural partner in tomato sauce. Serves 4.

12 young leeks
3 large tomatoes, skinned and roughly chopped
30 ml [2 tablespoons] olive oil
a small garlic clove
a small handful of chopped fresh parsley
a few black olives
salt and freshly ground black pepper

Trim the leeks, split the leafy pale green tops for about 3 cm [an inch or so], fan open gently and hold under a cold running tap to rinse away any grit. Then stand the leeks upside down for a few minutes in a tall jug of cold water to draw out any remaining grit. If, after doing this, a tell-tale shadow of grey still remains beneath the skin, make a small nick near the dirt spot so trapped earth particles can be washed away under the tap.

Steam the leeks rather than boil them. They easily become waterlogged, and slimy leeks which slide around the plate are very unappetising. 15 minutes should be plenty if the leeks are slim and tender. To arrest cooking and to help keep their attractive colouring, plunge the steamed leeks briefly into cold water. Drain, pat dry gently and turn onto a serving dish.

To make the sauce, warm the oil in a heavy-based pan, add the skinned and chopped tomatoes and the crushed garlic and cook over fairly high heat for 2–3 minutes, stirring all the time. Away from the heat, season with salt and pepper. (If the tomatoes lack really good flavour, sharpen them with a pinch of caster sugar and a squeeze of lemon juice.) Pour the hot sauce over the leeks and scatter with olives and parsley. Serve warm as a first course with plenty of good bread to mop up the juices.

Leek & Tomato Salad: For a similar, but oil-less dish to serve cold, sprinkle the hot leeks with a spoonful or so of wine vinegar and leave for 10 minutes. Blend 225 g [½ lb] skinned raw tomatoes to a smooth purée, season generously with salt and pepper and pour over the leeks. Sprinkle with the sieved yolk and chopped white of a hard-boiled egg just before serving.

French beans: Are also very good served in both the above ways. However, when making a French bean and tomato salad for serving cold, I recommend adding half a dozen very finely chopped spring onions to the raw tomato purée.

Courgettes: Are excellent served warm or cold à la provençale. However, it is best to replace the parsley with a handful of fresh basil. Add finely chopped spring onions when serving courgettes with a raw tomato purée.

Courgettes à la Crème

Very quick, very easy and excellent with plain roasts and grills. Serves 6–8.

900 g [2 lb] courgettes
225 g [½ lb] cream cheese
a few tablespoons milk
salt and freshly ground black pepper
fresh chopped parsley and chives

Wipe the courgettes clean and top and tail them. Slice them and steam for 8–10 minutes. Pat them very gently with kitchen paper towels to mop up surface moisture and turn them into a warmed dish.

Break the cream cheese into small lumps. Put it into the rinsed-out saucepan with a few spoonfuls of milk and a seasoning of salt and pepper. Stir gently over very low heat until the ingredients are well blended, smooth and very hot. Thin with a little more milk if the sauce seems very thick. Pour the sauce over the vegetables and sprinkle with fresh chopped herbs.

Beetroot à la Crème: Small beetroots are also very good served this way. Boil them for 1–2 hours until tender, slip off the skins, cut into halves or quarters depending on size and sprinkle with a few drops of wine vinegar before pouring on the sauce and scattering with herbs.

Onions & Almonds à la Crème: Shallots or pickling onions arc also good à la crème. Simmer them in their skins in salted water for about 10 minutes until tender. As soon as cool enough to handle, cut off the root ends then peel away skins. Reheat gently in the sauce and stir in 125–175 g [4–6 oz] toasted almonds. Omit herbs.

Baked Courgettes

This courgette and cream cheese recipe is more fiddly and time-consuming to prepare, but the effort is amply rewarded by a delicately flavoured and very pretty dish. Serves 8.

16 small courgettes, weighing a total of 800 g [1¾ lb] or so
250 g [½ lb] cream cheese
75 g [3 oz] Parmesan cheese
50 g [2 oz] fresh white breadcrumbs
2 egg yolks
1 small garlic clove
30 ml [2 tablespoons] fresh chopped basil
salt and freshly ground black pepper

Top and tail the courgettes and blanch them in a pan of salted boiling water for 5 minutes. Drain the courgettes, and make them into little "boats". To do this, first cut each courgette in half lengthways, then carefully scoop out some of the soft central flesh with a coffee spoon. Dry the courgette boats by wiping them with kitchen paper towels, and set them aside.

To make the stuffing first squeeze the pieces of scooped-out courgette flesh between sheets of kitchen paper to get rid of excess moisture, then chop it fairly finely. Put the breadcrumbs into a small bowl, add the egg yolks and mash together. Add the freshly grated Parmesan cheese and cream cheese, the finely chopped courgette flesh, the garlic crushed with a little salt, basil and seasonings, and beat until smooth and well mixed.

Fill the courgette boats with the stuffing and lay them in a single layer in a well-oiled baking dish. All this can be done several hours in advance of the meal.

Bake without a lid for about 30 minutes at 190°C [375°F], gas mark 5, until the stuffing is golden and hot. Any leftovers are delicious cold.

Braised Lettuce

Cooked lettuce has a delicate flavour, and this recipe is a godsend when there is a glut of lettuces in the garden. Serves 6.

6 large well-hearted lettuces
150 g [5 oz] butter or melted bacon fat
a bunch of spring onions
a small bunch of parsley
a sprig of lemon thyme
1 small bay leaf
strong chicken stock
about 45 ml [3 tablespoons] double cream
salt and freshly ground black pepper

Trim lettuce roots and any yellowing leaves. Wash the whole lettuces by dunking them in cold water several times. Shake off excess water and plunge the lettuces, 2 at a time, in a very large pan of fast-boiling water. Boil, without a lid, for 5 minutes. Drain very thoroughly, squeeze dry with plenty of kitchen paper and pat each lettuce into a neat fat shape.

Grease a gratin dish very generously, sprinkle the base with the finely chopped spring onions and lay the lettuces side by side on top. Tie the herbs together with string and bury them among the vegetables. Sprinkle with salt and plenty of pepper and dot with the remaining fat. All this can be done well in advance of the meal.

Pour on enough boiling hot stock to come one-third up the sides of the lettuces. Cover the dish with a loose-fitting sheet of buttered foil and braise for 1 hour at 160°C [325°F], gas mark 3, turning the lettuces over at half time.

Discard the herbs, strain off the liquid with a bulb baster and reduce it by fast boiling until slightly syrupy. Stir in and warm the cream over low heat. Check seasoning, pour the sauce over the lettuces and serve. Should there be any leftovers, purée them to make a delicate, summery soup.

Cucumber Matchsticks

Cucumbers are another summer vegetable that make an unusual and delicate braise. Serves 6.

3 long, fat cucumbers
8 ml [1½ teaspoons] caster sugar
15 ml [1 tablespoon] tarragon vinegar
a few fresh tarragon leaves
butter
a squeeze of lemon juice
salt and freshly ground black pepper

Peel the cucumbers and seed them, then cut the flesh into match-stick strips about 40 mm [1½ inches] long and 6 mm [¼ inch] thick. Turn them into a shallow dish and sprinkle with the sugar, an equal quantity of salt and the vinegar. Toss lightly, cover and leave in a cool place for a minimum of 1 hour.

Drain the cucumbers and squeeze them lightly in a double

thickness of kitchen paper. Repeat twice, then turn into a gratin dish. Add a good grinding of pepper, a squeeze of lemon juice and 3–4 tablespoons of melted butter. Turn the cucumbers to coat them all over. Cover and braise at 180°C [350°F], gas mark 4, for 1 hour, stirring the cucumbers gently and removing the covering 15 minutes before the end of cooking time. Check seasoning before serving and scatter the dish with a little chopped fresh tarragon.

Braised Celery

Winter vegetables also respond very well to braising. Celery heads must be large and tightly packed, and they need to be washed and scraped very thoroughly. Serves 6.

3 large heads of celery
150 g [5 oz] butter
7 ml [5 tablespoons] good stock
15 ml [1 generous tablespoon] dry white vermouth
celery salt
salt and freshly ground black pepper

Trim the roots and then the tops to give fine fat heads of celery about 18–20 cm [7–8 inches] long. Wash under cold running water and remove any stringy threads from the tougher outside sticks — a light scraping with a potato peeler is most effective. Stand the whole heads upside down in a tall jug of cold water for a few minutes to help wash out any particles of soil that may remain between layers.

Blanch by dropping the whole heads into a large pan of boiling, salted water and simmer gently for 12 minutes. Drain well. When cool enough to handle, cut each head in half lengthways and pat dry with kitchen paper towels.

Choose a gratin or baking dish that will take the 6 pieces of celery in a single layer. Butter the base and sides very generously. Lay the celery flat side down in the dish and dot with the remaining butter. Sprinkle with salt, pepper and celery salt, and pour on the stock and vermouth. Cut out a piece of greaseproof paper just smaller than the top of the dish, butter it well and lay it directly on top of the vegetables. (All this can be prepared in the morning if you wish.)

To cook, place the dish in the centre of an oven preheated to 180°C [350°F], gas mark 4, and braise for 1 hour. Then turn the celery over, baste it well with the juices and continue braising — this time without the buttered paper — for a further 25 minutes or so until the celery is tender and most of the juices have been absorbed or evaporated.

Braised Chicory: Blanch 12 smallish chicons for 5–6 minutes in boiling water to which you have added a little sugar and the juice of half a lemon. Drain well and squeeze out excess moisture with plenty of kitchen paper. Omit stock and vermouth and use just 15 ml [1 tablespoon] lemon juice as the liquid for braising, which will take only 1 hour.

Braised Leeks: Choose 10–12 long, slim young leeks, clean them thoroughly and cut each one into two 10 cm [4 inch] lengths. Instead of blanching, part stew the leeks in the butter for 10 minutes, turning them as necessary. Season with a few lightly crushed coriander seeds and use a scant half glass of dry white wine or cider for liquid. Braising will take about 1¼ hours.

Primo with Mustard Cream Sauce

A far cry from the unappetisingly waterlogged cabbage of institutional cookery, cabbage is treated here to a brief and respectful turning in butter, then coated with a piquant sauce. Serves 4–6.

1 head of Primo or other tight green cabbage weighing 700–900 g [1½–2 lb]
50 g [2 oz] butter
150 ml [¼ pt] soured cream
10 ml [2 teaspoons] Dijon mustard
5 ml [1 teaspoon] concentrated tomato purée
salt and freshly ground black pepper

Cut the cabbage into quarters, remove the tough stem and shred the leaves finely. Beat the soured cream, Dijon mustard and concentrated tomato purée together in a cup.

Melt the butter in a large heavy-based saucepan over medium heat. When the butter foam dies down add the shredded cabbage. Turn it with a pair of wooden spoons or salad servers so that every leaf is coated with a little of the butter. Continue cooking quite gently, stirring and turning the cabbage fairly frequently, for 6 minutes or so until the cabbage has reduced in bulk and is tender but still retains a slight bite.

Tip the contents of the cup into the pan. Increase heat to medium-high and cook, stirring and turning the cabbage continuously, for 2–3 minutes more so that the cream sauce reduces and thickens a little and evenly coats the cabbage. Season with salt and pepper to taste and serve immediately.

Rosy Cabbage

Here is another way to make the Cinderella of vegetables look and taste really good. Serves 6.

1 tight head of Savoy or Dutch cabbage, weighing about 900 g [2 lb]
25 g [1 oz] butter
15 ml [1 tablespoon] plain flour
1 small garlic clove
a good pinch of sugar
1 × 225 g [8 oz] can of tomatoes
8 ml [1 generous teaspoon] concentrated tomato purée
150 ml [¼ pt] soured cream
fresh chopped parsley
salt and freshly ground black pepper

Cut the cabbage into 6 wedges, remove the hard stalk and any ragged outer leaves. Steam until tender — 15–18 minutes — then pat each wedge dry, squeezing gently with kitchen paper towels to remove excess moisture.

While the cabbage is steaming, make the sauce. Make a roux with the butter and flour, blend in the chopped-up tomatoes and their juices, the crushed garlic, sugar, tomato purée and a good seasoning of salt and pepper. When slightly thickened and piping hot, gently blend in the soured cream. To serve, pour the sauce over the cabbage wedges and sprinkle some chopped parsley on top.

Gratin of Cabbage: For an even simpler sauce, scald 150 ml [¼ pt] each double cream and soured cream, and stir in 75 g [3 oz] grated Cheddar cheese and a generous seasoning of pepper. Lay the steamed and dried cabbage in a hot gratin dish, pour on the sauce and scatter a little more cheese on top; flash under a hot grill until the cheese and sauce are bubbling hot.

Steamed leeks, cauliflower sprigs, boiled celery and *chicory* can also be finished this way.

Chinese Leaves with Walnuts

A good choice when you want a simple but slightly unusual vegetable dish that is really quick to prepare. This makes an admirable partner for grilled pork chops, or it can be served alone as a first course. Serves 3–4.

600 g [scant 1½ lb] Chinese leaves
40 g [1½ oz] walnut kernels
30 ml [2 tablespoons] sunflower, peanut or walnut oil
10 ml [2 teaspoons] cornflour
30 ml [2 tablespoons] tarragon or wine vinegar
30 ml [2 tablespoons] soft brown sugar
60 ml [4 tablespoons] cold water
salt and freshly ground black pepper

The stalk end of Chinese leaves is best for stir-frying — the proportion of juicy riblet to leaf area is high and this makes for a deliciously crunchy cooked vegetable. Save the leafier end for salads.

Shred the cabbage finely and chop the walnuts coarsely. In a cup blend the cornflour to a paste with a little of the vinegar. Stir in remaining vinegar, sugar, water and a seasoning of salt and pepper.

Heat the oil in a wok, paella or large frying pan over medium heat. When the oil is hot, add the cabbage and cook, stirring and turning continuously with a pair of spoons, for 2–3 minutes. Sprinkle on the walnut pieces. Give the sauce a quick stir and pour it into the pan. Continue stirring and turning for a further 2–3 minutes until the sauce is hot, thickened and clinging to the leaves. Serve immediately.

Fried Sprouts with Hazelnuts: Another combination of nuts and brassica, but a cheaper version. Steam 600 g [1½ lb] Brussels sprouts until just tender. Wearing oven gloves to protect your hands against burning, pat the sprouts dry then cut each one in half. Put the sprouts into a large frying pan containing 50 g

[2 oz] or so of hot melted butter, add 50 g [2 oz] hazelnuts and a good seasoning of salt and pepper and fry for a few minutes, stirring and turning the vegetables, until they are piping hot, glistening with fat and just beginning to colour at the edges.

Fennel with Bacon

The smoky flavour of bacon goes beautifully with fennel. I serve this as a first course with plenty of hot crusty bread, and it makes a good accompaniment to grilled fish, chicken or liver. Serves 3–4.

2 heads of Florentine fennel, weighing a total of about 700 g [1½ lb]
125 g [¼ lb] streaky bacon, cut into small pieces
40 g [1½ oz] melted bacon fat or clarified butter
salt and freshly ground black pepper

Trim the root and feathery fronds from the fennel (save the fronds to add to a salad) and cut the bulbs into chunks. Put the bacon into a 25 cm [10 inch] frying pan and cook over low heat until the fat begins to run. Increase the heat a little and fry the bacon until it is crisp. Remove from the pan with a slotted spoon and keep hot.

Add the bacon fat or clarified butter to the pan. When it is melted and hot add the chunks of fennel. Stir and turn them to coat them all over with fat, then cook for about 15–20 minutes over medium-low heat, turning the chunks occasionally during this time to encourage even cooking.

The vegetables are ready when they feel tender, yet still retain a little crunch, and the surfaces are lightly browned. Return the bacon to the pan, stirring well to distribute evenly. Season with a good grinding of pepper and some salt if necessary, remembering that the bacon will have salted the dish to some degree.

Jerusalem Artichokes with Bacon: Jerusalem artichokes are also excellent cooked this way, and are best if the skins are left on. Scrub the tubers well, thoroughly dry them and cut into chunks, then proceed as described for fennel with bacon.

Broad Beans with Fennel

This is a rather sophisticated dish with a lovely nutty flavour, and is an excellent means of converting those who claim to dislike pulses. Serves 4–6.

225 g [½ lb] dried broad beans
a small head of fennel
125 g [¼ lb] butter
about 250 ml [½ pt] milk
about 250 ml [½ pt] chicken stock
45–60 ml [3–4 tablespoons] cream
fresh chopped parsley
freshly grated nutmeg
salt and freshly ground black pepper

Soak the beans for several hours in cold water. Drain, rinse and drain again, then slip off the skins. Put them into a pan with half the butter and equal quantities of milk and chicken stock to just cover the beans — you will probably need a total of 450–600 ml [¾–1 pt] liquid. Add a good grating of nutmeg and a good grinding of pepper, but no salt. Half cover the pan and simmer gently until the beans are tender and most of the liquid has been absorbed or evaporated — about 1 hour.

Towards the end of this time, clean and cut the fennel into slivers. Fry it gently in the remaining butter for 8 minutes or so until slightly softened. Season the beans with salt. Put one-third of the beans and their liquid into a liquidiser with the cream, and reduce to a smooth sauce. Reheat gently, stir in the rest of the beans and their liquor and the fennel and its buttery juices. Check seasoning and serve garnished with a sprinkling of fresh chopped parsley.

Butter Beans with Celery: For a cheaper variation on this dish, replace broad beans and fennel with dried butter beans and celery.

Parsnip Purée

Buttery and sweet, yet peppery, this purée makes a change from mashed potatoes, and is particularly good with braised or casseroled game. Serves 4–5.

1 kg [2 lb] parsnips
75 g [2 oz] butter
30–45 ml [2–3 tablespoons] fresh or soured cream
salt and freshly ground black pepper

Scrape or very thinly peel the parsnips, and slice them. Put them into a saucepan and pour on enough boiling water to cover — but only just. Add a pinch of salt, cover with a lid and simmer gently for 15–20 minutes until tender.

Meanwhile dice the butter and put it into the top part of a double-boiling pan. Measure a little water into the bottom part and bring it to a bare simmer. Place the top part over the barely simmering water and allow the butter to melt.

Drain the cooked parsnips very thoroughly. Pass them through the finest blade of a vegetable mill into the top part of the double-boiler. Beat them with the melted butter, add the cream, a little salt and plenty of pepper. (All this can be prepared several hours in advance of the meal.)

Let the purée continue to cook in the double-boiler for 15–20 minutes so that texture and flavour become smooth — cook without a lid if you want a drier purée, but remember to stir the mixture occasionally. This final cooking will take slightly longer if the initial cooking was done well ahead and the purée has become cold.

Lentil Purée: Split red lentils cook faster than whole green-grey ones, but I prefer the appearance and taste of the latter. Whichever type is used, allow 175–225 g [6–8 oz] for 4 people. Rinse, pick them over well and drain. Soften 2 finely chopped onions in plenty of butter. Add the prepared lentils (and a crushed clove of garlic if you wish). Turn the lentils to coat well with fat before pouring on enough water to cover them generously. Bring to the boil, cover and simmer very gently for 60–90 minutes until the lentils are so tender that they are beginning to disintegrate. Drain off surplus liquid (save it for soup). Add extra butter, salt and pepper to taste and beat with a wooden spoon until creamy and smooth. Like parsnip purée this can be prepared ahead, reheated and finished in a double-boiler before serving, if more convenient.

Celeriac Purée: Boil 225 g [½ lb] peeled potatoes cut into chunks and a double quantity of similarly prepared celeriac, cooking them in the same pan. Drain them when tender and pass them through the finest blade of a vegetable mill. Beat in butter, cream, a seasoning of celery salt and black pepper and reheat as for parsnip purée.

Roast Parsnips & Celeriac

These make a delectable alternative to roast potatoes. Parsnips go particularly well with lamb, and celeriac with beef, but together they go very well with either. Serves 4.

700 g [1½ lb] parsnips and/or celeriac, peeled weight
a little lemon juice or vinegar
30–45 ml [2–3 tablespoons] good beef dripping or melted bacon fat

Cut the vegetables into large chunks. Drop them into a pan of fast-boiling water (to which you have added a spoonful or so of lemon juice or vinegar if cooking celeriac) and simmer for 7 minutes to soften slightly. Drain the vegetables very thoroughly and return them to the rinsed pan. Cover it with a lid and shake it a few times — this will roughen the surfaces of the vegetables which encourages them to crisp well during roasting.

   Thoroughly heat the dripping or bacon fat in a roasting tin in the oven. Then place it over a medium-low heat, add the vegetables and turn them to coat all over with hot fat. Transfer the tin to the oven and roast at 190°C [375°F], gas mark 5, for 1–1¼ hours, turning the vegetables once or twice.

By the end of this time the vegetables should be tender within and crunchy outside. If necessary, give them an extra blast of heat — increase the oven temperature to 220°C [425°F], gas mark 7, and roast the vegetables for an extra 10 minutes or so while the joint rests between cooking and carving.

Making a Meal of Vegetables

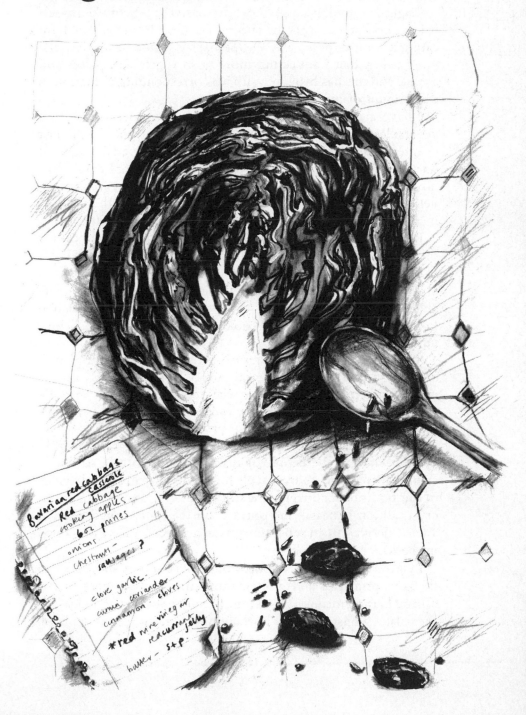

I love meat and have no intention of becoming a vegetarian. Nor do I find it necessary to become any sort of faddist in order to enjoy vegetables. But the growing awareness that the over-consumption of animal fats in western diets is a health hazard, the ecological arguments, and (most persuasive to a Scot like myself if I am honest about it) the sheer cost of meat, mean that I am eating less meat these days. Or, perhaps it would be more to the point to say that I am eating more fresh vegetables, pulses and grains, and this has brought with it a corresponding reduction in the amount of meat I consume.

I have argued throughout this book in favour of treating vegetables as worthy of a dish in their own right. In the last chapter I dealt in particular with the delicious advantages of serving a dish of vegetables before the meat course. I would like now to consider the idea of placing even greater emphasis on vegetables, by using them as the chief ingredient, the basis of main-course dishes that may or may not include just a little meat.

I recognise that this approach may not have instant appeal for those who have become accustomed to and love the British habit of serving generous slabs of meat with small quantities of veget-ables on the side, but I assure you that making a meal of veget-ables is not some cranky new-fangled scheme: it is very much in keeping with the traditions of cookery, and it can be very delicious indeed.

The barons of beef and other massive joints of "old England" about which we wax so lyrical, and which we regard as our rightful inheritance, are in fact relatively modern and were the privilege of a few (the Sunday joint is a phenomenon of very recent times). The richness of our pastures and our affluence as a nation enabled us to acquire the habit of eating considerably more meat than the people of many other countries, so that it eventually became for us a staple food. This distorted the balance of our traditional cookery towards meat. Our underlying cook-ery tradition is based, in contrast, on the same sound peasant values, derived from subsistence agriculture, that have remained in the forefront elsewhere.

In fact, the traditional cookery of most countries springs from the same principles and evolved quite simply as the most practi-cal and natural means of providing a nutritious diet and pleasing the palate, whilst carefully husbanding the resources of the land.

The traditional dishes of, say, France and Mexico taste quite unalike because the ingredients used and the mode of cooking are different, but the principles involved and the balance of foodstuffs are essentially the same — the abundant use of locally grown vegetables and cereals and the sparing use of meat.

The secret of making vegetables into a real meal lies in opening oneself up to the unashamed pleasure of cooking and eating vegetables, in nurturing their natural good qualities, in marrying them sympathetically with other ingredients, and in presenting them in ways that are nutritious, delicious and appropriate to their character. Avoid recipes which try to pretend that the vegetables are something else. Add a few herbs or spices, use grains, eggs or other dairy produce to add protein, or thriftily employ a little meat as a flavouring and enriching agent. If judiciously chosen and used, these ingredients can greatly enhance the taste and food value of vegetable dishes. It is wonderful, for example, how just a little pork added to a cabbage and cooked slowly will infuse the whole dish with richness.

There is no better way to find recipes for making vegetables into meals than to delve into the past, to rediscover the classic combinations evolved over centuries and appreciated by rich and poor alike. The pleasure of eating these dishes is such that you are quite unaware, unless you stop to analyse the ingredients used, that only a little (or no) meat is included.

The idea of using a little pork in cabbage dishes is much favoured all over Europe. The results can be mouthwateringly good and considerably varied, depending on the type of cabbage used, on whether the pork is fresh, simply salted or well spiced, and on what, if any, other ingredients are used. Pork meats are also traditionally used in conjunction with dried peas and beans, the fattiness of the meat complementing the mealy, earthy texture of pulses. Lentils with salamelle sausages is my favourite example of this combination; and a mixture of meats and haricot beans is used to similar effect in cassoulet. Potatoes also willingly imbibe other flavours, cooked, for example, with snippets of bacon and leeks and finished with cream they make a subtle-tasting and soothing "Welsh" pie.

Aubergines, or poor man's meat as it is nicknamed in the Middle East, are delectable simply cooked in very good olive oil, but I also commend them stuffed with rice and nuts as in the

classic Turkish dish Imam Bayaldi. Courgettes are well partnered by eggs, as are red and green peppers. Spinach is excellent
combined with nutty tasting chick-peas, garlic and yoghurt, and
is exquisite with cheese and eggs — flashed under a hot grill in the
Florentine manner, or poached and served as featherlight gnocchi. Cheese is a traditional ingredient for cooking with cauliflower in Italian, French and British cookery. In fact, cauliflower
cheese is one of the few traditional British ways of making a meal
of vegetables which we have faithfully continued to cook all
through the "meat years".

Chinese Pork & Cabbage

The easiest way to stuff a cabbage is to shred it and layer it with
pork meat. This version uses Chinese leaves for delicate brassica
flavour; certainly not a grand dish, but exceedingly good. Serves
4–5.

1 kg [generous 2 lb] Chinese leaves
450 g [1 lb] lean belly of pork
125 g [¼ lb] streaky bacon
a large onion
3 fat garlic cloves
butter
dried thyme
salt and freshly ground black pepper

Mince the pork and bacon coarsely. Fry it in a little butter,
together with the finely chopped onion, until lightly coloured.
Mix in the crushed garlic, and season very generously with salt,
pepper and thyme.

Shred the cabbage (Chinese leaves) and steam for 3–4 minutes.
Butter the base and sides of a casserole very generously and layer
it with the prepared ingredients — cabbage, pork mixture, cabbage, pork mixture, cabbage. Press the ingredients well down
into the dish with a potato masher. Lay a sheet of buttered
greaseproof paper on top, cover with a lid and bake at 160°C
[325°F], gas mark 3, for about 1½ hours. Serve with lots of mashed
potatoes or good bread to mop up the delicious juices.

Juniper Pork with Cabbage

A dish along similar lines to Chinese pork and cabbage, this uses white cabbage and is flavoured with juniper berries. Serves 4–5.

1 kg [generous 2 lb] white cabbage
500 g [generous 1 lb] belly of pork, boned and de-rinded weight
3 large carrots
1 large onion
2 garlic cloves
12 juniper berries
melted bacon fat or good dripping
salt and freshly ground black pepper

Heat a little fat in a flameproof casserole until sizzling hot. Add half the pork cut into cubes and brown it all over. Colour the remaining meat in the same way.

Away from the heat, add the shredded cabbage to the casserole together with the thinly sliced carrots, finely chopped onion and the browned pork. Crush the juniper berries and garlic into plenty of salt and pepper and stir them into the casserole. When the flavourings are evenly distributed and the vegetables glisten with a thin film of fat, press the mixture well down into the dish, cover with a circle of buttered greaseproof paper and a lid. Cook on the centre shelf of the oven at 150°C [300°F], gas mark 2, for 2½ hours.

Small potatoes can be baked simultaneously and go well with this dish. Choose potatoes weighing about 175 g [6 oz] each, allowing 2 or 3 per person depending on appetite. Prick the skins and rub with a mixture of oil and salt. Lay them on a baking sheet and put it on the top shelf of the oven as soon as you turn it on — don't wait for it to heat up.

Bavarian Red Cabbage Casserole

This recipe uses red cabbage and is aromatic with mixed spices. It reheats extremely well. To serve the cabbage as a vegetable dish rather than as a main course in its own right, omit the sausages or chestnuts and reduce the prunes by half. Serves 4–5.

700–900 g [1½–2 lb] red cabbage
1 cooking apple
175 g [6 oz] prunes
175 g [6 oz] dried chestnuts or 450 g [1 lb] best pork sausages
225 g [½ lb] onions
1 garlic clove
5 ml [1 teaspoon] each cumin and coriander seeds
a good pinch each ground cinnamon and cloves
30 ml [2 tablespoons] each red wine vinegar and redcurrant jelly
a little butter
salt and freshly ground black pepper

Shred the cabbage, chop the onions finely and cut the peeled apple into chunks. Put all three ingredients into a buttered casserole. Add the prunes (and chestnuts if using) — there is no need to soak either in advance. Add the cumin and coriander seeds, lightly crushed with mortar and pestle, and all remaining ingredients except the sausages. Season very generously with salt and pepper and mix everything well — using your hands is messy but most effective. Dot with a few flakes of butter, lay a sheet of buttered paper on top and cover with a lid.

Cook in the oven at 150°C [300°F], gas mark 2, for 2½ hours. If using sausages, fry them for 5–8 minutes to brown them, bury them in the cabbage mixture and cook for a further half hour. Check seasoning and transfer to a smaller dish for serving — the ingredients will have reduced quite a lot during cooking.

Nutty Stuffed Cabbage

A whole stuffed cabbage looks very elegant. It does involve more work for the cook, but is not as difficult to do as you may fear. I particularly like the buttery, lemon-flavoured nut stuffing given here, but a mixture of minced pork meats and brown rice makes an agreeable alternative. Serves 4.

1.1 kg [2½ lb] Savoy or other green cabbage with large, firm, crinkly leaves
75 g [3 oz] hazelnuts
75 g [3 oz] butter
a small onion
a bunch of parsley
the finely grated zest of a lemon
45 ml [3 tablespoons] fresh breadcrumbs
2 eggs
salt and freshly ground black pepper

Trim the cabbage stalk, reserve 8 fine large outside leaves and shred the remainder. Cook the shredded cabbage and finely chopped onion very gently in the butter over low heat for about 20 minutes. Away from the heat, beat in the breadcrumbs, roughly chopped nuts, parsley, lemon zest, lightly beaten eggs and a generous seasoning of salt and pepper.

Line a sieve with a large piece of butter muslin, and suspend it over a mixing bowl. Arrange the reserved cabbage leaves, stalk end downwards, in the sieve, overlapping the leaves slightly so that there are no gaps. Pile the filling mixture into the centre. Pull the cloth tightly round the cabbage, so that the original neat cabbage shape is re-formed, and tie it securely with string.

Lower the parcel into a large pan of salted boiling water. Bring quickly back to the boil, cover with a lid and simmer for about 20 minutes. Drain very thoroughly before carefully unwrapping and turning the cabbage out onto a hot serving dish.

Sicilian Cauliflower Cheese

Not suitable for those with delicate digestions (and too pungently flavoured for the taste of most children), but the sort of lunch dish that is very welcome, and suitably robust, after a long morning's blustery walk. Serves 4.

a large cauliflower
250 g [½ lb] onions
2 garlic cloves
50 g [2 oz] black olives
half a can of anchovy fillets
120 ml [8 tablespoons] olive oil
200 ml [7 fl oz] red wine
50 g [2 oz] grated cheese — strong Cheddar and Parmesan mixed together
a bunch of parsley.

Choose a flameproof casserole or heavy-based saucepan into which the whole cauliflower (trimmed of leaves and tough stalk end) will fit snugly. Warm the olive oil in it and cook the chopped onions gently for about 10 minutes to soften them slightly.

Meanwhile, stone and slice the olives. Mix them in a bowl with the crushed garlic, snipped anchovy fillets (reserve the anchovy oil) and the wine.

Tip the contents of the bowl into the casserole and bring to the

boil stirring. Lay the whole trimmed cauliflower in the casserole
— stalk end down — drizzle on the anchovy oil and sprinkle on
the cheese. Cover the casserole with a lid and cook over very low
heat for about half an hour until the cauliflower is perfectly
tender — the thick cauliflower base will cook in the liquid while
the delicate florets cook in the steam without fear of disintegration.

Lift out the cauliflower onto a hot serving dish. Boil the sauce
for a few minutes to reduce it a little. Pour it over the cauliflower,
scatter generously with chopped parsley, and serve with lots of
crusty bread and a fairly coarse wine.

Gratin of Cauliflower Cheese

In complete contrast to the last recipe, this version of cauliflower
cheese is creamy and soothing. Serves 4.

1 large cauliflower
a bunch of watercress
125 g [¼ lb] mixed freshly grated Gruyère and Parmesan cheese (or Cheddar)
3 eggs
150 ml [¼ pt] double cream
8 rashers streaky bacon
salt, pepper and nutmeg

Break the cauliflower into sprigs and steam until tender. Put
them into a liquidiser and season with plenty of pepper, nutmeg
and a little salt. Pour on the cream and reduce to a purée. Strip the
leaves from the watercress and roughly chop them. Stir them
into the cauliflower purée together with three-quarters of the
cheese and the lightly beaten eggs. Turn the mixture into a
buttered gratin dish, stand it on a preheated baking tray and cook
in the oven at 200°C [400°F], gas mark 6, for 20–25 minutes.

Remove the rind and halve the bacon rashers. Stretch each
piece with the back of a knife, roll it up and lay it, seam-side
down, on a baking tray. Cook on the bottom shelf of the oven
while the gratin cooks at the top.

Serve the gratin topped with bacon rolls. Triangles of fried
bread also go very well with this dish.

Crêpes Florentine with Mushrooms

Both pancakes and filling can be made ahead for this simple but excellent dish. Serves 4.

For the pancakes:
1 × 225 g [8 oz] packet frozen whole leaf spinach
50 g [2 oz] wholewheat flour
50 g [2 oz] plain white flour
2 eggs
125 ml [4 fl oz] milk
175 ml [6 fl oz] water
25 g [1 oz] melted butter
salt, pepper and nutmeg

For the filling and topping:
700 g [1½ lb] cap mushrooms, thickly sliced
65 g [2½ oz] butter
225 ml [8 fl oz] double cream
65 g [2½ oz] mature Cheddar cheese
salt and freshly ground black pepper

Puréed spinach makes rather dull eating; it is well worth seeking out the whole leaf variety. Defrost it in a sieve placed over a bowl (this takes several hours) then squeeze it with your hands to extract as much moisture as possible, and chop fairly finely. Put it into a measuring jug — 65 ml [2½ fl oz] are needed for this recipe.

To make the pancakes, beat the eggs, spinach, milk and water together and blend them gradually into the flours (well-seasoned with salt, pepper and a little nutmeg) to make a creamy batter. Stir in the cool melted butter. Use the batter to make 16–18 thin pancakes, each 15 cm [6 inches] in diameter, cooking them over medium-low heat for about 30–45 seconds on one side and for less than 30 seconds on the other. Stir the batter well from time to time or the bran and spinach may sink to the bottom of the mixture.

Cool the pancakes on a cake rack, then stack, interleaving them with greaseproof paper. They may then be wrapped in foil and refrigerated for up to 5 days. Remove the pancake parcel from the fridge a good hour before stuffing.

To make the filling, heat a large frying pan over medium-high heat. Add half the butter and, when it stops foaming, add half the mushrooms. Turn the mushrooms briskly, to coat each with a little fat, and fry for 5–7 minutes. (The small quantity of fat makes for very mushroomy tasting results.) Fry the second batch of mushrooms in the same way, then return all the mushrooms to the pan. Pour on 150 ml [¼ pt] cream and add a very generous seasoning of salt and pepper. Let the cream bubble up and reduce for 3–5 minutes while you stir and turn the mushrooms — each slice should be coated with a thin veneer of rich, seasoned cream. Cool completely, cover and chill if preparing ahead.

To serve, divide the mushroom mixture between the pancakes. Roll them up neatly and pile them into a lightly buttered gratin dish. Cover the dish with a dome of foil and heat through in the oven for 20 minutes at 200°C [400°F], gas mark 6. Mix the grated cheese and remaining cream to a paste. Spread it over the top of the pancakes and return the dish to the oven, without the foil covering, for 7–10 minutes until the topping has melted to a hot cheesy glaze.

Pancakes with Chicory & Ham

This is a lighter variation on the popular but rather heavy supper dish of chicory and ham rolls coated in a floury cheese sauce. Serves 4.

For the pancakes:
50 g [2 oz] plain flour
50 g [2 oz] wholewheat flour
2 eggs
150 ml [¼ pt] each milk and water
25 g [1 oz] melted butter
salt, pepper and nutmeg

For the filling and topping:
6 small chicons
12 thin slices of ham
a little Dijon mustard
125 g [¼ lb] Cheddar cheese
150 ml [¼ pt] soured cream
150 ml [¼ pt] double cream
salt and freshly ground black pepper

Make the batter along the lines described in the previous recipe and use it to make 12 fairly thick, English-style pancakes.

Steam the whole chicons for about 18 minutes until tender. When cool, squeeze gently in paper towels to extract excess juice, and cut each one in half lengthways.

Lay a slice of ham on each pancake. Smear it with mustard and sprinkle with a little grated cheese. Lay a piece of chicory on top, roll up and place in a buttered gratin dish. Cover the dish with foil and bake for 15–20 minutes at 200°C [400°F], gas mark 6. Pour on the soured and fresh double creams beaten together with some of the cheese, a little salt and plenty of pepper. Scatter the remaining grated cheese over the top and bake, without the foil covering, for a further 10–15 minutes.

Pancakes with Celery & Ham: For a different flavour replace chicory with steamed celery hearts. Save the outer stalks for salads or crudités, or to serve with cheese.

Imam Bayaldi

This famous Turkish dish makes a lovely item for the cold buffet table. Be sure to salt the aubergines or they will absorb an extravagant quantity of oil and the final dish may be greasy. Serves 6.

3 large aubergines
350 g [¾ lb] onions
350 g [¾ lb] tomatoes
2 fat garlic cloves
50 g [2 oz] raisins
50 g [2 oz] pinenuts or split almonds
3 ml [½ teaspoon] each cumin seeds and ground cinnamon
150 ml [¼ pt] olive oil
5 ml [1 teaspoon] caster sugar
a large lemon
parsley
salt and freshly ground black pepper
lemon wedges to garnish

Halve the aubergines lengthways. Scoop out the pulp, taking care not to pierce the skins. Dice the pulp, put it into a colander, sprinkle coarse salt between layers, cover with a plate and weigh it down lightly. Set aside for about 1 hour to draw out excess juices. Salt the aubergine shells as well. Rinse and dry pulp and shells.

To prepare the stuffing warm half the olive oil in a wide saucepan. Add the crushed garlic and cumin seeds, the finely chopped onions and the prepared aubergine pulp. Fry gently for 10 minutes or so until the onions are softened and slightly coloured. Stir in the cinnamon, and the skinned and chopped tomatoes. Increase the heat a little and cook, stirring often, for another 10 minutes or so until the tomatoes have pulped down and most of their moisture has evaporated. Away from the heat stir in the raisins and nuts, and add salt, pepper and lemon juice to taste.

Choose a baking dish large enough to take the aubergine shells in one layer, but without leaving much space in-between — it is best if the aubergines just touch each other. Fill the aubergine shells with the stuffing, and place them side by side in the dish. Carefully pour more lemon juice and the remaining olive oil round the aubergine shells (but not into them). Add the sugar, some crushed parsley stalks and enough hot water to come at least halfway up the sides of the aubergine shells.

Cover the dish with a dome of foil and cook in an oven preheated to 160°C [325°F], gas mark 3, for about 1 hour. Remove the dish from the oven as soon as the aubergines are cooked, but leave them in the cooking liquor until quite cold.

Once cold, carefully lift the aubergines out of the dish onto a serving plate, using a slotted spoon and a fish slice. (Or, if the dish is pretty enough to use for serving, simply drain off the cooking liquor using a bulb baster.) Cover the aubergines once more with foil and refrigerate until about 30 minutes before serving. Garnish with fresh chopped parsley and wedges of lemon.

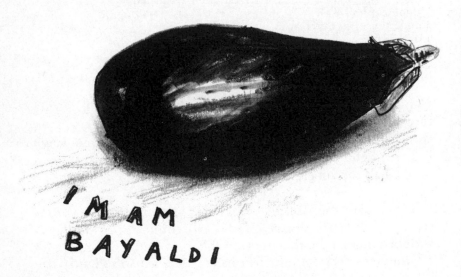

'M AM
BAYALDI

Isfahan Aubergines with Lamb

Another rather special aubergine dish, using many of the same ingredients as the last recipe, but this one is served hot. Again, it involves quite a bit of work for the cook, but most of the preparations can be done in the morning, leaving you only to layer the dish and to put it into the oven in the evening. Serves 6.

700 g [1½ lb] lean boneless lamb
a generous kilo [2½ lb] aubergines
2 large onions
1 fat garlic clove
5 ml [1 teaspoon] each cumin seeds and turmeric
25 g [1 oz] pinenuts or blanched and roughly chopped almonds
450 ml [generous ¾ pt] chicken stock
225 g [½ lb] long-grain rice
a little olive and sunflower oil
salt and freshly ground black pepper

Cut the aubergines into large dice without peeling them. Divide between 2 colanders, sprinkling coarse salt between layers, top with a plate apiece, weigh down and leave for at least 30 minutes to draw off some of the liquid.

Meanwhile chop the onions and cook gently in a little oil until slightly softened, then increase heat and fry until coloured. Set aside and cool. Cut the lamb into 1 cm [½ inch] squares. Mix the raw meat with the cumin seeds, nuts, crushed garlic and lots of pepper. When the onion is cold, stir it into the meat.

Drain the salted aubergine and squeeze it dry with your hands. Fry in batches in very hot oil over medium-high heat, stirring and turning occasionally until golden. Lift out the aubergines with a slotted spoon and let them drain and cool on a baking sheet lined with kitchen paper. Add the rice to the fat remaining in the pan and stir over low heat for 2–3 minutes until transparent. Season with salt and pepper and spread the rice over the base of a large casserole.

In the evening, salt the cold lamb mixture and spread it over the rice. Bring the stock to the boil, stir in the turmeric, and pour it into the casserole — the liquid should barely cover the meat. Pile the cold aubergine on top and cook, without a lid, for 1–1¼ hours at 160°C [325°F], gas mark 3.

Persian Spinach with Chick-Peas & Meatballs

Spinach is one of my favourite vegetables. Here it is combined with chick-peas and smooth-textured meatballs for a pleasing contrast of flavours and textures. Serves 6.

1½ kg [3 lb] spinach
175–225 g [6–8 oz] chick-peas
450 g [1 lb] braising steak or lean boneless lamb
2 garlic cloves
5 ml [1 teaspoon] turmeric
a few spoonfuls of yoghurt
salt and freshly ground black pepper
butter and oil for frying

Soak the chick-peas overnight. Drain and simmer in fresh water for about 2 hours until tender.

Mince the meat very finely and turn it into a bowl. Add 1 garlic clove crushed with 5 ml [1 teaspoon] salt, the turmeric and plenty of pepper. Mix together until well blended and very smooth, and shape into about 40 marble-sized balls.

Thoroughly wash the spinach in several changes of cold salted water and remove any tough stalks. Shake the spinach dry and pack it into a very large saucepan — you may find it easier to cook it in batches. Cover and cook over medium heat for 2–3 minutes until the leaves have wilted (turn the leaves once or twice during this time to encourage even cooking). Then remove the lid and continue cooking, still stirring occasionally, for another 3 minutes or so until the spinach is just tender and most of the moisture has been driven off. Turn off the heat, add a good seasoning of salt and pepper, a crushed garlic clove and 3 or 4 spoonfuls of yoghurt. Toss gently.

Keep the spinach hot while you fry the meatballs for 3–4 minutes in a large heavy-based pan over fairly high heat until crisp and golden brown. Drain the meatballs well, mix them with the cooked chick-peas and pile them onto the bed of spinach. Serve with bowls of chilled yoghurt.

Lentils with Salamelle

Salamelle is a highly spiced boiling sausage, similar to salami, which you can buy from Italian shops and good delicatessens. I think it is the best of all sausages, and particularly well partnered by the earthy flavour of puréed lentils. Serves 6.

500–700 g [1–1½ lb] salamelle sausages
700 g [1½ lb] whole green-grey lentils
2 onions
50 g [2 oz] butter
a bunch of coriander or parsley
salt and freshly ground black pepper
warm water or tomato juice

Rinse the lentils in a sieve under a cold running tap. Pick them over carefully and remove any little sticks and pieces of grit. Cook the finely chopped onions in the melted butter for 5 minutes. Add the well-drained lentils and stir for a minute or two to coat with fat. Pour on warm water or tomato juice to cover them and bring to the boil. Cover with a lid and simmer very gently for about 1¼ hours or until the lentils begin to disintegrate. Drain off most of the liquid (it has a delicious flavour so save it for a soup). Return the lentils to the pan, place over very low heat and beat briefly with a balloon whisk or wooden spoon until slightly dried out and reduced to a semi-purée — generally smooth yet retaining a little knobbly texture, like good tweed. Season with salt and pepper (not heavily in view of the spiciness of the sausages) and pile onto a hot serving dish.

When the vegetables are nearly ready, drop the whole sausages into a pan of boiling water and cook at a bare simmer for 10–15 minutes. Drain and slice them thickly (cut them up on a plate so you catch the richly flavoured meat juices that escape as you slice). Pile the sausages on top of the lentils, pour on their juices and scatter with plenty of coarsely chopped fresh herbs. Serve with good bread and a plain green salad.

Garbanzos y Chorizo: This is a Spanish variation of the pulses and sausages theme. Cabanos can be used if chorizo is not available. Soak 500-700 g [1-1½ lb] chick-peas overnight, then simmer them in fresh unsalted water for about 2½ hours until really tender. Season and reduce to a purée, moistening them with a generous lump of butter and some of their cooking liquor. Mound on a serving dish, pour on 150 ml [¼ pt] yoghurt beaten with 3 or 4 crushed garlic cloves, dust with paprika and surround with hot slices of sausage.

Courgette Flan

The nutty flavour of wholewheat pastry goes well with courgettes. Like all savoury custard flans, this is best eaten warm — not the moment it comes out of the oven but 5–10 minutes later. Serves 4.

shortcrust pastry made with 75 g [3 oz] each butter, plain and wholewheat flour
350 g [¾ lb] courgettes
1 small onion
2 eggs
25 g [1 oz] butter
150 ml [¼ pt] single cream
15 ml [1 tablespoon] freshly grated Parmesan cheese
nutmeg, salt and freshly ground black pepper

Make the pastry and use it to line a 20 cm [8 inch] fluted flan tin with a removable base. Partially blind-bake the pastry at 200°C [400°F], gas mark 6, standing the flan tin on a preheated baking tray, and using a little egg white from the filling ingredients to brush the pastry base and sides.

Chop the onion finely and soften it in the butter over low heat for 5 minutes. Slice the courgettes and add them to the pan. Increase heat slightly and fry for 5–6 minutes until lightly coloured. Beat the eggs in a bowl, then add the cream, Parmesan, a little nutmeg and some salt and pepper and beat again.

Reduce the oven temperature to 180°C [350°F], gas mark 4. Fill the pastry case with the courgette and onion mixture and pour on the custard. Bake on the preheated baking sheet for 25–30 minutes until the custard is slightly puffed, pale gold and just set firm.

Eggah Omelette

An Egyptian recipe for courgettes, this is quite different from a French omelette, and not as heavy as a Spanish tortilla. It is equally good hot or cold. For picnics, cut the cold omelette into

wedges and wrap in lettuce leaves to make breadless sandwiches.
Serves 4.

8 fairly small courgettes
8 eggs
30 ml [2 tablespoons] each fresh chopped parsley and chives
25 g [1 oz] butter
15 ml [1 tablespoon] oil
60 ml [4 tablespoons] freshly grated Parmesan cheese
salt and freshly ground black pepper

Top, tail and slice the courgettes, but do not peel them. Fry them
in the butter and oil in a 25 cm [10 inch] frying pan until golden,
then drain most of the fat from the pan.

Beat the eggs and season with the herbs, salt and pepper. Pour
the mixture over the courgettes. Don't touch it at all, just leave it
alone to cook fairly gently until the bottom of the omelette is set.

Sprinkle on the cheese, and transfer the pan to a preheated grill.
Continue cooking until the omelette is set (quite firmly set if the
omelette is to be eaten cold) and the top is golden brown.

Piperade

I serve this summery vegetable and egg dish for lunch with
plenty of fried bread triangles and a crisp green salad. Serves 2–3.

1 large Spanish onion
1–2 garlic cloves
2 large red peppers
450 g [1 lb] firm tomatoes
6–8 eggs
a few slices of Bayonne ham (optional)
fresh chopped basil or marjoram
15 ml [1 tablespoon] olive oil
40 g [1½ oz] butter
salt and freshly ground black pepper

Cut the peppers into quarters, lengthways, remove seeds and
pith, and flatten the flesh as much as possible. Cook under a very
hot grill until the papery-thin skins blacken and blister. Peel
away the skins as soon as the peppers are cool enough to handle,
then cut the flesh into strips. Quarter the onion, then slice very
thinly. Chop the garlic very finely. Skin, seed and cut the tomato
flesh into large chunks. Break the eggs into a bowl: beat lightly

and season with salt, pepper and fresh chopped herbs. (All these preparations can be done well in advance, but be sure to keep each vegetable in a separate covered bowl. Mixing the herbs with the eggs an hour or so before cooking will heighten the herb flavour.)

Melt the butter and the olive oil in a large saucepan. Add the garlic and onion and cook over low heat for 7–10 minutes until softened. Increase the heat a little and cook the onion and garlic for a further 2–3 minutes until beginning to colour. Add the peppers and cook, stirring occasionally, for 5 minutes. Then add the tomatoes and cook for a further 5 minutes, again stirring occasionally. Pour the eggs into the pan and cook, stirring, until they are thick and creamy like lightly scrambled eggs. Serve immediately, spooning the mixture straight from the pan onto warmed plates — on which you may have placed some slices of ham.

Spinach Gnocchi

These feathery light vegetable dumplings are best eaten as soon as possible after cooking so I don't recommend making more than this quantity at a time. Serves 4 as a first course, or 2 people as a lunch or supper dish.

450 g [1 lb] fresh spinach or 225 g [½ lb] frozen whole leaf spinach
225 g [½ lb] ricotta or cottage cheese
2 egg yolks
45 ml [3 tablespoons] plain flour
60 ml [4 tablespoons] freshly grated Parmesan cheese
salt, pepper and nutmeg

If using frozen spinach, thaw it completely and squeeze out all moisture; then chop it. There is no need to cook the spinach.

Thoroughly wash fresh spinach, discarding any tough stalks and yellowing leaves. Weigh out 350 g [¾ lb] spinach (save the rest for a salad). Pack it into a saucepan. Cover and cook over medium-low heat, turning the leaves occasionally, for 6–7 minutes, until quite tender. Turn the spinach into a sieve and press with a wooden spoon to extract as much moisture as possible, then chop it finely. Set aside to cool.

Sieve the ricotta or cottage cheese into a mixing bowl. Add the

spinach and beat to mix well. Lightly whisk the egg yolks and beat them into the mixture. Sift in 30 ml [2 tablespoons] plain flour, and the same quantity of grated Parmesan cheese and beat again. Season to taste with salt, pepper and nutmeg. Spread the mixture on a plate and chill for at least 2 hours, or overnight if more convenient.

Sprinkle a tablespoon of flour on a working surface. Drop small blobs of the mixture onto it, one at a time. Turn them over, then roll them between the palms of your hands and shape into small balls — about 32 in all.

Bring some salted water to the boil in a large sauté pan. Reduce the heat to a bare simmer. Drop about half the gnocchi into the pan and cook them, uncovered, at the gentlest simmer for about 5 minutes (if the water is boiling or the pan overcrowded, the gnocchi will disintegrate).

Lift out with a draining spoon, blot on kitchen paper and keep warm in a low oven while you cook the rest. Sprinkle the remaining 30 ml [2 tablespoons] Parmesan cheese over the gnocchi and serve with extra grated cheese and a bowl of melted butter.

Hot Potato & Frankfurter Salad

This is a quick, easy and very good lunch dish, which lends itself well to additions and variations. I sometimes include slivers of Florentine fennel and/or diced cucumber, or garnish the dish with clumps of mustard and cress, for example, and I have used canned tuna fish instead of sausages. The excellent and rapidly made mustardy sauce also goes very well with such fish as smoked mackerel and smoked trout. Serves 6.

1.3 kg [3 lb] waxy new potatoes
450 g [1 lb] frankfurter sausages
at least 120 ml [8 tablespoons] fresh snipped chives

For the sauce:
2 egg yolks
25 ml [2 scant tablespoons] caster sugar
45–60 ml [3–4 tablespoons] Dijon mustard
45 ml [3 tablespoons] wine vinegar
275 ml [½ pt] oil — ideally a little olive oil and mostly sunflower or safflower oil
salt and freshly ground black pepper

Choose even-sized potatoes. Lightly scrub them, but do not rub away the skins. Drop them into fast-boiling salted water and simmer until tender. Take great care not to overcook — mushiness ruins potato salads.

Meanwhile make the sauce. Beat the egg yolks, sugar and mustard together in a bowl. Add the vinegar, a spoonful at a time, whisking it in with a balloon whisk. Then add the oils, pouring them from a jug in a thin stream and whisking them into the egg mixture all the time as you pour. Continue whisking for a minute or so until the sauce is a homogeneous thick cream, then season with salt and pepper.

Heat the sausages by dropping them into a pan of freshly boiled water, cover and set aside for 5 minutes or so. Drain and slice thickly.

Thoroughly drain the potatoes, turn them into a pretty serving bowl and cut them up into bite-sized chunks if large. Add the sausages and sprinkle on most of the chives. Pour on the sauce and toss lightly to coat all the ingredients well. Scatter on the remaining chives and serve the salad while still fairly hot.

Welsh Leek & Potato Pie

I have to be forcibly restrained from third helpings of this comforting supper dish. A favourite for Sunday evenings with a green salad and cheese to follow. Serves 4.

900 g [2 lb] potatoes
600 g [1¼ lb] leeks
1 small onion
250 g [generous ½ lb] streaky bacon rashers
about 75 g [3 oz] butter
about 150 ml [¼ pt] hot chicken stock
about 150 ml [¼ pt] single cream
a little fresh chopped parsley
salt and freshly ground black pepper

Finely chop the onion, and thinly slice the leeks (tender green parts as well as white). Cut the bacon into matchstick strips. Cook all three ingredients in the butter in a covered pan over low heat for 5–7 minutes. Strain off and reserve the buttery juices. Season the bacon and leek mixture with a little salt (taste bacon to check saltiness) and plenty of pepper.

Preheat the oven to 200°C [400°F], gas mark 6, and peel and slice the potatoes very thinly. Butter a gratin dish measuring 20 cm × 28 cm [7½ in × 11½ in]. Layer it with potatoes and the bacon and leek mixture, beginning and ending with the potatoes, and seasoning each potato layer with salt and pepper. Press the ingredients down with a potato masher. Pour on the reserved buttery juices and enough hot stock to come more or less level with the top layer of potatoes.

Bake uncovered for 45–50 minutes until the potatoes are tender, but not disintegrated, and the liquid has been absorbed or evaporated. Switch off the oven. Dribble the cream over the vegetables and shake the dish so that the cream trickles down through the layers. Return the dish to the residual heat of the oven for 10–15 minutes, then sprinkle with chopped parsley and serve.

Potato Gratin with Herbs & Cheese: For a similar dish omit the leeks, onion, bacon and cream. Replace them with a bunch each of parsley and chives, 100 g [¼ lb] ham cut into matchstick strips, and 75 g [3 oz] mature grated Cheddar. Butter the gratin dish very generously and interlayer the sliced potatoes with a mixture of chopped herbs, snippets of ham and grated cheese, plus a good seasoning of pepper. Pour on 300 ml [½ pt] boiling stock, sprinkle on a final handful of grated cheese and bake as described.

Rice & Pasta

tagliatelle

ruote

spaghetti

fusilli

conchiglie

stellini

arborio

farfalle

patna rice

Rice and Pasta:
some examples

brown long grain

basmati

The main grain crop in Britain is *Triticum vulgare*, or common wheat, and we use it almost exclusively in its ground form — as flour for making pastry and bread.

Over the past decade or so, however, general recognition of the importance of fibre in the diet has brought about changes in our attitudes and tastes. Flour that is bleached and refined until it is as fine, snowy white and soft as icing sugar is now held in less esteem. We have come to appreciate the virtues of rougher flours that include *all* the goodness and fibre of wheat (in fact everything except the inedible outer husk of the grain). The pappy sliced white loaf is gradually being ousted; growing numbers demand real bread with the natural flavour of wholewheat and a texture you can get your teeth into.

Paralleling this trend towards healthier home-produced wheat products is a growing awareness of, and interest in, other grains. Foreign travel and the new richness and diversity of restaurants based on foreign cuisines, have introduced us to the grains and grain products that are staple foods in other parts of the world. We are beginning to appreciate that using these alternatives at home can bring welcome variety to our own cooking, now that modern trading and communications have made them available to us.

Millet, buckwheat and rye (and products made from them) have not yet won the hearts of or even seriously caught the imagination of the British public as a whole, and I confess I am not greatly enamoured of the dishes using them which I have tried. Moreover, these ingredients remain somewhat difficult to buy at present, unless you live near an exceptional delicatessen, a specialist grocer or a health food shop. On the other hand, whole toasted and rolled or flaked oats, corn, barley and wheat have gained considerable popularity and are widely available, loose or made up into muesli-type breakfast foods. However, the grain products which have been adopted with the most whole-hearted enthusiasm are rice and pasta, and it is with these two items that this chapter is concerned.

Vegetarians and anyone who is seriously trying to reduce the meat products and thus animal fats in their diet will always want to choose wholegrains, and to avoid refined products completely, so as to get maximum nutrients from grains. But others, who like me merely seek to make their cooking as varied and interesting as possible, but would like to increase the fibre in their diet, will take pleasure in using pasta and rice in all their forms.

Rice.   It seems only very few years ago that rice was solely identified in Britain with milk puddings, but today even supermarkets offer a selection of different types of rice, and we have come to value this grain as an excellent foundation for the creation of many varied and imaginative savoury dishes which cost little in time or money.

White long-grain rice, or Patna rice as it is sometimes called, is probably the most popular rice on sale today. It is certainly the most versatile, having an almost chameleon-like quality that enables it to blend into and bulk out composite dishes with ease. When white rice is plainly boiled and fluffed with a fork it makes an attractive and suitably bland accompaniment to many meat dishes in lieu of the ubiquitous potato purée. Plain boiled long-grain rice, incidentally, does not have to be served immediately. Providing the rice is cooked until just tender you can drain, fluff and turn it into a warmed and well-buttered casserole, place a folded teatowel on top, cover the dish with a well-fitting lid and keep it hot in a low oven for 20–30 minutes without spoiling.

Basmati is a type of long-grain rice I use comparatively rarely. It is not particularly cheap and, perhaps because of this, it is not as widely available as other types. It does, however, have superb flavour and is the traditional top quality rice of India, which makes it the obvious choice for authentic curries and kormas, and for Indian-inspired dishes such as my recipe for boxwallah's kedgeree.

Brown long-grain rice (i.e. long-grain rice that has not been subjected to refining treatments and polishings) is much denser than white rice in texture and is agreeably nutty. I find you need less per serving. Because it has much more character, and because it is richer in fibre and nutrients, it is not so suited to playing a secondary role. But it is the perfect choice for recipes such as mildly spiced rice or green rice salad. These dishes can be served alone as light main courses, or made more substantial by garnishing with additional ingredients.

Italian rice, usually called avorio or arborio, is slightly plumper and shorter. It is a medium-grain rice which, like brown rice, is best served as a dish in its own right. Unlike other rices, it should be stirred as it cooks and it develops a characteristic creaminess on the outside whilst remaining firm in the kernel. It is my favourite of all rices — in fact risotto alla milanese is a dish I cannot live without for more than a few weeks at a stretch!

Pasta is essentially friendly food. I always associate it with happy, relaxed occasions, perhaps partly because the Italians have the happy knack of regarding cooking as a joyous occupation which culminates in the gathering together of family and friends, not only to share the meal, but to recount the day's events with animated rapture. Pasta is made from *Triticum durum*, the wheat from which semolina is made, a much harder grain than the common wheat, from which ordinary baking flour is produced. Pasta is an earthy brown colour when made from the whole wheat, pale cream when made from refined grains, a deeper yellow when enriched with eggs, and pale green when spinach has been added. All kinds are delicious and I think it a pity to use one sort exclusively, just as it would be boring always to cook spaghetti and never to try any of the other, often amazing and intriguingly named, shapes.

I must admit, however, that there are certain pasta shapes I deliberately avoid — shell shapes, for example, are exceedingly difficult to drain completely of all the water in which they have been cooked. The recipes given here are based on using the tubular shapes and twists and the long thin pasta strands. I find these so generally useful that I keep them in permanent stock in my store-cupboard.

Short tubular shapes or spirals, such as macaroni, fusilli and bucatini, are excellent for buffet dishes. These pasta pieces are short enough to be eaten tidily with a fork when standing, and even quite small children seem to cope well. They are also perfect for layering with other ingredients in composite dishes such as pastitsio and Roman pie. (The latter is served cold, incidentally.)

Long pasta strands, whether flat ribbons or rounded shapes, such as tagliatelle (or fettucine as the Romans call it), spaghetti, trenette and so on, are the most successful vehicles for the greatest variety of sauces. Providing you choose a sauce which is quickly cooked, as are most of those in this chapter, these pasta dishes are very speedily prepared. They make satisfying main courses if you allow about 115 g [4 oz] pasta per person, which need only be followed by a simple salad and cheese or a fruit pudding.

Plenty of water is needed for cooking pasta — about 4 litres [7 pt] for every 450 g [1 lb] of pasta. Salt it and add a dribble of oil to prevent sticking. Cook the pasta at a rapid boil, without covering the pan, until it is al dente, that is tender yet still slightly firm to the bite. How long this takes depends on the type and shape of the pasta and on the manufacturer: the only way to gauge it correctly is to test and taste the pasta frequently as it cooks. If in doubt, draw the pan away from the heat sooner rather than later as pasta continues to soften slightly even when removed from the source of heat. Drain pasta quickly but thoroughly in a colander and serve it as soon as possible. I find the best way to ensure everything is fresh, piping hot and served with minimum delay is to make the sauce in a large flameproof casserole while the pasta is cooking. The drained pasta can then be turned directly into the heated casserole, lightly tossed with salad servers to coat every strand with the sauce and carried straight to the table. Using one and the same dish for sauce making and serving clearly also saves on washing up.

Perhaps my favourite of all pasta dishes, and certainly the most useful, is garlic-buttered tagliatelle (fruity flavoured virgin olive oil can be used instead of butter if you wish to serve this dish in the Roman manner). It is a classic example of how very few, very simple ingredients can be made into an exquisite dish, if thought rather than much time — or money — is spent on its making.

Green Rice Salad

A pretty salad which can be served as a first course, or as part of a buffet, or as an accompaniment to cold roast duck. To make the salad into a more substantial lunch dish, omit the cucumber and garnish with extra ingredients such as sliced raw mushrooms with freshly steamed mussels or boiled prawns. Another delicious combination to add to the basic salad is a few slivers of fennel, some watercress sprigs, the segments of a grapefruit or orange and plenty of crunchy whole, toasted almonds.

250 g [½ lb] brown rice
2 green peppers
half a cucumber

For the dressing:
a fat garlic clove
two-thirds of a lemon
30 ml [2 tablespoons] capers
a bunch of parsley
a bunch of chives
about 125 ml [4 fl oz] oil, preferably half olive oil and half peanut or sunflower
   oil
salt and freshly ground black pepper

Simmer the rice in well-salted water in a tight-lidded pan until tender — about 40 minutes.

Meanwhile make the dressing. Crush the garlic with plenty of salt. Put it into a liquidiser with a good grinding of pepper, the juice and grated zest of the lemon, the parsley, chives, capers and most of the oil. Reduce to a green-flecked purée. Taste and add extra oil and/or seasonings as necessary.

Turn the cooked rice into a bowl. Fluff it with a fork and stir in as much of the dressing as the rice is willing to soak up. Fold in slivers of green pepper and diced and seeded (but unpeeled) cucumber.

Mildly Spiced Rice

If white rice is used, this delicately spiced dish makes a good accompaniment to curried meats and poultry. Using brown rice, you can top it with hot hard-boiled eggs just before serving, and this makes a main-course dish in its own right. Bowls of fresh chopped mint and coriander leaves, sliced bananas, deep-fried onions, good chutney, chilled yoghurt and poppadoms make attractive and appetising side-dishes. Serves 8–10.

600 g [1¼ lb] long-grain white or brown rice
2 onions
ghee or clarified butter
10 ml [2 teaspoons] turmeric
10 ml [2 teaspoons] ground cinnamon
5 ml [1 teaspoon] allspice
plenty of salt and freshly ground black pepper
chicken stock or water

Chop the onions finely and soften them in a generous quantity of fat for 10–15 minutes. Add the spices and stir them for a few seconds before adding the rice. Turn the rice in the fat for a couple of minutes then pour on boiling liquid equal to twice the volume of the rice — either salted water or, preferably, chicken stock. Stir the pan once, cover it with a well-fitting lid and leave over the lowest possible heat for 15 minutes (or 40 minutes for brown rice), by the end of which time the rice will be swollen and tender and no liquid will remain in the pan. Check seasoning and fluff the rice before serving.

Risotto alla Milanese

Fragrant and distinguished, yet quick, easy and inexpensive, risotto is my idea of the perfect dish for Sunday supper, or any other meal when you want something light, but more substantial than, say, an omelette. It is also invaluable for emergencies because its few ingredients are all store-cupboard items. Serves 4–6 as a main course.

450 g [1 lb] arborio or avorio rice
a few saffron strands
100 g [¼ lb] butter
1 small onion
a small glass of white wine or very dry cider (optional)
about 2 litres [3½ pt] piping hot chicken or fish stock
freshly grated Parmesan cheese
salt and freshly ground black pepper

Melt half the butter in a flameproof casserole or heavy-based saucepan. Add the finely chopped onion and cook gently for about 5 minutes. Meanwhile, pound then soak the saffron in a little of the very hot stock.

Tip the rice into the pan and cook, stirring continuously for a minute or two, until coated all over with fat. Keeping the heat low, add the wine or cider, if you wish, or a small ladleful of the hot stock (if your stock is made from a commercial stock cube, the inclusion of wine or cider will greatly improve the risotto). Let the rice simmer, uncovered, until the liquid is almost completely absorbed. Stir the rice lightly to prevent it sticking to the pan base and add another ladleful of stock.

Continue adding more stock each time the previous ladleful is absorbed, adding the saffron-flavoured stock towards the end. Stir lightly as necessary; don't cover the pan. The rice is ready when it is creamy and tender with just a hint of bite to the centre of each grain — about 20–25 minutes' cooking time.

Switch off the heat but keep the pan on the stove. Stir in the remaining butter cut into small dice. Add a good seasoning of pepper, some salt and a few spoonfuls of grated Parmesan cheese. Stir again and serve the risotto as soon as the cheese has melted. Put a bowl of Parmesan cheese on the table so that people can help themselves to more.

Variations: Meat, fish or vegetables can be incorporated into a risotto, but remember that risotto is essentially a simple dish of fragrant rice, so treat any "extras" accordingly, more as a garnish than a major ingredient. Add just a few fried mushroom slices, steamed mussels, or sautéed chicken livers, for example. Always use fresh foods, never pre-cooked leftovers. Cook them in a separate pan while the rice simmers and stir them into the risotto just before serving.

Indonesian Fried Rice with Spring Omelettes

Great fun to cook and eat, and pleasantly cheap on the pocket, this is very popular for a young people's supper party. Don't be daunted by the length of the recipe, it is really quite simple, but I

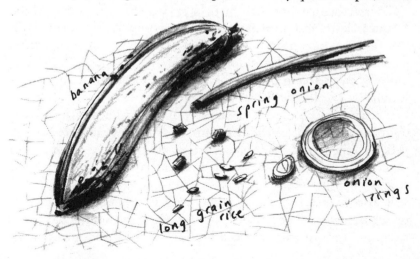

have described everything in detail so that two teenagers can organise and do all the cooking for themselves. They will need two large frying pans. Serves 6–8.

For the Indonesian rice:
450 g [1 lb] long-grain rice
225 g [½ lb] onions, peeled weight
6 fat garlic cloves
150 ml [¼ pt] peanut oil
30 ml [2 tablespoons] anchovy essence
10 ml [2 teaspoons] coriander seeds
5 ml [1 teaspoon] chilli powder
250–350 g [½–¾ lb] ham or cold cooked pork
60 ml [4 tablespoons] soy souce
salt

For the side-dishes:
2 large cucumbers
8 large bananas
450 g [1 lb] onions
225 g [½lb] dry roasted or salted peanuts
12 eggs
1 bunch spring onions
lots of poppadoms
a little butter and peanut oil
the juice of 1 lemon
soy sauce
salt and freshly ground black pepper

The main part of the dish is the rice. This must be boiled a day, or at least several hours, ahead so that it is completely cold for frying just before serving.

To boil the rice, bring 1.1 litres [2 pt] water to the boil. Add the rice and a large spoonful of salt and bring quickly back to the boil. Stir once, reduce heat as low as possible, cover the pan with a well-fitting lid and let it simmer very gently for 15 minutes, without any stirring or peeking. By the end of this time the rice should be swollen and tender.

Uncover the pan and tilt it slightly: if any water remains, cover the pan again and let the rice simmer for a few minutes more. When all the liquid has been absorbed, tip the cooked rice onto a shallow dish, fluff it with a fork and set it aside until completely cold.

It also makes sense to prepare well in advance the paste in which the rice will be fried. To do this, chop the onions and garlic roughly, and put them into a liquidiser. Add the oil, anchovy essence, coriander seeds and chilli powder. Blend until reduced to a thick, smooth and pungent paste. Divide the mixture between two small bowls and set aside in a cool place.

Cut the ham or pork into strips. (The smaller quantity is usually sufficient, but use more if you're feeling generous.) Divide between two plates, cover and chill until required.

To save any last-minute panic, measure the soy sauce for the rice into two egg cups and set them aside. Once all this has been done, you can relax until a little while before you plan to serve supper.

About 45 minutes before serving, put some plates and a serving dish into the plate warmer and turn the oven to 220°C [425°F], gas mark 7. Then, with the assistance of your helper, start preparing the side-dishes. I suggest one person takes charge of the cucumber, frying the onions and baking the bananas, while the other prepares the peanuts, spring omelettes and poppadoms.

The salted peanuts simply need to be put into a pretty bowl.

The cucumbers need to be wiped (leave the peel on), diced and piled into a separate bowl.

The onions should be sliced, pushed into rings, fried in oil until very crisp, thoroughly drained on kitchen paper, then piled into a bowl and kept hot in the plate warmer (don't cover the bowl or the onions will lose their crispness).

To make crisp little one-egg spring omelettes, first break an egg into a cup, add a good shake of soy sauce, a little grinding of black pepper and 2 finely chopped spring onions (green parts as well as white). Beat lightly together.

Put a 15–18 cm [6–7 inch] omelette pan over medium heat. When hot, add a knob of butter or a little oil. When the fat is hot and coating the entire base of the pan, pour in the egg mixture. When the egg begins to set, tilt the pan slightly away from you and draw the cooked egg up towards you with a palette knife: the raw egg will run down the pan to take its place. Lay the pan down again and continue cooking until all the egg is firmly set. Turn the omelette out of the pan onto a plate, laying it flat like a pancake, and keep it hot in the plate warmer.

Prepare and cook the rest of the omelettes in the same way, adding each to the stack as it is ready. Then roll up each omelette tightly, like a cigar, and cut it into ribbons with kitchen scissors. Pile the omelette ribbons into a hot dish, sprinkle any leftover chopped spring onions on top, and keep hot.

To bake the bananas, first peel and slice each in half lengthways, then across to make short lengths. Arrange them in a single layer in a lightly buttered baking or roasting pan, brush with lemon juice and dot with flakes of butter. Bake in the preheated oven for 10 minutes or until hot and just tender, turning the bananas carefully halfway through. Cover the dish with foil and keep it warm.

The cleanest and easiest way to cook poppadoms is in the oven. When the bananas have cooked, increase the oven temperature to 230°C [450°F], gas mark 8. When this temperature is reached, simply lay the poppadoms in a single layer on the top two oven shelves (don't put them too close to the source of heat — the sides in some ovens, the back in others — or they might burn at the edges). They will only take a minute or so to become hot and crisp. Pile most of them into a basket, but reserve one or two to crumble over the fried rice.

And so, finally, to the frying of the main dish. Pour the prepared paste into two large frying pans. Set over medium heat and cook steadily for several minutes until the mixture is bubbling hot and smelling delicious. Then divide the rice between the two pans and increase the heat slightly. Fry, stirring fairly frequently (use wooden salad servers if possible) for 8–10 minutes until the rice is hot and slightly coloured. Add a little extra oil to the pans if necessary.

Stir in the strips of ham or pork and the soy sauce. Reduce the heat slightly and continue cooking and stirring for another 5 minutes or so until everything is well mixed and piping hot. Turn the contents of both pans onto one large serving dish, crumble a couple of poppadoms over the top, and serve immediately with all the hot and cold side-dishes.

Mississippi Shrimp with Rice

This rice and shellfish dish, given to me by a friend from Mississippi, is not cheap, but it is rich and showy, and it takes agreeably little effort to prepare. Large fresh prawns (or shrimps as they are called in America) are hard to find in Britain, but this recipe makes the best of frozen varieties. Serves 8.

900 g [2 lb] prawns, shelled weight
350 g [¾ lb] long-grain rice
30 ml [2 tablespoons] lemon juice
olive oil
1 very large onion
2 green peppers
1 × 400 g [14 oz] can of tomatoes
10 ml [2 teaspoons] concentrated tomato purée
125 ml [4 fl oz] sherry
250 ml [scant ½ pt] double cream
125 g [¼ lb] split almonds
salt, paprika and freshly ground black pepper

Drop the prawns into a pan of well-salted, fast-boiling water and simmer for 5 minutes. Drain well, reserving the liquid, and turn the prawns into a ceramic bowl. Sprinkle the prawns with the lemon juice, twice as much olive oil and a very generous grinding of black pepper. Boil the rice in the prawn liquid, drain it, pile it on top of the prawns, cover the bowl with a teatowel and set aside in a cold place or fridge for at least 2 hours or overnight.

Chop the onion and green peppers and sauté them in a little olive oil in a flameproof casserole for 5 minutes over moderate heat. Cover and set aside.

About an hour before serving, reheat the vegetables over a very low flame. When they are warmed through, add the prepared prawns and rice to the casserole, together with all remaining ingredients except for 25 g [1 oz] of the almonds. Season generously, stir gently but thoroughly to mix all the ingredients well and bring slowly to simmering point.

Cover the casserole with a tight-fitting lid and leave it to cook as gently as possible until everything is thoroughly hot and flavours are well blended — about 45 minutes in an oven preheated to 160°C [325°F], gas mark 3, or 30 minutes on top of the stove. If possible give the casserole an occasional gentle stir during this time, particularly if cooking on top of the stove as ingredients may begin to stick to the base of the casserole. Check seasoning and top with the reserved almonds and a good shake of paprika just before serving.

Cut-Price Mississippi Rice: I have made a successful every-day version of this dish by replacing most of the prawns with a mixture of pork and chicken — diced and sautéed salt pork plus poached, skinned and boned chicken cut into big chunks — and by substituting soured cream for fresh.

Persian Lamb & Apricot Pilaf

Spicy and fruity, this is a lovely dish for a not-so-warm summer's day, and most of the cooking can be done well ahead if you wish. Dried apricots seem to vary greatly in flavour; for top quality I find health food shops the most reliable. Serves 10–12.

1.1–1.4 kg [2½–3 lb] lean boneless lamb cut into cubes
250–350 g [½–¾ lb] dried apricots, chopped but not soaked
350–450 g [¾–1 lb] chopped onions
550 g [1¼ lb] long-grain rice
a little butter and oil
25 ml [5 teaspoons] coriander seeds
20 ml [4 teaspoons] cumin seeds
7 ml [1 heaped teaspoon] ground cinnamon
75 g [3 oz] flaked almonds
salt and freshly ground black pepper

Brown and seal the lamb in batches in a small quantity of butter and oil in a large flameproof casserole. Remove with a slotted spoon. Melt another lump of butter in the casserole, add the rice and stir it continuously over low heat for 2–3 minutes until glistening with fat. Scrape the rice into a bowl and reserve.

Add a little more butter and oil to the casserole and fry the chopped onions gently for 5 minutes. Stir in the pounded coriander and cumin seeds and the cinnamon; when they begin to release their aroma pour on 1.7 litres [3 pt] hot water and bring to the boil.

Return the meat to the casserole, stir in the chopped apricots and a generous seasoning of salt and pepper. Cover the casserole with a well-fitting lid and cook for 1 hour in an oven preheated to 150°C [300°F], gas mark 2. (All this can be done in the morning or a day ahead of serving.)

About half an hour before serving, place the covered casserole over low heat on top of the stove and bring it slowly back to simmering point. Tip in the rice, increase the heat a little and stir continuously until it returns to simmering point. Cover the casserole, transfer it to an oven preheated to 160°C [325°F], gas mark 3, and cook for 25 minutes or so until the rice has absorbed most of the liquid and become quite tender. Spread the almonds on a baking sheet and toast them on the top shelf of the oven at the same time.

Stir the pilaf to mix the ingredients well, turn it out onto a hot serving dish and sprinkle the toasted almonds over the top.

Buey a la Catalana

A hearty dish of beef and rice, generously spiked with saffron, fennel, thyme and bay, this tastes very different from the previous recipe, but the cooking method is exactly the same. Make your own blend of spices, pounding them with mortar and pestle, or use the prepared mixture which is sold under the Culpepper label as "herbs for grilled fish". Serves 8.

1.4 kg [3 lb] chuck steak, cut into cubes
450 g [1 lb] onions
5–6 fat garlic cloves
450 g [1 lb] long-grain rice
a little olive oil and clarified butter
12 ml [1 scant tablespoon] mixture of saffron, fennel, thyme and bay, pounded
2 × 400 g [14 oz] cans of tomatoes
850 ml [1½ pt] beef stock
a generous fistful of small black olives
plenty of fresh chopped parsley
salt and freshly ground black pepper

Thoroughly brown and seal the cubes of beef, just a few at a time, in very hot fat in a flameproof casserole. Remove with a slotted spoon. Add a little extra fat and, when hot, tip in the rice. Stir the rice continuously over fairly low heat for about 2 minutes, or until every grain looks milky. Remove the rice from the pan and reserve it for later.

Add a little more fat to the casserole, increase the heat and fry the roughly chopped onions briskly until they begin to brown at the edges. Lower the heat, stir in the finely chopped garlic and spices. When they are warmed through and aromatic, add the canned tomatoes and stock and a generous seasoning of salt and pepper. Return the beef and onions to the casserole, pushing them well down into the liquid, cover and cook for about 2¼ hours in an oven preheated to 150°C [300°F], gas mark 2. (All this can be done in the morning or a day ahead of serving.)

About half an hour before serving, place the covered casserole over low heat on top of the stove, and bring it slowly back to simmering point. Tip in the rice, increase the heat a little and stir continuously until simmering point is reached. Cover the casserole, transfer it to an oven preheated to 160°C [325°F], gas mark 3, and cook for 25 minutes or so until the rice has absorbed most of the liquid and become quite tender. Check seasoning, gently stir in the olives and parsley and serve with a large green salad.

Dolmades

Preparing dolmades is a bit fiddly and time-consuming, but the resulting savoury parcels are so delectable to nibble with pre-dinner glasses of wine, to serve as part of a cold lunch or supper, and to take on picnics that I cannot resist making them occasionally. It makes sense, I think, to make a good quantity while you are at it — this meatless version keeps well in a cold place for several days. Makes about 50.

at least 60 fresh vine leaves or 2 cans or packets of vine leaves in brine
225 g [½ lb] long-grain rice
175 ml [6 fl oz] olive oil
225 g [½ lb] onions
2 fat garlic cloves
2 × 225 g [8 oz] cans of tomatoes
2 lemons
25 g [1 oz] pinenuts
a bunch of mint
caster sugar
concentrated tomato purée
1 litre [2 pt] chicken stock
salt and freshly ground black pepper

Warm the olive oil in a heavy-based pan over low heat and cook the finely chopped onions for 5 minutes or so. Add the rice and very finely chopped garlic and cook as gently as possible for a further 15 minutes, stirring frequently. Add the roughly chopped canned tomatoes and their juices, 10 ml [2 teaspoons] lemon juice and an equal quantity of caster sugar. Stir them into the rice, cover and leave to simmer for 15–20 minutes. Strain off and reserve any liquid remaining in the pan. Turn the rice into a shallow dish and leave until cold.

Meanwhile prepare the vine leaves. Drop them, in a stack, into

a large saucepan of boiling water (heavily salted if you are using fresh vine leaves) and blanch for 1 minute if fresh leaves are used, or for 5 minutes if canned leaves are used. In either case, flip the stack over halfway through blanching. Drain and rinse the leaves in a sinkful of cold water. Separate them carefully. This is the trickiest part of the operation — if the leaves were folded to fit into the can, it is easy to tear them. Dry them with kitchen paper towels and lay the best-shaped whole leaves, vein side up, in a single layer on a work surface.

Stir the nuts and at least 6 tablespoons of chopped mint into the cold rice mixture, and season it generously with salt and pepper. Spoon a little bit of stuffing onto each vine leaf near the stalk end. Fold the stalk end over the stuffing, fold the sides of the leaf inwards, then roll up tightly and neatly to make a miniature cigar-shaped parcel — certainly no longer than 2.5 × 5 cm [1 × 2 inches], the smaller they are the more attractive they are. Choose large gratin or shallow baking dishes that are attractive enough for serving. Arrange the dolmades in them, seam-side down and in a single layer. Wedge them fairly close together to prevent unrolling.

Bring the stock to the boil, together with any liquid leftover from cooking the rice, the juice of a lemon, a couple of large spoonfuls of concentrated tomato purée and a good seasoning of salt and pepper. Pour on as much boiling liquid as is needed to cover the dolmades. Arrange any leftover or broken vine leaves on top, cover the dishes with foil and bake in an oven preheated to 150°C [300°F], gas mark 2, for 1¾ hours.

When the cooked dolmades are quite cold, remove the layer of leftover leaves and use a bulb baster to drain off any liquid remaining in the dishes. Cover with fresh foil and store in a cold place (better than the fridge) for 12–24 hours before serving.

Hot Dolmades: Dolmades which contain meat are better than meatless ones for serving hot. Use 350 g [¾ lb] lean minced lamb and only 120 g [¼ lb] rice; add the lamb to the pan at the same time as the onions, otherwise follow the recipe given above, but use only one can of tomatoes. To make an accompanying sauce, strain off the liquid after cooking and boil briskly until well flavoured and syrupy. Stir in a few spoonfuls of yoghurt just before serving.

Boxwallah's Kedgeree

This spicy, warm kedgeree can be kept in a low oven for an hour or so without coming to harm. Or it can be made a day ahead and reheated when required. Fresh ginger is increasingly easy to buy these days, but if you cannot find any, use the finely grated zest of a lemon instead. Serves 6 generously.

1.1 kg [2½ lb] smoked haddock
350 g [12 oz] Basmati rice
3 large onions
125–150 g [4–5 oz] butter
fresh root ginger
20 ml [4 teaspoons] each lightly crushed cumin and coriander seeds
5 ml [scant 1 teaspoon] each chilli powder and turmeric
Worcestershire sauce
mango chutney
175 g [6 oz] sultanas
a bunch of parsley or coriander leaves
3 hard-boiled eggs
salt and freshly ground black pepper

Soak the rice for an hour in a bowl of cold water.

Chop the onions and sweat them gently in a good quantity of butter. Meanwhile, put the fish into a pan with some crushed parsley or coriander stalks and pour on enough water to cover. Bring to the boil, remove from the heat, cover and leave to stand for 5 minutes. Drain, reserving the liquor and fish separately.

Add a spoonful of grated ginger, the crushed cumin and coriander seeds, chilli and turmeric to the onion pan, and cook, stirring over medium heat, for 2–3 minutes. Stir in the rice and, when it is well coated with butter and spices, pour on the fish liquor plus boiling water to make a total of 850 ml [1½ pt] of liquid. Add a little salt and bring to the boil, then leave the rice to cook, without a lid, over medium heat until almost all the liquid is absorbed and holes begin to appear in the mass — about 10 minutes.

At this point, turn the heat off. Leave the pan where it is, but place a double thickness of kitchen paper directly on top of the rice and cover the pan with a well-fitting lid. In 15 minutes time the rice should be perfectly tender and each grain separate.

Fluff the rice with a fork. Stir in the sultanas, plenty of Worcestershire sauce and mango chutney, and salt and pepper to taste. Butter the base and sides of a casserole very generously. Turn the rice mixture into it, scattering chunks of the skinned and boned fish between layers. Lay a sheet of well-buttered paper on top and cover with the lid.

To reheat for serving, stand the casserole in a roasting pan and pour in enough boiling water to come halfway up the sides of the casserole; put the pan in a slow oven until the kedgeree is thoroughly hot — about 20 minutes if freshly cooked. Stir in lavish quantities of coarsely chopped fresh parsley or coriander just before serving, and top with chopped hard-boiled eggs.

Salmon & Fennel Kedgeree

Quicker to make, richer and more delicately flavoured, this kedgeree is an excellent means of stretching a small quantity of cold poached salmon or salmon trout. It is also very good indeed when made with canned salmon. Serves 4.

about 350 g [¾ lb] cooked salmon or salmon trout
2 Florentine fennel
225 g [½ lb] long-grain rice
200 ml [7 fl oz] double cream
a little butter
3 hard-boiled eggs
a bunch of parsley
salt and freshly ground black pepper

Trim the fennel, reserving the feathery fronds. Cut the bulb into 3 or 4 very thick vertical slices. Drop the slice(s) containing the hard fennel heart into a pan of boiling salted water and cook for 2–3 minutes before adding the other slices. Bring back to simmering point, cover and cook gently until tender but still with a slight bite — about 6–10 minutes. Drain, reserving the liquid, cool the fennel, squeeze it dry and cut into chunks.

Boil the rice in the fennel liquid. When it is nearly cooked, fry the chunks of fennel in a little butter over medium-high heat until nicely coloured and well heated through. Scald the cream in a separate small pan and season it very generously indeed with salt and pepper.

Mix the cooked and fluffed rice with the fennel. Add the chopped parsley and pour on the hot cream. Toss gently to mix well, then lightly fold in the coarsely chopped hard-boiled eggs and the salmon broken into large chunks. Pile the kedgeree onto a hot serving dish and sprinkle the chopped feathery fennel fronds on top.

Pastitsio with Chicken Livers

This comforting and inexpensive Greek dish is, in effect, a cross between macaroni cheese and lasagne. It is more interesting than plain macaroni cheese and decidedly less fiddly to prepare than lasagne. Like lasagne, it can be cooked ahead and reheated for serving. Serves 6–8.

For the chicken liver sauce:
450 g [1 lb] chicken livers
225 g [½ lb] streaky bacon
2 fat garlic cloves
2 large onions
a little well-seasoned flour
a little oil
225 ml [8 fl oz] red wine
225 ml [8 fl oz] chicken stock
5 ml [1 teaspoon] tomato purée
5 ml [1 teaspoon] each dried rosemary and thyme
2.5 ml [½ teaspoon] dried marjoram
salt and freshly ground black pepper

For the macaroni:
250 g [9 oz] macaroni
75 g [3 oz] butter
50 g [2 oz] plain flour
425 ml [¾ pt] milk
275 ml [½ pt] yoghurt
175 g [6 oz] mature Cheddar cheese
salt, pepper and nutmeg
a few spoonfuls of dry breadcrumbs

Clean and halve the chicken livers. Dust them with a little well-seasoned flour and sauté them briefly in a little hot oil. Remove and reserve them. Fry the chopped onions until they begin to brown. Add the bacon, cut into matchstick strips, and colour them. Add the crushed garlic and wine and cook for 5–10 minutes until the wine has reduced considerably.

Return the chicken livers to the pan. Stir in the tomato purée, seasonings and herbs and pour on the hot stock. Cook over low heat, without a lid, for about 20 minutes, just stirring the pan occasionally, until the meat sauce is rich and fragrant.

While the meat sauce reduces, boil the macaroni until al dente; and make a thick white sauce with the butter, flour and milk. Let it simmer for several minutes.

Away from the heat, stir half the cheese into the sauce, blend in the yoghurt and season to taste with salt, pepper and nutmeg. Then stir in the cooked and drained macaroni.

Spread half the macaroni mixture over the base of a large gratin or soufflé dish, cover with the meat filling and top with the rest of the macaroni.

To reheat for serving, sprinkle the rest of the cheese and a few breadcrumbs over the pastitsio and bake in the oven at 190°C [375°F], gas mark 5, for about 45 minutes. A little longer will do no harm.

Pastitsio with Mince: Minced beef or lamb can be used instead of chicken livers. Do not flour minced meat but brown it very thoroughly. Remove it from the pan while colouring the onions and bacon, and return it to the pan when adding the garlic and wine.

Roman Pie

A spectacular cold dish, requiring remarkably little effort, this is an admirable recipe for revitalising leftover Christmas turkey. Despite the implications of the name, Roman pie is in fact an old English recipe, the word Roman indicating that pasta is used rather than pastry. Serves 5–6.

For the macaroni:
125 g [¼ lb] macaroni
22 ml [1½ tablespoons] plain flour
25 g [¾ oz] butter
225 ml [8 fl oz] milk
125 ml [¼ pt] single cream
65 g [2½ oz] freshly grated Parmesan cheese
freshly grated nutmeg
salt and freshly ground black pepper

For the meat layers:
350–450 g [¾–1 lb] cooked turkey meat, skinned and boned weight
350 g [¾ lb] mushrooms
125 g [¼ lb] ham
125 g [¼ lb] tongue
1 × 50 g [2 oz] can of anchovy fillets
a little olive oil
a large bunch of parsley
a handful of small black olives
canned consommé, or good clear stock and a little gelatine powder
lemon juice
salt and freshly ground black pepper

Boil the macaroni until al dente. Meanwhile, make a white sauce with the butter, flour and milk. Away from the heat, beat in the Parmesan cheese, some nutmeg and the cream, and season with salt and pepper. Go gently with the salt throughout remembering the salt content of the ham, anchovies and cheese. Stir in the cooked and drained macaroni and allow to cool.

Slice the mushrooms thickly and sauté them in a little oil. Season them with a good squeeze of lemon juice, some salt and pepper, and allow them to become cold before mixing them with the turkey meat, which should be cut into bite-sized slivers.

Cut the ham and tongue into matchstick strips. Mix them with the anchovy fillets, also cut into matchstick strips, and a generous quantity of fairly coarsely chopped parsley.

Arrange half the ham mixture over the base of a 2.4 litre [4 pt] soufflé dish. Cover it with half the macaroni mixture, then all the turkey and mushroom mixture, then the rest of the macaroni mixture. Pack it quite, but not too firmly and level the top. Arrange the remaining ham mixture on top together with the olives — it is worth taking a little time and trouble to arrange this top layer decoratively so it will glow like a mosaic under the jelly.

Pour on enough barely melted consommé or cool jellied stock to cover. The amount you will need depends on the surface area of your dish, but I allow 5 ml [1 teaspoon] gelatine powder for every 275 ml [½ pt] well-flavoured stock. Cover with clingfilm or foil and refrigerate until set, but allow the Roman pie to come back to room temperature at least 2 hours before serving.

Variations: I sometimes use freshly poached chicken breasts instead of turkey (they only need half an hour's simmering with an onion, carrot and herbs), and mature Cheddar cheese instead of Parmesan to keep costs down. A plump roast pheasant or partridge makes a delicious alternative for a special occasion.

Garlic-Buttered Tagliatelle

This is one of the quickest and simplest dishes. It makes an agreeable change from boiled or puréed potatoes with grilled meats and casseroles. It can also be served as a main course simply accompanied by a large bowl of freshly grated Parmesan cheese and a green or tomato salad.

350 g [¾ lb] tagliatelle
100 g [3½–4 oz] butter
2–3 garlic cloves
45 ml [3 tablespoons] freshly grated Parmesan cheese
salt and freshly ground black pepper

Cook the pasta in plenty of boiling salted water until al dente. Meanwhile cut the butter into dice and put it into a flameproof casserole. Add a good grinding of black pepper, and the garlic crushed with some salt. Place the casserole over low heat and allow the butter to melt — but don't let it brown.

Switch off the heat, add the cooked and drained pasta and the Parmesan cheese. Toss the pasta lightly until it glistens with a fine coating of butter, and serve immediately.

Fettucine with Garlic: In Rome (where tagliatelle are called fettucine), and throughout southern Italy, a fruity flavoured virgin olive oil would be used instead of butter — healthier and every bit as delicious.

Tagliatelle with Cream Cheese & Walnuts

Subtly flavoured and very rich, this recipe is plenty for 4 people as a lunch or supper dish.

350 g [¾ lb] plain or green tagliatelle
225 g [½ lb] cream cheese
about 150 ml [¼ pt] milk
75 g [3 oz] walnut pieces
15 g [½ oz] butter
60 ml [4 tablespoons] freshly grated Parmesan cheese
salt and freshly ground black pepper

Cook the pasta in plenty of boiling salted water until al dente. Meanwhile, chop the walnuts finely, then melt the butter in a flameproof casserole over the lowest possible heat. Break the cream cheese into small lumps and add it to the casserole with most of the milk. Cook very gently indeed, stirring and mashing the mixture until it becomes a smooth, hot, thick and creamy sauce. Add extra milk as necessary to produce the correct consistency.

Tip the cooked pasta into a colander and leave it to drain for a minute or so while you stir the walnuts, Parmesan cheese and a good seasoning of salt and pepper into the sauce.

Away from the heat, add the pasta to the casserole and turn it lightly with wooden spoons until every strand is well coated with the sauce. Serve immediately with a bowl of grated Parmesan cheese for the table.

Spaghetti with Anchovy & Parsley

Another excellent and very quick pasta sauce: subtle, smoky and creamy. Serves 3–4.

350 g [¾ lb] spaghetti
2 × 50 g [2 oz] cans of anchovies
butter
150 ml [¼ pt] double cream
90 ml [6 tablespoons] soured cream
a large bunch of parsley
freshly ground black pepper

Cook the pasta until al dente in plenty of salted boiling water.

Melt a lump of butter the size of a hazelnut in a flameproof casserole. Add the anchovies and their oil, and mash and stir with a wooden spoon until they disintegrate. Pour on the creams and add a good seasoning of pepper. Cook over gentle heat, stirring continuously, until the ingredients are well blended. Simmer for a few minutes to make a pungently flavoured, smooth, thick, hot sauce.

Away from the heat, add the cooked and drained pasta and very generous quantities of coarsely chopped parsley. Toss to coat every strand with the sauce and to fleck the pasta with parsley.

Spaghetti alla Carbonara

Based on ingredients to be found in every fridge and store-cupboard, I find this dish invaluable when friends arrive unexpectedly, and a regular standby to turn to on the occasions (happily rare) when I am a grass widow. Serves 3–4.

350 g [¾ lb] spaghetti
175 g [6 oz] streaky bacon rashers
3 eggs
90 ml [6 tablespoons] cream or top of the milk
45 ml [3 tablespoons] freshly grated Parmesan cheese
salt and freshly ground black pepper

Cook the spaghetti in an uncovered pan of boiling salted water until al dente.

Meanwhile, remove the rind from the bacon and cut it into matchstick strips. Put it into a flameproof casserole and place over low heat. Cook gently until the bacon fat begins to run, then increase the heat a little and cook the bacon for a few minutes longer, stirring occasionally. Break the eggs into a bowl. Add a generous seasoning of salt and pepper, the grated Parmesan cheese and the cream or top of the milk. Beat the ingredients together lightly with a fork.

Remove the casserole from the heat. Add the cooked and drained pasta to it, and pour on the egg mixture. Turn the pasta gently, over and over, until every strand is coated with the bacon-flecked sauce. Serve immediately with extra Parmesan cheese.

Trenette al Pesto

Basil is my favourite herb and well worth growing just to make this exquisite sauce. Pesto is also delicious with new potatoes steamed in their skins, and can be used to top grilled meat and fish. Serves 5–6.

500 g [18 oz] trenette (or linguine, tagliatelle or spaghetti)
a little olive oil

For the pesto:
75 g [3 oz] fresh basil leaves (weighed after stripping the leaves from the stalks)
40 g [1½ oz] pinenuts
3–4 garlic cloves
about 90 ml [6 tablespoons] olive oil
60 g [2¼ oz] freshly grated Parmesan cheese
salt and freshly ground black pepper

It is best to make the pesto a good half an hour before using, so flavours have time to blend and develop to the full. It can be made in seconds using a liquidiser (reduce all ingredients except Parmesan cheese to a purée, then beat in the cheese), but I find a wasteful amount sticks irrevocably to the blades. Pounding the sweet smelling ingredients with mortar and pestle is, for me at any rate, an essential part of the pleasure of pesto.

Tear the basil leaves into small pieces with your fingers to reduce their bulk. Chop the nuts and garlic into small pieces — a mezzaluna knife and curved wooden bowl are best for this. Tip all three ingredients into a mortar and pound with a pestle until reduced to a smooth, thick, rich green paste. This takes 10–15 minutes.

Carefully blend in half the oil, adding it a spoonful at a time. Beat in the cheese, then blend in the rest of the oil, adding it in a slow drizzle this time. Season with a little salt and pepper to taste.

Cook the pasta until al dente in boiling salted water. Drain well and toss in a spoonful or so of olive oil so each strand glistens. Serve topped with the sauce, which can be diluted with a few spoonfuls of the pasta water if wished (this encourages the sauce to coat the pasta evenly). Accompany it with a bowl of Parmesan cheese.

Joints, Poultry & Game

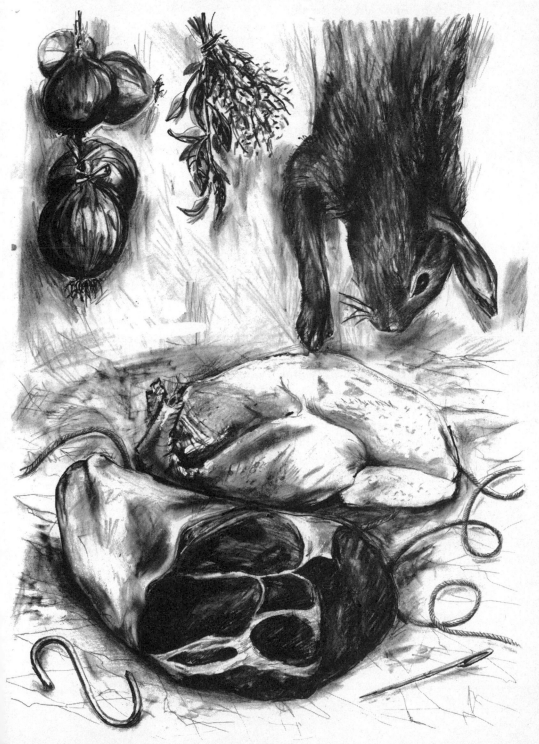

A joint of meat is a treat. It is never cheap, but I no longer regard it as the extravagant indulgence the puritanical streak in my nature once led me to think.

This may at first sound at odds with today's ecological arguments, and imprudent in view of the ever-spiralling cost of meat. But it seems to me that, whilst it obviously makes sense to use the cheaper cuts of meat most of the time, to relearn how to use meat sparingly in the traditional peasant manner, and sometimes to use no meat at all in cooking, it is perfectly right and proper to relish the sheer excellence of high quality meat, plain and unadorned, on occasion. *When* we do so, we should enjoy it to the maximum, serving it in all its glory as the celebratory centrepiece of a meal, without any feelings of guilt. In summary, the motto is to serve prime cuts of meat (joints, game, steaks and chops) less often, but when they are served to enjoy them all the more.

Few things awaken the appetite faster than the sizzling sounds and delectable aroma which waft from the oven when a joint is roasting, and nothing beats the flavour of fine quality meat that has been well hung and cooked to perfection.

Only a decade or so ago, when the Sunday roast featured regularly in every household, a joint might have seemed rather ordinary fare to offer to guests. Today it is rightly regarded as special by both family and friends, and automatically creates a wonderful sense of occasion. Moreover, a joint is a gratifyingly practical meat from the cook's point of view.

It is true that buying a good joint involves paying out a large sum of money, but a joint in fact costs several pence less per gram than do prime small cuts such as steaks and chops. Moreover, the initial outlay of, say £10, on a large joint of beef can be regarded as an investment to enjoy over several days. Whereas chops or steaks will be eaten at one sitting, a large joint will always yield a great many servings, not only a hot feast, but at least one cold meal as well. And a cold meal has the inestimable virtue of giving the cook a night off.

A joint obviously takes longer to cook than steaks or chops, but once in the oven it requires little or no attention, which makes it ideal for occasions when you would rather be relaxing, talking over a pre-dinner drink than busy with last-minute cooking. Joints of pork, beef and lamb are particularly good in this respect: the natural layer of fat they contain makes it unnecessary to baste them at all during roasting. Very lean meats, such as veal and game birds, need to be larded or barded and will benefit greatly from occasional basting.

Gravy, of course, can never be made until roasting is completed, but that takes only a couple of minutes and can easily be done during the few minutes every cook expects to spend in the kitchen between pre-prandial drinks and sitting down at table. The gravy will keep hot without spoiling while you eat the first course, and so will the joint. In fact, joints should always be "rested" in a warm place for up to 30 minutes between roasting and carving. Resting a joint allows juices brought to the surface by high temperature to flood back through the meat and settle, and this, in turn, makes the meat more uniformly succulent and much easier to carve into neat slices. The resting period should be built into your timing plan if no first course is to be served.

It may seem old hat to say that a good butcher is the cook's best friend, but I believe it more strongly than ever today. Supermarket shopping is convenient, quick and a boon for buying foods such as butter or flour where quality is easily identified by brand labels. The quality of meat, however, is not so easy to judge, particularly if it is pre-wrapped in a sealed package. A good butcher will sensibly spend time advising and helping you, because it is in his interest to do so. He will know what is currently best value. He can tell you how many days gammon has been brined, and whether the brine was heavy or light. He can tell you how long beef has been hung, or when a game bird was shot and can demonstrate whether it is young and tender enough to roast by checking the pliability of its feet.

I rarely buy frozen or imported joints. They may cost a little less but I think home-produced meat in season is best. I do, however, consider it worthwhile to buy home-produced fresh legs and shoulders of lamb in late summer, when they are cheap, largish and well flavoured, and to freeze them at home. Although never quite so delectable as fresh roast lamb, they bring a welcome taste of summer to the winter months. To get good results it is essential to defrost the joint very slowly in a refrigerator and, once thoroughly defrosted, to marinate it for at least 24 hours before roasting.

Marinating meat before cooking is more often associated with

cheap stewing meat than with roasting joints, but I always marinate roasting joints of beef and lamb for 24–48 hours, using a
mixture of good olive oil, lemon juice or wine, generous grind-
ings of black pepper and a few herbs or spices such as crushed
rosemary or coriander seeds. This helps to flavour and tenderise
the meat, and generally to counteract today's common fault of
selling meat which is less well hung than one would wish.

As to the actual roasting of meat, I belong to the school that
believes best results are usually obtained by an initial fierce blast
of heat followed by a moderate roasting temperature. To
encourage a crusty surface and even cooking, I always place the
meat on a rack suspended across the top of the roasting pan so
that heat circulates freely all round the joint. If the joint is placed
on the base of the pan, heat cannot circulate properly and the
underside of the joint will fry in the fat exuded during cooking.
Purpose-designed racks for roasting meat can now be bought
quite cheaply from most kitchenware shops but the rack from
your grill pan will serve the same purpose.

As well as the crisp and crackling roasts we love so much in
Britain, I have included a number of recipes for pot-roasted and
braised joints. These slower and gentler methods, which are
popular in France and Italy for cooking pork and veal, make for
the most tender mouth watering results. Dishes such as pork
with pistachio and green herbs, for example, are so excellent that
I have readily abandoned the sacred English belief that pork
always means crackling! (These slower, gentler methods do not
produce it.)

Boiling is another cooking method included in this chapter. It
is spurned by many cooks today but I feel it deserves fresh
appraisal. The Victorian passion for doing nothing by halves is
probably responsible for our tendency to associate boiling with
intolerably steamy kitchens and food with about as much texture
and taste as a face flannel.

But this picture is very distorted. One has only to think of that
great British delicacy, boiled ham, to see how delicious boiled
meat can be. Boiled meats are, in fact, boiled only for an instant,
and thereafter barely simmered. To keep the liquid at boiling
point throughout is a waste of fuel, and, more to the point, the
fast movement of the boiling liquid will coarsen the texture of
the meat into a tough, stringy consistency.

"Boiled" meats are certainly plain, but only in the sense that they are not rich, and this does not mean that they are dull. On the contrary, they offer a fresh, clean succulence and delicate flavour unobtainable by other cooking methods. Try Easter chicken, for example, and you will find that a refreshing new dimension has been added to the normal round of chicken dishes.

Roast Beef with Yorkshire Pudding

If your butcher has really high quality beef and he hangs it well, topside can be used for this (and the next) recipe. However, whereas marinading sirloin can be regarded as optional, it is always important to marinade topside for at least 24 hours before roasting. A watercress salad goes beautifully with plain roast beef, is less "obvious" and involves less work then the usual brussel sprouts et al. Roast celeriac and parsnips (see page 91) make a delicious alternative to Yorkshire pudding. Serves 8–10.

1.4–1.8 kg [3–4 lb] boned and rolled sirloin
a garlic clove (optional)
175 ml [6 fl oz] good beef stock
120 ml [scant 4 fl oz] red wine
salt and freshly ground black pepper

For the Yorkshire pudding:
125 g [¼ lb] plain flour
2 eggs
125 ml [4 fl oz] milk
150 ml [¼ pt] cold water
salt and freshly ground black pepper

Weigh the joint and calculate the roasting time, then arrange your timetable so that the joint will complete roasting half an hour before you plan to serve it. We like fairly rare beef so I allow 13–15 minutes per 450 g [1 lb] when roasting a 1.8 kg [4 lb] sirloin (allow more if you like well-cooked beef). If, however, the piece of sirloin were half this weight, I would allow about 20 minutes per 450 g [1 lb], because the thickness and shape of the joint need to be considered, as well as its weight, when calculating the roasting time.

Preheat the oven to 220°C [425°F], gas mark 7. Cut the garlic into tiny slivers and stud the joint with them, or, for a mild garlic flavour, simply rub the surface of the meat with a cut garlic clove. Rub the meat all over with pepper, and rub the fat with some salt. Lay the joint on a rack in a roasting pan and roast in the hot oven for 15 minutes. Then reduce the oven temperature to 190°C [375°F], gas mark 5, and continue roasting. I find basting unnecessary.

Meanwhile, make the Yorkshire pudding batter by blending the ingredients together in a liquidiser until they are smoothly mixed and creamy in texture.

Ten minutes before the end of roasting time spoon a little fat from the meat pan into a second roasting pan. Move the meat pan down to a lower oven shelf and place the pan containing the dripping on an upper shelf. Increase the oven temperature to 230°C [450°F], gas mark 8.

When roasting time is up, remove the joint from the oven and let it rest in a warm place. Give the pudding batter a brisk stir and pour it into the pan of sizzling dripping on the top shelf of the oven. Bake the pudding for 30 minutes until puffed up and crisp.

Meanwhile make the gravy. Skim surplus fat from the meat roasting pan. Pour on the wine and stock, and stir to mix them well with the remaining fat, juices and meat sediment in the pan. Cook over high heat for several minutes until well blended, slightly reduced and well flavoured.

Horseradish sauce: This takes only a couple of minutes to make at home and is far superior to the branded versions. In addition to being the classic English accompaniment to roast beef with Yorkshire pudding it is excellent with smoked trout, mackerel and eel. Beat the contents of 2 tubs of soured cream with a little French mustard and a pinch of salt. When creamy and well blended, beat in a few spoonfuls of grated horseradish — either home-grown horseradish, or the grated horseradish which can be bought in jars from good delicatessens. Let the sauce stand for an hour or so to allow flavours to blend and develop, then try it and add extra seasonings to taste.

Sirloin with Shallot Sauce

In the previous recipe roast beef is garnished with Yorkshire pudding and horseradish sauce to provide classic Sunday lunch-time fare. In this recipe the same roast is finished and dressed with a rich wine and shallot sauce to make a handsome dish for an evening celebration. Pickling onions are cheaper and often easier to find than shallots, and they are suitable for use here. Serves 6–8.

1.1–1.4 kg [2½–3 lb] boned and rolled sirloin
125 g [¼ lb] unsalted butter
12–14 shallots or pickling onions
150 ml [¼ pt] red wine
100 ml [3½ fl oz] good beef stock
20 ml [1½ tablespoons] Dijon mustard, or more to taste
150 ml [¼ pt] double cream
salt and freshly ground black pepper

Chop the onions finely and cook them gently in half the butter in a covered saucepan for 12 minutes or so until they are soft and golden. Pour on the wine and stock. Let the mixture bubble up over fairly high heat for a minute or so, then let it simmer, just stirring occasionally, for about 6 minutes until reduced and well flavoured. Set the pan aside. Pour the cream into a cup. Add the mustard and a good seasoning of salt and pepper. Stir to mix well and set the cup aside.

Preheat the oven to 220°C [425°F], gas mark 7. Rub the meat all over with pepper, and rub the fat with a little salt. Lay the joint on a rack in a roasting pan, and roast it in the hot oven for 20 minutes. Then reduce the oven temperature to 190°C [375°F], gas mark 5, and complete roasting at this temperature. Allow about 17 minutes per 450 g [1 lb] for fairly rare beef, more for medium or well-done meat.

When the beef is cooked to your liking, transfer the joint to a carving dish and let it rest in a warm place for 20 minutes or so before carving, saucing and serving.

To finish the sauce, scrape the meat juices and sediment from the roasting pan into the saucepan containing the wine and onion mixture. Add the remaining butter, cut into dice, and place the pan over fairly high heat. Cook briskly, stirring continuously, for a few minutes until the ingredients are well blended. Stir in the seasoned cream and let the sauce simmer for a further few minutes until it is very hot and smooth.

Carve the beef, arrange the slices on a warmed serving dish, pour on the sauce, and serve immediately. Good bread, steamed new potatoes or a potato purée go well with this dish. If you want to serve green vegetables with the meat, do not butter them; the shallot and wine sauce will flavour the vegetables richly.

Roast Lamb with Redcurrant Glaze

Leg and best end of lamb can be cooked this way, but the fresh flavourings of redcurrant, orange and mint go particularly well with sweet, but fatty, shoulder. Serves 8.

whole shoulder of lamb
1 orange
10 ml [2 teaspoons] coriander seeds
45 ml [3 tablespoons] redcurrant jelly
a little fresh chopped mint
salt and freshly ground black pepper

Pierce the joint at intervals with a small skewer and insert the coriander seeds. Grate the zest of the orange finely into a cup, add 45 ml [3 tablespoons] of water and set aside. Squeeze the orange juice over the lamb. Turn the joint to moisten it on all sides, and leave in a cool place for at least 2 hours before cooking.

Preheat the oven to 220°C [425°F], gas mark 7. Drain the lamb and add the orange juice to the cup containing the water and orange zest. Place the joint on a rack in a roasting pan. Rub the lamb fat with a little salt and pepper.

Roast the joint in the hot oven for 20 minutes, then reduce the oven temperature to 190°C [375°F], gas mark 5, and complete roasting (I allow a total of 18–20 minutes per 450 g [1 lb] for whole leg of lamb; shoulder, being a shallower cut than leg, takes about 15–17 minutes per 450 g [1 lb] for the same pinkish meat result). Twenty minutes before the end of cooking time sieve then melt the redcurrant jelly with a tablespoon of water in a small pan and brush the entire surface of the joint with it.

Let the roasted joint rest while you make the gravy. Add the cup of orange to the roasting pan juices, let them bubble up for a few minutes, season to taste and stir in the chopped fresh mint. Turn the gravy into a small sauceboat and, when the meat has been carved, stir into the gravy any meat juices that collect in the carving dish.

Gigot with Garlic Potatoes

French friends in Beaune introduced me to this wonderful alternative to lamb with roast potatoes. Serves 8.

whole leg of lamb weighing about 2 kg [4½ lb]
1½ kg [3 lb] potatoes, or more
3 fat garlic cloves
50 g [2 oz] butter
salt and freshly ground black pepper

Weigh the joint, calculate the roasting time and aim to finish roasting about 15 minutes before serving to give the joint a chance to rest between cooking and carving. We like juicy lamb with a hint of pink so I allow 18–20 minutes per 450 g [1 lb] for whole leg of lamb weighing 1.8–2.3 kg [4–5 lb]. I allow slightly more time — about 25 minutes per 450 g [1 lb] — for a half leg of lamb weighing 1.1–1.4 kg [2–3 lb].

The potatoes will take a good 1½ hours to cook so you will need to start cooking them first in order to complete vegetables and meat simultaneously. Peel and slice the potatoes very thinly indeed — a food processor or mandolin is the only really quick and easy way to get uniformly thin slices. Layer them in a large gratin dish, the base and sides of which have been generously buttered, sprinkling salt, pepper and most of the crushed garlic between layers. Top with flakes of butter. Place the dish of potatoes on the centre shelf of an oven preheated to 220°C [425°F], gas mark 7.

Stab the joint here and there with the point of a sharp knife and insert tiny slivers of garlic. Rub the surface fat generously with salt and freshly ground black pepper. When it is time to start cooking the lamb, lay the joint directly onto the oven shelf immediately above the dish of potatoes, so the meat juices drip down onto, and flavour, the potatoes during cooking. Roast for 20 minutes at the high temperature, then complete roasting at 190°C [375°F], gas mark 5.

Augustin's Lamb

Another recipe in which lamb is roasted over a dish of vegetables which absorb the rich meaty juices that drip from the joint. This is a very good-tempered dish and will not come to any harm if kept in the oven for an extra 20 minutes or so. Serves 4–6.

knuckle end leg of lamb weighing about 1½ kg [2½–3 lb]
15 ml [1 tablespoon] lemon thyme, or ordinary thyme plus a little lemon zest
2 fat garlic cloves
7 ml [1½ teaspoons] coriander seeds
350 g [¾ lb] aubergines
350 g [¾ lb] courgettes
350 g [¾ lb] red or green peppers
350 g [¾ lb] tomatoes
75 ml [3 fl oz] good stock or wine
50 g [2 oz] butter
fresh chopped basil and marjoram
salt and freshly ground black pepper

Pound the garlic, thyme and coriander with mortar and pestle to make an aromatic paste. Make deep cuts here and there in the joint and push the herb mixture into them with your fingers. Set the joint aside at room temperature for 1 hour.

Meanwhile, cut the aubergines and courgettes into 6 mm [¼ inch] slices, layer them in a colander with coarse salt and weigh down for at least 40 minutes to drain off excess liquid. Seed the peppers and cut into chunks; skin and roughly chop the tomatoes.

Rub the skin of the joint with salt and pepper, stand the joint on a rack and balance the rack across a roasting tin. Roast at 220°C [425°F], gas mark 7, for 15 minutes. Remove the tin from the oven and reduce the oven temperature to 160°C [325°F], gas mark 3.

Mix the rinsed and dried aubergines and courgettes with the peppers. Spread them over the base of the roasting tin. Put the prepared tomatoes, butter and stock or wine into a small pan. Bring to the boil, season with salt, pepper, basil and marjoram, and pour the contents of the pan over the aubergine mixture. Lay

the rack of meat across the top of the roasting tin again. Return it to the oven and cook for 1½–1¾ hours depending on the weight of the joint and how well cooked you like lamb. Give the vegetable mixture a good stir once or twice during this time. Good bread goes better with this dish than potatoes.

Mutton with Fennel

Mutton is difficult to buy these days (although you can get it from halal butchers) but end-of-summer New Zealand lamb is cheap, on the large side and, when boiled, tastes almost as good as the mutton of yesteryear. Cooking in liquid keeps the meat beautifully moist (leftovers thus make excellent cold eating) and the inclusion of fennel adds a subtle, smoky flavour. Serves 10.

whole leg of lamb (or mutton) weighing about 2¼ kg [5 lb]
5 bulbs of Florentine fennel
120 g [¼ lb] butter
20 g [scant 1 oz] plain flour
150 ml [¼ pt] milk
150 ml [¼ pt] cream
French mustard
white wine vinegar
salt and freshly ground black pepper

Choose a large oval heavy-based pan and place the joint in it. Pour on warm water or stock to cover the meat completely. Place over medium heat and bring to the boil. Skim away scum as it forms.

As soon as boiling point is reached, reduce heat to very low. Add salt and pepper, cover the pan and start timing. The joint will take 15–20 minutes per 450 g [1 lb] depending on how well cooked you like it. Cut off and reserve the feathery fennel fronds. Scrub and trim the bulbous roots and add the trimmings to the cooking pot.

About 25–30 minutes before the lamb is due to complete cooking, drop the whole fennel bulbs into the cooking pot. (Increase the heat briefly to bring the liquid back to simmering point as quickly as possible.)

When cooking time is up remove the pan from the heat. Lift out the whole fennel, ladle out 150 ml [¼ pt] stock to use for making the sauce and leave the joint to rest in the uncovered pan.

Dry the fennel, cut each bulb into 4 slices and lay in a single layer in a gratin dish which has been greased with 45 g [1½ oz] butter. Top with an equal quantity of flaked butter and finish cooking under a hot grill, turning and basting the slices as necessary until lightly coloured.

Meanwhile, make a white sauce with the remaining 30 g [1 oz] butter, the flour, reserved stock, milk and cream. Stir in the chopped feathery fennel fronds, and leave to simmer uncovered for 5–10 minutes. Season to taste by stirring in salt, pepper and a dash each of mustard and vinegar just before serving.

Carve the meat and serve with the fennel and sauce.

Mutton with Onion Sauce: For a more traditional sauce, omit fennel and cook 350 g [¾ lb] small whole onions with the lamb. Drain, chop and reduce them to a purée with a few spoonfuls of the cooking liquor. Blend in 150 ml [¼ pt] scalded double cream. Reheat gently, season well and thin with extra lamb broth to taste. Stir in a handful of coarse chopped parsley for colour just before serving.

Easter Chicken

Like the previous recipe, this one disproves the theory that boiled meats make dull eating. A plump fresh chicken and a good selection of tender young vegetables, displayed on one large dish, look truly enticing and taste delicately fresh. I suggest using roasting chicken rather than boiling fowl, because the latter is often very disappointing. To use a roasting bird has other advantages: first, you will obtain a good well-flavoured stock that needs no further reducing (because the quantity of water is limited to that needed to cover the thighs of the bird); second, a roaster can be briefly fried in butter before poaching, which rids the skin of that anaemic, goose-pimpled look. Serves 6–8.

1 × 2.3 kg [5 lb] roasting chicken
1 large onion
a little butter
a bouquet garni
salt and freshly ground black pepper

For the vegetable accompaniment:
700–900 g [1½–2 lb] new potatoes
350 g [¾ lb] baby carrots
700 g [1½ lb] young leeks
350 g [¾ lb] stringless French beans
350 g [¾ lb] mangetout peas
350 g [¾ lb] cauliflower sprigs
2–3 bunches of watercress

For the egg and herb vinaigrette:
275 ml [½ pt] vinaigrette dressing
2 × 3½-minute boiled eggs
the juice and zest of a lemon
a handful of fresh chopped parsley and chives, and a little tarragon if possible
a few spoonfuls of chopped capers

Rub the chicken skin all over with salt and pepper. Choose a heavy-based pan into which the bird will fit snugly. Heat it, melt a little butter in it and fry the chicken briefly until the skin is golden all over. Lay the chicken on its back, tuck the quartered onion and bouquet of herbs round it, and pour on enough hot water to cover the chicken thighs completely. Bring quickly to the boil, cover the pan and poach at a very gentle simmer until the chicken is quite tender — about 1¼–1½ hours.

About half an hour before the chicken is ready, start cooking the vegetables. The new potatoes, carrots and beans can be cooked in the chicken pan; the potatoes will take about 20 minutes, the others will need less than half that time, so add them later. Leeks, cauliflower and mangetout peas are better steamed and can be cooked together in one steamer basket — put the slower cooking vegetables into the basket first and systematically add those that cook more quickly.

To make the sauce, simply chop the egg whites and beat the runny yolks into the vinaigrette dressing. Stir in the herbs and capers and sharpen the flavour (which will have been muted by the eggs) by adding the zest and some juice of a lemon.

Drain the chicken well, tilting it so the liquid runs out of the body cavity, and place it in the centre of a really large hot dish. Arrange the watercress and cooked vegetables round the chicken in colourful clumps. Season the broth and pour a spoonful or so over the vegetables just before serving. Hand round the egg and herb vinaigrette in a jug. (Save the rest of the broth for another meal.) A first course is quite unnecessary before Easter chicken, but bread and a good selection of cheese go well after it.

Bollitto Misto: Italians make a real feast of boiled meats, serving a selection of meats as well as lots of different vegetables. I find cooking several meats at a time too complicated a conjuring trick to master, but it is no trouble to add a boiling sausage to the chicken pot, and I sometimes ring the changes by using another meat instead of chicken. Gammon, tongue and salt beef make good alternatives. Allow 20 minutes per 450 g [1 lb] and 20 minutes over for gammon. A large ox tongue will take about 4 hours to cook. Beef will take 2–4 hours depending on cut and weight. Try using cider as part of the liquid when cooking salt meat.

Vegetables can be as varied as the meats. Small turnips or kohlrabi, whole onions, wedges of very crisp cabbage and dumplings, for example, all go well with the brisket and make a substantial and economic dish for winter eating.

Mustard-Glazed Gammon with Marsala Sauce

New potatoes and young French beans are the best vegetables to serve with this dish. Steam the vegetables, but don't dress them with butter — the Marsala-flavoured Hollandaise sauce will anoint them beautifully. Serves 6–8.

1.1 kg [2½ lb] corner gammon
35 ml [2 heaped tablespoons] mustard powder
35 ml [2 heaped tablespoons] soft brown sugar

For the sauce:
45 ml [3 tablespoons] Marsala
15 ml [1 tablespoon] lemon juice
3 egg yolks
175 g [6 oz] butter
salt and freshly ground black pepper

Soak the gammon in cold water for 4–24 hours depending on how salty it is — a sip of the soaking water will act as a guide.

Choose a heavy-based saucepan into which the joint will fit snugly. Put the gammon into it. Pour on fresh cold water and bring slowly to the boil. Cover the pan and simmer gently for 55 minutes. Towards the end of this time, preheat the oven to 180°C [350°F], gas mark 4, and mix the mustard powder and sugar together in a cup.

Drain and dry the partially cooked gammon. As soon as it is cool enough to handle, strip off the rind and score the fat with a criss–cross pattern. Stand the joint, fat side up, on a sheet of foil in a roasting pan. Press the mustard and sugar mixture firmly onto the fat and draw the foil up to cover the meaty sides of the joint, leaving only the mustard–coated fat exposed. Bake for 55 minutes, basting occasionally, by the end of which time the meat should be juicy and tender, and the fat glazed.

To make the sauce, first melt 125 g [¼ lb] butter in a small pan, cover and set aside. Put the Marsala, lemon juice and egg yolks into the top part of a double-boiler and whisk for a few seconds. Add 25 g [1 oz] chilled butter and place the pan over barely simmering water. Cook very gently, whisking continuously until the mixture thickens.

Remove the pan from the heat and quickly whisk in the remaining 25 g [1 oz] chilled butter. When absorbed, gradually beat in the hot melted butter to make a thick, smooth Hollandaise-type sauce. Check seasoning and beat in a little of the mustardy juices that have collected in the foil packet in which the gammon was cooked.

Larger joints can be cooked in exactly the same way. Allow 20 minutes per 450 g [1 lb] and 30 minutes over. Half the total cooking time should be allocated to boiling, and half to baking in the oven.

Crackling Pork with Spiced Apples & Cider Sauce

Leg or hand of pork can be used for this recipe, but loin looks best and is sure to produce the really crisp crackling that is synonymous with pork in most people's minds. Potato purée and watercress make good accompaniments. Serves 6.

loin of pork weighing 1.4–1.6 kg [3–3½ lb] chined and with scored rind
a small garlic clove
a sprig or two of rosemary
6 Cox's apples
25 g [scant 1 oz] butter
ground cinnamon and allspice
225 ml [8 fl oz] dry cider
salt and freshly ground black pepper
7 ml [1 heaped teaspoon] plain flour

Preheat the oven to 230°C [450°F], gas mark 8. Weigh the joint. Rub the meat with a cut garlic clove, or make small incisions in the flesh and insert slivers of garlic. Check that the pork rind and fat are completely dry, and rub the rind generously with salt. Lay the pork, rind side up, on a rosemary sprig or two on a rack in a roasting pan. The rind should stand proud of the rim so heat can penetrate it well and transform it to perfect crackling.

Roast in the hot oven for 20 minutes irrespective of the weight of the joint. Then reduce the oven temperature to 190°C [375°F], gas mark 5, and complete roasting, allowing 35 minutes per 450 g [1 lb] weight.

Dice the butter, put it into a gratin dish and place the dish on the floor of the oven. When the butter has melted, stir in about 2.5 ml [½ teaspoon] each ground cinnamon and allspice. Peel and core the apples and roll them in the spiced butter. Place the dish of apples on the floor of the oven to cook for the last hour of roasting time.

Simmer the apple trimmings in the cider, in a covered pan for 10 minutes, then strain and reserve.

If the crackling is not as crunchy as you would like when roasting time is up, increase the oven temperature to 230°C [450°F], gas mark 8, remove the cooked apples to a warm place and roast the joint for an extra 10 minutes or so.

Rest the joint while you make the gravy. Skim most of the fat from the roasting pan. Stir in the buttery apple juices and the flour. Pour on the cider and add a good seasoning of salt and pepper. Boil and stir for a few minutes until the sauce is well flavoured and slightly thickened.

Pork with Pistachio & Green Herbs

In this recipe pork is slow-roasted in the French manner to succulent perfection. Good served hot but even more delicious served cold. Serves 8–10.

loin of pork weighing about 2 kg [4–4½ lb]
a fat garlic clove
10 ml [2 teaspoons] coriander seeds
50 g [2 oz] pistachio nuts
300 ml [½ pt] clear meat stock
150 ml [¼ pt] dry cider or white wine

1 onion
a large bunch of parsley
a bunch of chives
a little fresh basil
salt and freshly ground black pepper

Bone and rind the pork. Lay the meat fat side down and rub the flesh with pepper. Use a knife to insert tiny slivers of garlic and whole coriander seeds here and there. Sprinkle a handful of coarse chopped parsley leaves down the centre of the joint, and add the pistachio nuts. Roll it up from one long side to the other, and tie into a neat bolster shape with string. Rub the fatty outside of the bolster with plenty of salt and lay the joint on a bed of sliced onion in a roasting pan. Arrange the bones and rind either side of the meat. Cook in the centre of an oven preheated to 180°C [350°F], gas mark 4, for 45 minutes until the pork fat turns pale gold.

Bring the stock and cider or wine to the boil. Pour the liquid over the meat and bury a bunch of crushed parsley stalks in the liquid. Cover the roasting pan with a double layer of foil, reduce the oven temperature to 160°C [325°F], gas mark 3, and cook for a further 2 hours.

Discard the bones, rind and vegetables, letting the juices drip back into the roasting pan. Leave the meat in the liquid, cover the pan again and place it in a cold place overnight — the liquid will set to a beautiful amber jelly with a layer of fat on top.

Next day scrape off the fat (save it for spreading on bread). Carve the pork and arrange the slices on a large dish. Sprinkle fresh snipped chives, parsley and basil over the meat and surround it with the chopped jelly. Serve with a simple salad of lettuce hearts and plenty of good crusty bread.

Note: Although at its best served cold, this roast can be served hot. Lift the joint out of the roasting pan and let it rest in a warm place for 20 minutes or so before carving. Meanwhile use a bulb baster to skim as much fat as possible from the cooking liquor. Ladle half the liquor from the roasting pan and just boil it for a few minutes to make a well-flavoured gravy.

Pork or Veal Tonnato

Vitello tonnato is surely one of the loveliest of summer dishes. It used to figure on my menus all too rarely, because of the price of veal, but I've now discovered that it works just as well using boned, rinded and rolled loin or leg of pork. The joint is browned on top of the stove and laid on a bed of vegetables, then cooked slowly in the oven and cooled in the pan as in the previous recipe. Serves 6.

1.2 kg [2½ lb] roasting veal or pork, boned weight
25 g [1 oz] butter
2 carrots
2 onions
2 celery stalks
a bunch of parsley
1 bay leaf
275 ml [½ pt] dry white wine or cider
freshly ground black pepper

For the tuna and anchovy sauce:
3 egg yolks
320–425 ml [12–15 fl oz] olive oil
150 g [5 oz] canned tuna fish
2 × 50 g [2 oz] cans anchovy fillets
2 large lemons
75 ml [5 tablespoons] capers
salt and freshly ground black pepper

Preheat the oven to 160°C [325°F], gas mark 3. Rub the boned, rolled and neatly tied joint with plenty of pepper. Heat the butter in a roasting pan on top of the stove. Turn the joint in it to colour it lightly on all sides. Remove the meat and cook the sliced vegetables until coloured. Drain the fat from the pan and lay the meat on the bed of vegetables. Add the bay leaf and crushed parsley stalks. Pour on the wine or cider and as much water as is necessary to come halfway up the vegetables. Cover the pan with foil and braise in the oven for 2¼–2½ hours (allow the longer time for pork). Let the cooked joint cool completely in the covered pan; this will keep the meat beautifully moist and is particularly important if veal is used.

To make the tonnato sauce, first make a mayonnaise with the egg yolks and olive oil. Season it with plenty of lemon juice and pepper and very little salt. Pound the anchovies and tuna to a paste with a few drops of lemon juice. A food processor makes fast work of this; mortar and pestle take time, but will produce equally smooth results with patience. Carefully and gradually beat the mayonnaise into the fish paste. Dilute the sauce to the consistency of thick cream by blending in up to 150 ml [¼ pt] of the cold, strained braising liquor. Check and adjust seasoning to taste.

Carve the cold meat into slices and arrange them, slightly overlapping, in a dish. Pour the sauce over the meat to coat it. Cover with clingfilm or foil and refrigerate for at least 8 hours (and up to 24 hours) to allow flavours to amalgamate.

Bring the dish back to room temperature about 1 hour before serving and sprinkle it lavishly with chopped parsley, capers and slices of lemon. Serve with a green salad and plenty of good bread to mop up the delicious sauce.

Chicken Tonnato: An inexpensive dish can be made by poaching a 2.3 kg [5 lb] roasting chicken (as described in detail in the recipe for Easter chicken, page 150). Let the bird cool completely in the cooking liquor. Skin, bone and cut the meat into chunks and coat it with tonnato sauce several hours before serving.

Chicken or Turkey à la Tapenade

A more unusual sauce than tonnato, this includes many of the same ingredients. The piquant flavour somehow suggests that hours of work are needed to make this sauce. In fact, it involves no cooking and takes less than 5 minutes to make. An excellent dish when made with freshly poached chicken, and very useful for revitalising the dried-out remains of a Christmas roast turkey. Serves 6.

2.3 kg [5 lb] roasting chicken, poached and cooled in its stock, or 500–700 g
  [1¼–1½ lb] cold roast turkey meat, skinned and boned weight
1 large crisp lettuce or 4 heads of chicory
2 avocado pears
1 head of celery and/or 1 green pepper
fresh snipped chives and parsley

For the tapenade sauce:
1 × 50 g [2 oz] can of anchovy fillets
25 g [1 oz] capers
125 g [¼ lb] pimento-stuffed green olives
150 ml [¼ pt] each olive and peanut oil
2 egg yolks
1 lemon
freshly ground black pepper

To poach the chicken see recipe for Easter chicken (page 150).

To make the sauce, put the anchovy fillets and their oil into a liquidiser. Add the capers and stuffed olives and a little olive oil, and blend to a thick, very smooth and savoury purée. Add the egg yolks and the rest of the oils and blend again to make a heavy mayonnaise-type sauce. Season with pepper (no salt) and beat in a spoonful or so of lemon juice and a little cold stock or water to dilute the sauce to a cream.

Skin, bone and cut the poached and cooled chicken, or cold roast turkey, into bite-size chunks. Toss in the sauce, cover and set it aside in a cold place for an hour or so if time permits. Just before serving, pile the poultry and its sauce onto a bed of crisp shredded lettuce or chicory, to which you have added slivers of avocado, strips of green pepper and/or sliced celery. Scatter generous quantities of fresh chopped herbs over the top and serve with plenty of good bread.

Pork or Veal à la Tapenade: Tapenade sauce is excellent poured over pork or veal which has been slowly cooked, cooled and carved as described in the recipe for pork or veal tonnato.

Oeufs à la Tapenade: A very good appetiser or light lunch dish can be made by coating hard-boiled eggs and crescents of celery with tapenade sauce.

Pot-Roast Pork

In this recipe a boned and rolled joint is slow- roasted on top of the stove. This is slightly quicker than the French oven method and produces similar succulent results. Meat cooked this way is delectable served hot and very good served cold. Fennel is a lovely accompaniment. Serves 6.

1.2 kg [2½ lb] loin of pork, boned and rinded weight
3 garlic cloves
5 ml [1 teaspoon] coriander seeds
5 ml [1 teaspoon] dried thyme or fresh basil leaves
30 ml [2 tablespoons] oil
15 g [½ oz] unsalted butter
200 ml [7 fl oz] white wine or still, very dry cider, or 45 ml [3 tablespoons] dry
    vermouth plus 150 ml [¼ pt] clear meat stock
salt and freshly ground black pepper

Choose a lean joint for this recipe. If the meat is covered with a thick layer of fat, pare some of it away with a sharp knife.

Crush the garlic, coriander seeds and thyme or basil to a smooth paste with pestle and mortar. Lay the boned joint fat side down. Rub the flesh with plenty of pepper and spread the aromatic paste over it. Roll up the joint from one long side to the other, and tie it into a neat bolster shape.

Warm a flameproof casserole just large enough for the meat. Add the oil and diced butter. When the butter foam begins to subside, add the rolled joint and cook it over medium-high heat until browned all over.

Pour on the wine (or cider or vermouth) and stock and let it come to the boil. Immediately reduce heat so the liquid barely simmers. Add a seasoning of salt and pepper, place the lid askew on top of the dish and cook very gently, until the meat is quite tender — about 1½–2 hours depending on the thickness of the joint. Turn the meat occasionally and, if the cooking liquid dries up, add a few tablespoonfuls of warm water.

Let the roast rest in a warm place for about 15 minutes before carving it into fairly thin slices.

The gravy remaining in the casserole will be richly flavoured. There should be a tablespoon or so for each serving. Scrape the meaty sediment off the casserole base with a wooden spoon, dilute it with a few tablespoonfuls of hot water and stir it into the gravy. If there is too much liquid, fast boil it briefly to concentrate flavour and reduce quantity.

Pot–Roast Veal: Loin or boned and rolled shoulder of veal is luscious cooked this way, particularly if seasoned with garlic and crushed rosemary. Add an extra 25 g [1 oz] butter to the casserole. Otherwise method and timing remain as for pork.

Roast Venison with Cumberland Sauce

Venison is a delicious but very lean meat. It needs to be larded with strips of pork back fat and to be covered during roasting to prevent drying out. Traditionally the larded joint was sealed in a flour and water paste, which had to be chipped away after cooking. A roasting bag will protect the joint equally effectively, and will also allow the meat to brown. A tart, home-made rowan or elderberry jelly makes a good alternative to Cumberland sauce when available. Braised celery is a good accompaniment. Serves 6–8.

1.4 kg [3 lb] well-hung haunch of venison
150–175 g [5–6 oz] pork back fat, cut into strips
30–45 ml [2–3 tablespoons] good dripping or softened butter
salt and freshly ground black pepper

For the marinade:
5 ml [1 teaspoon] black peppercorns
1 dozen juniper berries
the zest of an orange
a sprig of thyme
60 ml [4 tablespoons] oil
275 ml [½ pt] red wine

For the Cumberland sauce:
1 Seville orange (or half a lemon and half an orange)
115 g [¼ lb] redcurrant jelly
45 ml [3 tablespoons] port
5 ml [1 teaspoon] French mustard
generous pinch each of ground ginger and cinnamon
a little salt and plenty of pepper

Lightly crush the juniper berries and peppercorns with mortar and pestle. Mix them with the rest of the marinade ingredients and bathe the venison in it. Leave to marinate in a cold place for 24–36 hours, turning the meat occasionally.

To make the Cumberland sauce (which will keep for at least 10 days if stored in a fridge in an airtight jar), first grate the citrus zest into a small saucepan. Pour on boiling water to cover, and simmer for 5 minutes to tenderise the zest. Drain well and reserve. Sieve the redcurrant jelly into the rinsed pan. Add the port, mustard, spices and seasonings, and stir over gentle heat until the jelly has melted and blended well with the other ingredients. Away from the heat, stir in the citrus juice and blanched zest. Chill the sauce.

Drain the joint from the marinade and use a larding needle to lace the meat with the strips of pork fat, threading the fat evenly through the joint to keep it succulent during roasting. Smear the entire surface of the joint with dripping or butter and sprinkle it with salt and freshly ground black pepper.

Dust the inside of a roasting bag with a thin film of flour, then slide the joint into the bag, as though packing a pillow into a pillowcase. Tie the mouth of the bag securely, leaving an airspace round the joint inside the bag. Place the parcel in a roasting tin and prick the top of the bag once or twice with a fork.

Roast the venison in an oven preheated to 180°C [350°F], gas mark 4, allowing 20 minutes per 450 g [1 lb] and 25 minutes over. Let the joint rest for 15 minutes or so before carving then pour the cooking juices over, and serve. Serve the chilled Cumberland sauce separately.

Roast Pheasant with Cream Cheese & Herbs

The breasts of game birds are usually covered with bacon rashers to keep the flesh moist during roasting. I prefer to slip some butter or cream cheese mixed with fresh herbs between the breast skin and flesh. As an added precaution against drying out, and also for extra flavour, I put more butter or bacon fat (or slices of lemon or orange) into the body cavity. Serves 3–4.

1 plump hen pheasant
50 g [2 oz] Petit Suisse
30 ml [2 tablespoons] fresh chopped parsley
15 ml [1 tablespoon] fresh chopped chives
5 ml [1 teaspoon] fresh chopped tarragon, if available
15 ml [1 tablespoon] freshly grated Parmesan cheese
butter
a few slices of lemon
salt and freshly ground black pepper

Mash the herbs with the cream cheese, Parmesan and plenty of pepper to make a smooth paste. Put your fingers under the neck skin and gently and gradually ease the skin away from the breast. Spread the herb mixture over the breast meat, taking care not to pack it too tightly: if the breast skin is stretched too taut over the stuffing, it may burst during cooking. Seal the stuffing by sewing the flap of neck skin under the bird with a few stitches, or secure it with a small wooden skewer. (Personally, I don't truss game birds or poultry: I find the leg meat cooks better if the heat can circulate freely all round the body.) Put the slices of lemon and/or lumps of butter in the body cavity of the bird.

Melt 25 g [1 oz] butter in a hot roasting pan on top of the stove, and briefly brown the pheasant all over. Season the skin with salt and pepper and transfer the pan to an oven preheated to 200°C [400°F], gas mark 6. Roasting will take about 45–60 minutes depending on the weight of the bird, but allow more time as frequent basting is necessary. To check that the bird is cooked, pierce the thickest part of the inside of the leg with a skewer: the juices should be clear.

Clear gravy with a squeeze of lemon juice in it, straw potatoes and plenty of watercress are my favourite accompaniments. Fried mushrooms, braised chicory or celery, a purée of fresh chestnuts or celeriac are also good choices.

Roast Guinea Fowl: An under-rated bird with a mild gamey flavour, like very briefly hung pheasant. I put apple slices and crushed juniper berries into the body cavity, and find 40 minutes roasting is usually enough.

Roast Partridge: Partridge must be young for roasting; allow 1 bird per person; 35 minutes, roasting should be enough.

Roast Chicken: Fresh chicken is well worth serving simply stuffed and roasted as for pheasant. I put tarragon sprigs and a slice of lemon inside the bird and cook it breast down on a rack for two-thirds of roasting time, which takes a total of 1 hour for a 1.35 kg [3 lb] bird.

Faisan à la Normande

Pheasant with fried apples, bathed in a cream and Calvados sauce, is richer than plain roast pheasant, and will feed more people. The dish can be prepared a few hours ahead and reheated for serving, but, when I once prepared it a day ahead and refrigerated it overnight, the sauce separated on reheating. Serves 4–5.

1 plump roasting pheasant
225 g [½ lb] Cox's apples
unsalted butter
a little lemon juice
125 ml [4 fl oz] Calvados
250 ml [8 fl oz] double cream
salt and freshly ground black pepper

Peel and core the apples. Brush them with lemon juice to prevent

discolouration and set aside. Put the apple trimmings into the body cavity of the pheasant to keep the flesh juicy and moist during roasting. Brown the bird all over in 25 g [1 oz] butter in a roasting pan on top of the stove. Season the skin with salt and pepper, place the bird on a rack over the roasting pan, and roast it in the oven at 200°C [400°F], gas mark 6, for 45 minutes, or until the juices run clear when you prick the thickest part of the leg. Baste frequently and roast the bird breast downwards for most of the time.

Remove the pheasant and let it rest. Add an extra 25 g [1 oz] or so of butter to the roasting pan and sauté the sliced apples until golden. Carve the pheasant. Lay it in a shallow dish and arrange the apples on top.

Warm the Calvados in a small pan, then pour it into the buttery pheasant and apple juices in the roasting pan. Set light to it and, when the flames have died down, pour on the cream. Cook, stirring continuously, until the ingredients are smoothly blended and the sauce is bubbling hot and slightly thickened — about 5 minutes. Season the sauce, pour it over the pheasant and return the dish to a low oven for 15–20 minutes before serving.

This dish is best served with triangles of crisply fried bread, without accompanying vegetables.

Poulet à la Normande: For a delicious cheaper version, use 1.35 kg [3 lb] roasting chicken instead of pheasant. Allow 1 hour for roasting the chicken (*Guinea fowl* can also be used and will take about 40 minutes to roast).

Costs can be further reduced by omitting the Calvados. Instead, boil 300 ml [½ pt] still, dry cider until reduced to 75 ml [3 fl oz]. Then stir in 30 ml [2 tablespoons] brandy or, failing that, 15 ml [1 tablespoon] lemon juice. Use the resulting mixture to make the sauce.

Pheasant with Celery & Almonds

Fried almonds and celery make crunchy and well-flavoured partners for game birds and poultry. A good recipe for roasting chicken and guinea fowl as well as for pheasant. Serves 4–5.

1 plump pheasant
1 really large, or 2 medium-sized, heads of celery
1 small onion
50 g [2 oz] split almonds
unsalted butter
350 ml [12 fl oz] giblet stock
5 ml [1 teaspoon] lemon juice
15 ml [scant 1 tablespoon] plain flour
75–90 ml [5–6 tablespoons] cream
celery salt
salt and freshly ground black pepper

Choose a small flameproof casserole into which the bird will fit snugly, and melt a little butter in it. Fry the pheasant briefly to colour it all over and remove. Add the celery cut into crescents, turn to colour lightly for a couple of minutes, remove and reserve separately.

Measure the stock and lemon juice into the casserole. Add the finely chopped onion, a good seasoning of pepper and a little each of coarse salt and celery salt. When the mixture comes to the boil, return the pheasant to the pot, lying it on its back so that the thighs are immersed in liquid; the breast will cook in rising steam. Cover the breast of the bird with a sheet of buttered greaseproof paper; put on the lid and leave to cook at the gentlest simmer for 30 minutes.

Add the prepared celery, tucking it round the bird and pushing it down into the liquid. Cover the pot again and simmer for a further 20–25 minutes until both pheasant and vegetables are tender. Meanwhile, fry the almonds in a little butter until rich golden brown.

Drain the cooked pheasant and set it on a warmed serving dish. Arrange the celery round it, scatter with almonds and keep the dish hot while you make the sauce. Ladle 275 ml [½ pt] of the cooking liquor into a saucepan. Gradually stir in small nuggets of the flour mashed to a paste with an equal quantity of softened butter. Let it simmer for 2–3 minutes, stir in the cream and check seasoning. If necessary, continuing cooking the sauce for a few minutes until well flavoured and of good consistency.

Pour a little of the sauce over the celery. Serve the rest in a sauceboat or jug.

Hare or Rabbit with Orange & Olives

The syrupy rich sauce in this recipe is good with hare and wild rabbit. A good-sized rabbit will serve 4, a hare will serve 5.

1 hare (or rabbit), jointed
275 g [10 oz] green streaky bacon, cut into dice
275 g [10 oz] sliced onions
the finely grated zest of 2 oranges
a pinch of cloves
rosemary
30 g [1 oz] caster sugar
butter and olive oil
125 ml [4 fl oz] Marsala
2 dozen black olives
salt and freshly ground black pepper

For the marinade:
30 ml [2 tablespoons] olive oil
1 onion
2 fat garlic cloves
5 ml [1 teaspoon] thyme
parsley stalks and a bay leaf
250 ml [½ pt] dry cider

Put the hare joints into a large bowl and grind a good quantity of pepper over them. To prepare the marinade, cook the finely chopped onion and garlic in the oil for a few minutes over gentle heat. Away from the heat add the herbs and cider. Pour the mixture over the hare, cover the bowl with a clean cloth and leave to marinate in a cool place for 24–36 hours, turning the meat occasionally.

Drain the hare from the marinade, pat it dry and dust it with the sugar. Heat a knob of butter and a spoonful of oil in a flameproof casserole. Add the hare, a few pieces at a time, and brown and seal the meat well. Remove the hare joints with a slotted spoon, then lightly colour the diced bacon. Remove the bacon, then lightly colour the sliced onions.

Return the hare joints and bacon to the casserole, burying them among the onions. Pour on the strained marinade liquid and Marsala, and add the orange zest, cloves, rosemary and plenty of salt and pepper.

Bring the mixture to boiling point, then cover the casserole and transfer it to an oven preheated to 150°C [300°F], gas mark 2. Cook until the hare is tender — about 2 hours — adding the olives to the casserole for the last half hour.

Just before serving, strain off the liquid and fast boil it until reduced and thickened to a syrupy rich coating sauce. Spoon the sauce over the hare and serve with a dish of steamed potatoes or parsnip or celeriac purée.

Hare or Rabbit with Mustard Cream Sauce

This is even easier to prepare than the previous recipe because the raw ingredients are simply layered in a casserole and cooked from cold. Again, it is a very good recipe for rabbit as well. Serves 6–8.

1 kg [2¼ lb] hare (or rabbit) joints
1 kg [2¼ lb] belly of pork
600 g [1¼ lb] onions
175 g [6 oz] prunes
2 fat garlic cloves
plenty of parsley and thyme
45 ml [3 tablespoons] brandy
15 ml [1 tablespoon] wine vinegar
150 ml [¼ pt] strong chicken stock
French mustard
2 egg yolks
150 ml [¼ pt] double or soured cream
salt and freshly ground black pepper

Marinate the hare as described in the previous recipe. Drain it well and strain the liquid. Cut off the pork rind in one piece and reserve it. Bone and dice the pork meat. Slice the onions thinly and push them into rings.

Lay half the onions in a casserole, season them generously with chopped parsley, thyme, garlic, salt and pepper. Lay the hare joints on top and bury the prunes among them. Cover with the remaining onions, seasoning as before, then add the diced pork.

Heat the strained marinade liquid with the stock, brandy and vinegar. Pour it into the casserole, lay the pork rind on top and cover with a well-fitting lid.

Cook in the oven at 160°C [325°F], gas mark 3, for 1 hour. Reduce the temperature to 150°C [300°F], gas mark 2 and cook for a further 2 hours.

Discard the pork rind. Transfer the meats, onions and prunes to a warm serving dish and skim the fat from the cooking liquor with a bulb baster. Reduce the liquor by fast boiling while you beat the egg yolks and cream together in a cup. Blend a little of the hot liquor into the egg and cream liaison, then blend the contents of the cup into the pan. Cook very gently indeed, stirring continuously, until the sauce has thickened. Stir in a good spoonful of mustard, check seasoning, pour the sauce over the hare and serve with boiled rice, noodles or potatoes.

Gloucester Place Pigeon

Pigeon is usually too tough to roast successfully, but cooked slowly, breast down, in a little well-flavoured liquid, the meat is kept moist and becomes very tender. Serves 6.

6 pigeons
175 g [6 oz] diced salt pork or streaky bacon
24 shallots or pickling onions
225 g [½ lb] small mushrooms
60 ml [4 tablespoons] brandy
275 ml [½ pt] beef stock
15 ml [1 tablespoon] tomato purée
seasoned flour
a little butter
2 fat garlic cloves
thyme
salt and freshly ground black pepper

Cook the pork or bacon in a large frying pan over low heat until the fat begins to melt. Add the shallots or pickling onions and brown them slightly. Using a slotted spoon transfer the bacon and onions to a casserole or baking dish which is large enough to take all 6 pigeons in a single layer.

Sauté the whole mushrooms in the bacon fat, adding a little butter if necessary. Remove from the pan and reserve. Dust the birds with well-seasoned flour and brown them in hot butter. Transfer the birds to the casserole or baking dish, burying them breast down in the bacon and onions.

Add the brandy, stock, tomato purée, thyme, crushed garlic, salt and pepper to the frying pan and bring to the boil stirring. Pour the sauce over the pigeons. Cover with a well-fitting lid and braise at 160°C [325°F], gas mark 3, for 1 hour. Reduce the heat to 150°C [300°F], gas mark 2, and cook for a further 20 minutes.

Add the sautéed mushrooms and braise for a further 30 minutes, until the pigeon meat is very tender. Lift the birds out of the pot, and arrange them on fluted rounds of fried bread. Arrange the drained onion, mushroom and bacon round them, together with clumps of watercress. Pour the juices into a sauceboat and serve with puréed potatoes or lentils.

Pigeon Cassoulet

This is my anglicised version of the traditional Languedoc recipe. A substantial, cheering and comforting dish, and a favourite for a supper party in bleakest February. No first course, no pudding, but lots of piping hot cassoulet, plenty of vin ordinaire, generous salads, ripe cheeses and the company of good friends.

Start preparations at least a day ahead. Alter proportions of beans to meats according to budget and taste, but be sure to include some fatty and some spicy meat, and to use a really well-flavoured stock. Serves 8–10.

600–700 g [1¼–1½ lb] dried haricot beans
1.1 kg [2½ lb] belly of pork
225 g [½ lb] Salamelle or Toulouse sausages or chorizo or cabanos
2 pigeons (or 1 pheasant or partridge)
1 onion
1 carrot
a large bouquet garni
4 fat garlic cloves
1 × 400 g [14 oz] can of tomatoes
1 white loaf reduced to crumbs
dried marjoram and thyme
salt and freshly ground black pepper
black peppercorns

Bone the pork and cut off the pigeon breasts. If using larger game birds, take legs and other meat off the bone as well. Make a good stock with the carcasses, pork bones, onion, carrot, bouquet garni and a few peppercorns — but no salt. Soak the beans in plenty of cold water for about 3 hours.

Turn the drained beans into a large heavy-based saucepan, and bury the cubes of pork among them (leave the pork rind on). Add the crushed garlic, tomatoes and enough unsalted stock to cover the beans completely. Do not add any salt at this stage, it is liable to toughen the bean skins. Bring to the boil, cover and simmer gently for 1 hour, adding the sausages about 10 minutes before the end of the cooking time.

Lift out the sausages and slice them thickly. Season the beanpot generously. Using a slotted spoon, transfer half the pork and bean mixture into a large, deep, buttered baking dish or casserole. Cover with the sausages and sliced pigeons or other game. Top with remaining pork and bean mixture, adding a ladleful of the stock. Sprinkle on half the breadcrumbs mixed with plenty of dried marjoram and thyme. Bake uncovered at 180°C [350°F], gas mark 4, for 1¼ hours, after which the beans should be tender and the crumbs will have formed a golden crust.

Press the crust down into the beans and add a little more stock if the beans seem dry. Top with remaining breadcrumbs mixed with another generous spoonful each of marjoram and thyme. Continue baking, this time at 150°C [300°F], gas mark 2, for about 1 hour.

The cassoulet is now ready to eat, but can remain in a low oven for a further 1–1½ hours. Or it can be cooled and refrigerated, then reheated when needed.

Raised Chicken Pie

The time-consuming part of making a raised pie is preparing the filling, but it is well worth the effort. Raised pies always look exceedingly handsome — homely yet elegant — and they are such a useful cut-and-come-again food. Hot water-crust pastry is exceptionally quick and easy to make, but you could use short-crust if you prefer, made with 225 g [½ lb] each wholewheat flour, plain flour and butter. Serves 8–10.

For the hot water-crust pastry:
450 g [1 lb] plain flour
5 ml [1 teaspoon] each salt and freshly ground black pepper
75 g [3 oz] lard
25 g [1 oz] dripping or butter
175 ml [6 fl oz] water
2 eggs

For the filling:
1 × 2 kg [4½ lb] roasting chicken
450 g [1 lb] unsmoked streaky bacon
225 g [½ lb] pie veal
225 g [½ lb] mushrooms
the juice and zest of 2 lemons
a bunch each of parsley, chives and tarragon
5 ml [1 teaspoon] allspice
275 ml [½ pt] well-flavoured jellied stock made with the chicken carcass and a
   pig's trotter
a little butter
salt and freshly ground black pepper

Skin and bone the chicken, and reserve the giblets. Cut the raw meat into slivers and put it into a large bowl. Sprinkle on the allspice, add the lemon juice and zest, mix well, cover and set aside in a cool place. Use the chicken carcass, giblets (except the liver) and pig's trotter to make stock.

Chop the mushrooms into large pieces. Sauté them in a very little butter over fairly high heat for a few minutes. Chop the chicken liver and add it to the frying pan for the last minute or so. Turn the mixture into a bowl and cool.

To make the pastry, first separate one of the eggs and put the egg yolk into a large mixing bowl. Cover it with the sifted flour, salt and pepper. Heat the diced fats and the water together in a small pan. When the fats have melted, bring to a brisk boil. Quickly pour the contents of the pan into the flour bowl, stirring the flour with a wooden spoon as you pour. When the mixture forms a ball leaving the sides of the bowl clean, turn it out and knead lightly for a minute or so to make a smooth dough. Cover the dough with the upturned bowl and leave it for **exactly** 15 minutes. (Timing is important as the key to moulding hot water crust lies in using the dough when it is just warm enough to be malleable. If it is too hot, it will slide down the pie tin; if too cold, it is very difficult to shape.)

Meanwhile, lightly grease a traditional hinged and fluted pie mould, or a 23 cm [9 inch] round cake tin with springclip sides and removable base. Preheat the oven to 220°C [425°F], gas mark 7, and finish the filling: first mince the bacon and veal very coarsely (or chop finely). Mix them with the sautéed mushrooms and chicken liver, the chopped herbs and chicken meat. Season generously with salt and pepper and mix everything well with your hands.

Leaving a generous quarter of the dough to keep warm under the upturned bowl, put the rest into the mould. Use your hands to shape it over the base, then work it gradually up the sides of the mould and extend it nearly 12 mm [½ inch] above the rim at the top. Try to work fairly quickly, pressing lightly but firmly, and be sure to make the pastry lining as smooth and even as possible — the slightest crack will encourage precious meat juices to leak out during cooking, and a thin patch of wall may collapse when the pie is unmoulded.

As an added precaution against seepage, brush the pastry lining all over with the leftover egg white. Then spoon in the filling, packing it well into the corners and mounding the top nicely in the centre. Roll out the pastry lid and place it on top of the pie. Damp the edges of the lid and press and seal them to the edges of the pastry walls. Then gently ease the sealed pastry edges slightly inwards and upwards to make a rim that stands proud of the mould. This is important because, if the pastry is sealed against the mould, it may stick as it cooks and subsequently tear during unmoulding.

Make a large steam hole in the centre of the lid and hold it open by half inserting a rolled postcard. Glaze the top of the pie with beaten egg, decorate with pastry trimmings and glaze again. Stand the pie on a baking tray and bake for 20 minutes at 220°C [425°F], gas mark 7, then for 1¾ hours at 180°C [350°F], gas mark 4, reglazing the pie top at regular intervals.

Remove the pie from the oven and let it stand at room temperature for 30 minutes. If the pie is made using hot water-crust pastry, then very carefully and gently ease the sides of the mould away from the pie. Glaze the sides of the pastry and return the pie to the oven for 10 minutes or so to colour the sides. (NB. If using shortcrust pastry, omit this step. The high fat content of shortcrust makes the pie walls liable to collapse if unmoulded before the filling is completely cold, which takes at least 5 hours.)

When the cooked pie has cooled for 5 minutes or so, carefully pour into it enough of the stock to fill any unseen gaps in the filling. The stock should be cool, but not set; if you made it a day ahead, you will have to melt it again gently. A jam funnel is useful here and using a large spoon instead of a jug means you add the liquid in a slow trickle which minimises the chances of flooding. Let the pie stand in a cold place overnight and serve it the next day. Don't cover the pie until it is completely cold.

Game Pie: For a splendidly rich pie, use pheasant, partridge, grouse or pigeon (singly or mixed) instead of chicken. You will need about 600 g [1 lb 6 oz] boned and skinned game meat. If the birds yield less meat then expected, make up the difference with snippets of tongue and ham or hard-boiled eggs. Replace lemon juice with 4 generous spoonfuls of brandy, and bacon with fat boneless belly of pork. Choose herbs and spices to complement the game used — I find juniper berries and thyme go well with all. Layer the filling, rather than mix the meats, for a spectacular effect when the pie is cut open.

Pieces of Meat

Grilled and pan-fried meats, casseroles and pies, these are the meat dishes most cooks like to cook most of the time — grilled and fried meats when time is of the essence, casseroles and pies for greater economy and a sense of homeliness.

I have devoted the first half of this chapter to dishes that are cooked on top of the stove. Most of them are rewardingly quick to cook and will therefore appeal to the cook in a hurry. Many have the not unmixed blessing of smelling so wonderfully inviting as they bubble in the pan or burnish under the grill, that they draw diners eagerly into the kitchen.

Best quality tender cuts of meat are essential for grilling and frying. Escallopes of veal, steaks and lamb cutlets are favourite choices, but very expensive. I have included a few recipes using these luxury items but, with a keen eye to the housekeeping budget, many of my grilled and fried recipes use the more modestly priced tender cuts, such as chicken joints, pork and offal.

All grilled and pan-fried dishes must be eaten more or less straight from the pan as delays between cooking and serving wilt their charm completely. It is probably for this reason that these dishes are usually avoided when entertaining. However, I would suggest that a meal which begins with one of these dishes (accompanied by good bread to mop up the juices), is followed by salad and cheese served together, and finishes with a cold cook-ahead pudding, will be much appreciated by guests and family alike. It makes a well-balanced feast and has the advantage of involving less work than the traditional three-course pattern demands. In fact such a menu is an exceptionally practical and attractive proposition for the cook–hostess who wants to have friends to dinner during the week, but whose working day rules out anything elaborate.

I have also included a few top-of-the-stove dishes which are not so quickly cooked but which are too good not to enjoy now and again. Amongst these are steak and kidney pudding, a wonderful dish that makes the onset of cold wintry weather seem almost welcome, and several variations on the meat pudding theme using pigeon and other fillings. Also in this section is osso buco, perhaps my favourite of all veal dishes, and a similar but cheaper version that I have devised for everyday occasions using oxtail instead of shin of veal.

The second half of the chapter is concerned with oven-cooked dishes. These range from traditional toad-in-the-hole (often rated as a children's dish, but irresistible to most adults if made with really good sausages) to Greek and South African minced beef dishes which make attractive alternatives when shepherd's pie otherwise seems inevitable.

There are lots of comforting casseroles, like oystered beef with green peppers, and fresh-tasting ragoûts, such as pork with basil and tomatoes, which are inexpensive and can be cooked ahead and reheated when needed. I usually make double quantities of this kind of dish and freeze some to serve the following week. I also include a few dishes, like French farmhouse steaks, which hold a special place in my affections. These are what I call cold-start dishes. They are exceptionally quick and effortless to prepare and enable you to go out for the day leaving the dish to start cooking by automatic timer. You come home to be greeted, for example, by the rich scent of a casserole that is ready and waiting to be eaten, a prospect I find as heartwarming as the thought of a log fire in the grate and my slippers warming beside it. Cold-start dishes only need the cook's attention for the 5 minutes or so it takes to put a few raw ingredients into an ovenproof dish, place the dish in the oven, and set timing and temperature controls. Such dishes are tailor-made for occasions when you are too tired, too lazy or too busy to cook, and they are an answer to the prayers of those who claim they cannot boil an egg, but are suddenly required to fend for themselves.

Lamb Steaks in Herb Blankets

If you grow your own herbs, this is a simple way to make grilled lamb taste and smell very special. Thick slices of meat, taken from the fillet end of a leg of lamb, make tender and generous steaks. Alternatively you could use large chump chops. Serves 4.

4 leg of lamb steaks
30 ml [2 tablespoons] lemon juice
60 ml [4 tablespoons] olive oil
90 ml [6 tablespoons] fresh chopped parsley
30 ml [2 tablespoons] each fresh chopped mint and chives
15 ml [1 tablespoon] each fresh chopped tarragon and marjoram
salt and freshly ground black pepper

Mix the lemon juice, oil and a good grinding of black pepper together in a gratin dish. Add the steaks, turn to coat them all over, cover the dish and set aside to marinate in a cold place for 1–8 hours.

Heat the grill until very hot. Lay the steaks on a grid suspended across the gratin dish and grill the meat for 1½ minutes on each side under fierce heat to seal and colour the meat. Then reduce heat to medium-low and continue grilling for a further 3–5 minutes on each side, depending on how pink or well cooked you like lamb.

Meanwhile, chop the fresh herbs and mix them together. Strew a few of them on a warm serving dish. Lay the cooked steaks on top, sprinkle them with salt, cover with the remaining herbs and pour on the pan juices. Serve immediately with plenty of good bread to mop up the herb-scented meat juices.

Winter Lamb Steaks: When fresh herbs are not available, a similar dish can be made using 1 garlic clove, 10 ml [2 teaspoons] each dried basil and thyme and 7 ml [scant 2 teaspoons] dried rosemary. Crush these flavouring with some peppercorns, add 30 ml [2 tablespoons] olive oil and half that quantity of lemon juice. Turn the lamb steaks in this and leave in a cold place for 3–9 hours. If left for more than 5 hours, scrape off and discard the herbs before grilling or flavours will be very strong. If grilling with the herb coating, allow slightly longer than usual for the heat to penetrate the herbs and cook the lamb properly.

Istanbul Cutlets

Another very easy and aromatic way to grill lamb. Noisettes can be used instead of cutlets if you prefer. Serves 4.

8–12 trimmed lamb cutlets
a bunch of mint

For the sauce:
a small cucumber
half a small onion
150 ml [¼ pt] plain yoghurt
fresh mint
salt and freshly ground black pepper

First make the sauce. Seed but do not peel the cucumber and cut the flesh into small dice. Grate the onion coarsely. Stir both vegetables into the yoghurt and season well with salt, pepper and a little chopped mint. Cover and chill very thoroughly.

Grill the cutlets under a very hot grill for a minute or so on each side to seal the meat. Continue grilling under more moderate heat for 3–5 minutes on each side, depending on how well cooked you like lamb.

Decorate the cutlets with paper frills and pile them onto a warmed serving dish that has been strewn with sprigs of fresh mint. Pour on the pan juices, sprinkle the meat with a seasoning of salt and pepper and serve with the well-chilled sauce.

Kotopoulo tis Skaras

This is the Greek way to grill chicken, for which I use the fresh portions of breast or thigh meat that can be bought at chain-stores. Whether you use fresh or dried herbs, the delicious cooking smells will very likely draw the whole family into the kitchen. Grilled tomatoes, bunches of watercress and a small dish of rice make admirable accompaniments. Serves 4.

1.1 kg [2½ lb] chicken breasts or thighs
60 ml [4 tablespoons] olive oil
30 ml [2 tablespoons] lemon juice
20 ml [4 teaspoons] fresh chopped marjoram or half quantity dried marjoram
20 ml [4 teaspoons] fresh chopped thyme or half quantity dried thyme
salt and freshly ground black pepper

Mix the oil, lemon juice and herbs in a shallow dish. Add a good grinding of pepper but no salt. Prick the chicken flesh all over with a fork, turn the pieces in the marinade and leave in a cool place for up to 8 hours whilst the chicken absorbs the flavours.

Lay the chicken pieces, skin side down, on a grid suspended over a gratin or baking dish. Pour on the marinade liquid. Grill under medium-high heat for 8–10 minutes, basting occasionally. Turn the chicken pieces over and grill them for a further 8–10 minutes, using fierce heat for the last 5 minutes so that the skin crisps to a rich golden brown while the flesh remains juicy and tender. Stir the pan juices into the accompanying dish of boiled rice just before serving.

Greek Skewered Lamb: 700 g [1½ lb] lean boneless lamb (fillet or shoulder meat carefully trimmed of excess fat) is delicious cut into large cubes, marinated as described in the main recipe, then threaded onto skewers and grilled for 8–12 minutes.

Dip small whole mushrooms and wedges of onion into the marinade mixture to moisten them, and thread them onto the skewers in between the chunks of meat. Do not pack the ingredients very tightly on the skewers unless you specifically want fairly rare lamb.

This recipe is excellent served hot with rice, or made into sandwiches for a picnic. To make the sandwiches, cut a French loaf into pieces as long as the skewers. Slice each piece lengthways, leaving a hinge down one side, and scoop out some of the crumb. Lay the hot, freshly cooked kebab (still on its skewer) in the hollow, sprinkle it with a little salt and pour on some of the pan juices. Close the bread, stick an old cork onto the protruding point of the skewer, then wrap the sandwich in foil, place it between two chopping boards and put weights on top. By the time the sandwich is cold and flattened, the meat, vegetable and herb juices will have seeped into the bread.

Tandoori Breast of Chicken

A "pretend" version as anyone who has eaten the real article will quickly recognise, but I have found tandoori lovers to be rather enthusiastic about it. Preparations and cooking take 10 and 20 minutes respectively; the preparations should be carried out a day ahead of cooking. Serves 6.

6 large pieces of chicken breast meat
7 ml [1 heaped teaspoon] chilli powder
30 ml [2 tablespoons] lemon juice
15 ml [1 tablespoon] each cumin and coriander seeds
the seeds from 3 cardamom pods
3 fat garlic cloves
90 ml [6 tablespoons] double cream
30 ml [2 tablespoons] concentrated tomato purée
40 g [1½ oz] butter

Carefully skin the chicken and remove any fat and bones. Prick the flesh all over with the point of a knife and make 2 or 3 slashes across the thickest part of the meat. Sprinkle on the chilli powder, pour on the lemon juice and brush the mixture all over the chicken and deep into the cuts.

Warm the cumin and coriander seeds in a small pan over low heat for a minute or so to bring out their aroma. Pound them together with the cardamom seeds and garlic with mortar and pestle. Stir in the tomato purée and blend in the cream to make a thick and aromatic paste. Spread this all over the chicken, cover the dish and leave it in a cold place for 24 hours.

To cook, lay the chicken on a grid over a gratin dish and cover with flakes of butter. Grill, several inches away from the heat, for about 8 minutes, basting occasionally with the pan drippings and more butter if necessary. Turn the chicken over and grill for a further 8 minutes, again basting occasionally, until the chicken flesh is very tender and the paste has formed a surface crust. Serve with spiced rice, poppadoms, and a bowl of iced yoghurt.

Veal, Pork or Chicken with Mushroom Cream

Not cheap, but useful when you want something special and rich-tasting that is very quick to cook. Fillet of pork, sliced and beaten very thin, can also be used, so can skinned, boned and beaten breast of chicken, but the latter takes slightly longer to cook. Serves 4.

4 escallopes of veal, beaten very thin and weighing 100–125 g [3½–4 oz] each
225 g [½ lb] mushrooms, thickly sliced
about 150 g [5 oz] unsalted butter
300 ml [½ pt] double cream
15 ml [1 tablespoon] lemon juice
salt and freshly ground black pepper

Melt a little butter in a hot frying pan. Add 2 escallopes and fry gently for 3–4 minutes on each side. Remove to a warm serving dish and keep hot. Add a little more butter if necessary and cook the remaining pieces of veal in the same way. Drain and add them to the warmed serving dish.

Increase heat under the pan. Add another knob of butter and, when it is sizzling hot, tip in the mushrooms. Sauté for several minutes over brisk heat to evaporate most of the juices. Lift the mushrooms out of the pan onto a plate and keep them hot.

Reduce heat to low again. Add 75 g [3 oz] butter, cut into small dice, to the frying pan. When it has melted, quickly pour in the cream and increase heat to medium. Cook, stirring continuously, for about 3 minutes or so until the cream and butter homogenise to make a smooth, hot and slightly reduced sauce.

Remove the pan from the heat. Tip in the mushrooms, add the lemon juice and a very generous seasoning of salt and pepper. Stir to blend everything well, then pour the sauce over the veal slices and serve the dish immediately. Hot crusty bread is the only accompaniment needed.

Veal, Pork or Chicken with Cucumber Cream: A delicately flavoured, slightly less rich dish, but it takes longer to prepare as some of the cucumber juices must be drained off before cooking. This dish can also be made with fillet of pork or breast of chicken.

Peel and seed 2 large cucumbers and cut the flesh into matchstick strips. Sprinkle with 5 ml [1 teaspoon] each caster sugar and salt and a double quantity of wine or tarragon vinegar. Leave for 1 hour, drain and squeeze dry with kitchen paper towels.

Fry the cucumber before the veal, cooking it in 40 g [1½ oz] butter for 8–10 minutes over medium heat until tender and hot. After cooking the veal, make the butter cream sauce but omit the lemon juice and add chopped fresh tarragon leaves or dill when seasoning with salt and pepper.

Fillet of Pork with Pimientos

An elegant little dish, similar to the previous recipe, but with a less rich sauce. Reasonably priced when made with pork fillet, it can also be made using escallopes of veal or skinned, boned and flattened breast of chicken. Serves 4.

600 g [1¼ lb] fillet of pork
1 × 190 g [7 oz] can of sweet red peppers
40 g [1½ oz] butter
250 ml [scant ½ pt] well-flavoured chicken stock
1 egg yolk
60 ml [4 tablespoons] double cream
coriander seeds
salt and freshly ground black pepper
black peppercorns

Trim fat and membrane from the pork. Cut the flesh across into 6 mm [¼ inch] thick slices, and beat each one flat between sheets of clingfilm or greaseproof paper. Pound 10 ml [2 teaspoons] coriander seeds with a few black peppercorns (using a mortar and pestle or grinding them in a peppermill) and dust the pork all over with this mixture. Warm the red peppers, draining them of the liquid in the can, and immersing them in the hot chicken stock for 5 minutes or so.

Melt the butter in a large frying pan. When it is foaming hot, add the slices of pork, a few at a time. When cooked, transfer the pork to a hot serving dish. Drain the red peppers, cut them into thin strips and arrange them on top of the pork.

Add the chicken stock to the frying pan and cook, stirring, over medium-high heat until reduced by about half. Beat the egg yolk and cream together in a cup with some salt, pepper and a few crushed coriander seeds. Blend a little of the hot sauce into the cream mixture, then carefully blend the contents of the cup into the pan and cook, stirring, over very low heat until the sauce is hot, creamy smooth and thickened. Pour the sauce over the pork and pimientos and serve immediately.

Afelia

Pork and coriander again, this is a wonderful, quick and easy dish, yet it always tastes as though hours of careful blending and cooking have gone into its making. Serves 4.

600–700 g [1¼–1½ lb] fillet, leg or blade of pork (boned and rinded weight)
coriander seeds
soft brown sugar
15 ml [1 tablespoon] olive oil
275 ml [½ pt] dry white or red wine
25 g [1 oz] butter
fresh chopped coriander leaves or parsley
salt and freshly ground black pepper

Trim away any sinew and cut the pork into cubes. Put the meat into a shallow dish. Sprinkle on equal quantities of crushed coriander seeds, pepper and soft brown sugar, using a total of about 20 ml [1 heaped tablespoon]. Toss the ingredients lightly and leave the dish in a cold place for at least half an hour and up to 4 hours.

Choose a frying pan large enough to take the pork cubes in one layer. Heat the olive oil in the pan over high heat. When the oil is sizzling hot, add the pork and fry it briskly until browned all over. Pour on the wine — stand back, it will bubble up — and, after a minute or so, reduce the heat to medium-low. Leave the pork to cook for about 20 minutes, turning the cubes occasionally to encourage even cooking.

By the time the wine has reduced to a syrupy consistency, the meat will be tender. Stir in the butter and coriander leaves or parsley. As soon as the butter has melted, season to taste with salt, pepper and crushed coriander seeds. Turn the pork and its sauce onto a bed of boiled and lightly buttered noodles, and serve.

If you don't have a bottle of wine open, use instead 200 ml [7 fl oz] very dry cider mixed with 15 ml [1 tablespoon] lemon juice and 45 ml [3 tablespoons] boiling water in which you have crushed half a chicken stock cube.

Garlic Pork: For a similar, but even quicker dish, dust the pork cubes with pepper only and cook immediately. Fry the pork briskly in 50 g [2 oz] butter until browned and sealed. Reduce heat to low, add an extra 50 g [2 oz] butter to the pan and 2 large very finely chopped garlic cloves. Half cover the pan and leave to cook very gently for 20 minutes or so until the meat is tender, stirring and turning the cubes occasionally to encourage even cooking. Season, sprinkle very lavishly with fresh chopped parsley and chives and serve the meat and its buttery juices on a bed of tagliatelle.

Quick Sweet & Sour Pork

A good dish for two people and particularly tasty if the pork is served on a large bed of crisp, shredded lettuce, accompanied by lots of good bread to mop up the sauce.

2 large pork chops
60 ml [4 tablespoons] tarragon vinegar
20 ml [1 slightly heaped tablespoon] soft brown sugar
1 garlic clove
peanut oil
soy sauce
freshly ground black pepper

Make deep cuts at intervals in the fat on the pork chops to prevent it curling up during cooking. Lay the chops in a shallow dish. Sprinkle on the finely chopped garlic and pour on the vinegar. Turn the pork to moisten it all over, cover the dish and leave in a cold place for at least 1 hour before cooking, or all day if you like.

Heat a heavy-based frying pan over medium–high heat. Add a little oil to film the bottom of the pan. Drain the chops very thoroughly, reserving their juices. Add the chops to the pan and cook for 1–1½ minutes to seal and brown the meat on both sides. Reduce the heat to medium–low and fry gently for another 7–8 minutes on each side. Lift the meat out of the pan and keep it hot.

Draw the pan away from the heat, and add the vinegar and garlic juices to the pan. Stand back, as the vinegar fumes are pretty powerful, and use a long-handled wooden spoon to scrape up the meaty sediment from the pan base. Return the pan to low heat and let the juices bubble up and reduce for a minute or so.

Switch off the heat, but leave the pan where it is. Add the sugar, a good grinding of pepper and a generous splash of soy sauce, and stir until the sugar has dissolved. Pour the rich brown sauce over the chops and serve immediately.

Note: For a very economical dish, replace pork chops with 350 g [¾ lb] lean belly of pork rashers. Cut off the pork rind and cube the meat, then marinate and cook as described above.

Steak Tartare

I love this famous dish of raw steak. Seasoning it is a matter of personal taste, so I prefer to make the basic meat mixture fairly mild in flavour (as here), and to place tiny bowls of extra chopped onions, etc., on the table, so that people can help themselves to more. Serves 4.

well-hung rump or fillet steak weighing 700 g [1½ lb] after all fat and gristle have
　been trimmed away
75 g [3 oz] onion, peeled weight
30 ml [2 tablespoons] capers
60 ml [4 tablespoons] fresh chopped parsley
10 ml [2 teaspoons] each olive oil and Worcestershire sauce
5 ml [1 teaspoon] lemon juice
4 small egg yolks
salt and freshly ground black pepper

The best ways to break down the raw meat fibre are to put the steak through a food processor, or to scrape the meat against the grain with the blade of a knife. If you do not own a food processor and do not have the time to reduce the meat by hand, put it through the fine blade of a mincer.

Chop the onion and capers very finely indeed. Put them into a mixing bowl, together with the prepared meat, the olive oil, lemon juice, Worcestershire sauce, parsley and a good seasoning of salt and pepper. Mix together very thoroughly. Divide into 4 portions, shape each into a disc, and make a hollow in the centre of each. Put an egg yolk into each hollow. Diners can stir the egg into the steak at table.

Skewered Kidneys with Nut Butter

A very good way to serve kidneys. The nut butter also goes well with grilled fish, chops, steaks and baked potatoes. Serves 4.

12 lambs' kidneys
25 ml [scant 2 tablespoons] olive oil
2.5 ml [½ teaspoon] each salt, cumin and coriander seeds
salt and freshly ground black pepper

For the nut butter:
75 g [3 oz] butter
40 g [1½ oz] dukka (see page 55) or toasted and chopped hazelnuts seasoned with pounded cumin and coriander
45 ml [3 tablespoons] fresh chopped chives
a little salt
watercress for garnish

First make the nut butter. Beat the softened butter until creamy. Mix in the chives and nut mixture and a little salt. Using wet hands mould the butter into a bolster shape, roll it up in damp greaseproof paper and chill until solid.

Skin, core and halve the kidneys. Grind the spices with mortar and pestle, and mix with salt and pepper in a gratin dish. Pour on the oil. Add the kidneys and turn them to coat them all over, then thread them ribbon fashion onto skewers. Suspend the skewers across the top of the dish.

Grill under high heat for a few minutes, turning the skewers and basting with oil as necessary, until the kidneys are browned on the surface, but still juicy and pink within.

Serve on a bed of plain boiled rice with the pan juices poured over. Top with pats of the chilled nut butter and garnish generously with watercress.

Fegato Alla Veneziana

Seasoning a traditional Venetian dish with English ketchup and Worcestershire sauce sounds sacrilegious, and you can, of course, omit these ingredients. But I think they make splendid additions, particularly when using lambs' liver. Serves 4.

500 g [1 lb] calves' or lambs' liver
500 g [1 lb] onions
butter and olive oil
tomato ketchup
Worcestershire sauce
salt and freshly ground black pepper

Rather than buying thick, uneven, badly butchered slices, it is often better to buy liver in one piece. Using a very sharp knife, cut it down the length of the lobe in thin slices. Remove the transparent membrane and cut out any tubes. Cut the liver into very thin slices, then cut the slices into matchstick strips.

Slice the onions very thinly, then push the slices into rings. Melt the fats in a large frying pan over very low heat. Add the onions, cover and cook, stirring the contents of the pan occasionally, for about 20 minutes until the onions are very tender.

Push the softened onions into a ring round the edge of the pan and increase the heat to medium-high. When hot, add the liver to the centre of the pan and cook it for just a minute or so, turning it more or less continuously with a pair of wooden spoons, so that it browns on all sides but remains tender and just pink inside.

Reduce the heat to low. Add a spoonful each of tomato ketchup and Worcestershire sauce and a good seasoning of salt and pepper. Stir for 1 minute to mix all the ingredients well. Serve immediately with a potato purée.

Foie aux Fines Herbes

Liver must be served as soon as it is cooked; if it is left in the oven while the rest of the meal is prepared or eaten, it will continue to cook and quickly turn to leather. I rarely precede offal dishes with a first course for this reason. But, if you do, I suggest you slice the liver and prepare the fines herbes before you start the meal, and cook the dish between courses. The cooking takes only 5 minutes or so, a natural interval after the first course. Serves 4.

450 g [1 lb] calves' or lambs' liver
175 g [6 oz] mushrooms
1 small garlic clove
90 ml [6 tablespoons] fresh chopped parsley
15 ml [1 tablespoon] fresh chopped tarragon
30 ml [2 tablespoons] fresh chopped chives
10–15 ml [2–3 teaspoons] lemon juice
a little well-seasoned flour
olive oil and butter
salt and freshly ground black pepper

Using a mezzaluna and bowl or a sharp knife, chop the mushrooms very finely. Crush the garlic and mix it with the mushrooms and chopped herbs. Slice the liver thinly, peel away the membrane and cut away any tubes. Dust a large square of work surface with a little very well-seasoned flour.

When ready to cook, heat a frying pan over medium-high heat. Add about 30 ml [2 tablespoons] of olive oil and 25 g [1 oz] butter. Quickly dry the liver slices by turning them in the seasoned flour. Add them, a few at a time, to the hot fat. Cook only long enough to seal and sear the meat on both sides: it should have a surface crust, but still be pliable to the touch and tender inside — faintly pink, but by no means raw. Transfer the cooked liver slices to a warmed serving dish. Tip the fines herbes mixture into the pan and reduce the heat slightly. Cook, stirring, for 2–3 minutes. Add the lemon juice and a good seasoning of salt and pepper. Stir to mix well and spoon the mixture over the liver slices.

Beignets de Cervelles

Deep-fat frying is my least favoured cooking method, but some fried foods are so good that greed overcomes my dislike of the process. A cheap dish, as well as a delectable one, and very popular with most professed offal haters, provided any preliminary advertising is discreet. Serves 4–5.

700 g [1½ lb] calves', sheep's or lambs' brains
1 large lemon
90 ml [6 tablespoons] oil
salt and freshly ground black pepper
oil for frying

For the fritter batter:
125 g [¼ lb] plain flour, well seasoned
30 ml [2 tablespoons] oil
150 ml [¼ pt] tepid water
2 egg whites

Soak the brains in cold salted water for at least 2 hours to wash away any little chips of bone and blood. Rinse in fresh cold water and gently pull away the opaque white material and as much membrane as you can without tearing the flesh. Put the brains into a saucepan, add a good spoonful of lemon juice and boiling water to cover. Poach at a bare simmer for 15–20 minutes.

Drain the brains well and turn them into a shallow dish. Pour on the remaining lemon juice, the oil and a good grinding of pepper and salt. Leave the brains to cool slightly before cutting them into thick slices. Toss gently to coat all the cut surfaces with the marinade, and leave until the brains are completely cold.

Make the batter by whisking the oil and tepid water into the sifted and well-seasoned flour, until smooth and creamy. Set the batter aside in a cold place for an hour or two.

When ready to cook, drain the brains very thoroughly. Heat good quality oil in a deep-fat fryer to 180°C [350°F]. Whisk the egg whites and fold them into the batter. Coat the brains with batter and deep-fry them, a few at a time, for 2–3 minutes until puffed up and golden. Drain on plenty of crumpled kitchen paper and serve piping hot. Wedges of lemon, good bread, a plain green salad and a bowl of mayonnaise (into which you have stirred plenty of fresh chopped herbs) will complete the feast.

Cervelles en Salade: One of the best ways to show off the soft creamy texture and delicate flavour of brains is to serve them as a salad — for a first course or as a light lunch dish.

Marinate the poached brains in plenty of olive oil and lemon juice with a good grinding of salt and pepper. When the brains are completely cold, stir in a generous handful of coarse chopped parsley and a few capers for extra colour and flavour. Serve the salad with plenty of crusty bread.

Cervelles au Beurre Noir: Poach, marinate and slice the brains as in the main recipe. Drain them when cold. Dust them in well-seasoned flour and shallow fry in a little clarified butter for about 3 minutes on each side until hot and pale gold. Pile onto a warmed serving dish. Quickly make and pour over them some beurre noir (see page 222).

Osso Buco alla Milanese

Perhaps the best of all veal dishes, traditionally served with a fragrant risotto (recipe page 120), this is fairly substantial. If you want to precede it with an appetiser, be sure to choose something really light and simple, such as melon or poor man's caviar. Serves 4.

4 × 5 cm [2 inch] thick slices of shin of young veal
40 g [1½ oz] butter
10 ml [2 teaspoons] olive oil
a small onion
2 celery stalks
150 ml [¼ pt] dry white wine
4 large tomatoes, skinned and chopped
275 ml [½ pt] veal or chicken stock
salt and freshly ground black pepper

For the gremolata:
a small bunch of parsley
1 fat garlic clove
1 lemon

Choose a sauté pan or flameproof casserole wide enough to take the slices of meat in a single layer. Heat it and add the butter and oil. Brown the meat all over, rolling the slices to brown and seal the sides. Then lay the meat flat so the bones stand upright and thus hold the delicious marrow in place. Finely chop the onion and celery. Push the vegetable pieces into the gaps between the pieces of meat and colour them too.

Pour on the wine and cook briskly for 10 minutes or so until it has reduced to a few spoonfuls. Add the skinned and chopped tomatoes and stock and bring the contents of the pan back to boiling point. Reduce the heat to the gentlest possible simmer, cover the pan with a well-fitting lid and cook for 1 hour 20 minutes. Turn the slices of meat once during this time.

Finally, uncover the pan and continue simmering for a further 20 minutes until the meat is tender and the sauce has reduced to a good consistency. Season it to taste with salt and pepper.

While the sauce reduces, prepare the gremolata. Chop the garlic finely, grate the lemon zest and chop the parsley. Mix the three ingredients together and sprinkle them over the veal immediately before serving.

Oxtail all' Osso Buco

This is my adaptation of osso buco for everyday entertaining and family occasions. This treatment lifts oxtail very successfully from the cheap and cheerful to the distinguished class. One practical advantage of this dish over true osso buco is that it is much better if cooked a day ahead and reheated for serving. Cooking oxtail ahead is important in order to remove all the fat, which is easy to scrape off the surface of the dish when cold and solid. If left in the dish it will taste unpleasantly greasy.

The flavour of oxtail is more robust than shin of veal, and it will overpower a delicate risotto. It is better to accompany the oxtail with a dish of long-grain rice that has been boiled in beef stock with a few slices of lemon, some salt and a generous lump of butter. Serves 4–5.

1.1 kg [2½ lb] oxtail cut into 5 cm [2 inch] pieces
2 onions
3 celery stalks
200 ml [7 fl oz] dry white wine or very dry cider
200 ml [7 fl oz] light beef stock
1 × 225 g [8 oz] can of tomatoes
a little butter and olive oil
salt and freshly ground black pepper

For the gremolata:
a small bunch of parsley
1 fat garlic clove
1 lemon

Trim the oxtail of surplus fat, wash and dry it thoroughly. Choose a flameproof casserole with a large surface area so that it will take the oxtail in a single layer. Heat a little butter and olive oil, add the oxtail in batches and colour it all over; add the finely chopped onions and celery to the casserole with the last batch.

Return all the meat to the casserole. Pour on the wine, or cider, and let it bubble up and simmer uncovered for 10 minutes until slightly reduced. Add the mashed tomatoes and their juices, the beef stock and a scant seasoning of salt and pepper. Bring back to simmering point, cover the dish with a lid and transfer it to the oven.

Cook gently at 140°–150°C [275°–300°F], gas mark 1–2, for 3–3½ hours, until the meat is tender and beginning to come away from the bones. Turn the pieces of meat over halfway through the cooking time.

Lift the meat out of the casserole, draining it well. Put it into a bowl, cover with foil and leave in a cold place overnight. Leave the rest of the ingredients in the casserole and chill overnight.

Next day, scrape off and discard the fat that has solidified on the surface of the casserole. Return the meat to the casserole. Place the dish over low heat and bring slowly back to simmering point. Cook it without a lid for 20–30 minutes until the meat is thoroughly reheated, and very tender. If the sauce is of good consistency just season it. If necessary, lift out the meat and let the liquid boil for a few minutes until sufficiently concentrated. Finely chop and grate the gremolata ingredients. Mix them together and sprinkle them over the meat just before serving.

Beefsteak & Kidney Pudding

A meat pudding is my favourite alternative to roast beef, and not only because it is so much cheaper. It is a splendid choice for Sunday lunch in winter, particularly when friends from abroad are visiting.

Avoid the mean and gristly mixtures of meats some butchers sell ready cubed for steak and kidney puddings and pies. Use well-hung chuck steak and plenty of ox kidney — the latter produces richly flavoured gravy and is very cheap, so it will offset the cost of using braising steak.

For very special occasions, I add a few oysters: don't cook them, just slip them into the pudding when the crust is cut open for serving. Serves 6.

750 g [generous 1½ lb] chuck steak
350 g [¾ lb] ox kidney

225 g [½ lb] small cap mushrooms
2 medium-sized onions
10 ml [2 teaspoons] lemon juice
5 ml [1 teaspoon] Worcestershire sauce
400 ml [14 fl oz] beef stock
50 g [2 oz] beef dripping
45 ml [3 tablespoons] plain flour
a bouquet garni
salt and freshly ground black pepper

For the suetcrust:
350 g [¾ lb] self-raising flour
5 ml [1 teaspoon] each baking powder, salt and dried mixed herbs
175 g [6 oz] shredded suet
about 175 ml [6 fl oz] water

It is best to prepare the filling a day ahead. This enables you to check the texture and flavour of the gravy before sealing the filling in the pastry, and makes for relatively brief boiling of the pudding, which will produce a particularly light suetcrust.

Heat half the dripping in a large flameproof casserole and sauté the mushrooms over high heat. Remove them with a slotted spoon and reserve. Add the rest of the dripping. When it is very hot, seal the steak and kidneys. Both meats should be cut into good-sized cubes and cooked in batches to make each cube really crusty and brown. When sealed, remove the meats from the casserole onto a plate.

Chop the onions finely. Add them to the casserole, together with a little extra fat if necessary, and cook them until slightly coloured. Sprinkle on the flour, pour on the stock and cook, stirring continuously, until you have a smooth, slightly thickened, simmering sauce. Season with salt and pepper, the lemon juice and Worcestershire sauce, and add the bouquet garni. Return the meats to the casserole — but not the mushrooms — pushing them well down into the gravy. Bring the ingredients quickly back to simmering point, cover with a lid and transfer the casserole to an oven preheated to 150°C [300°F], gas mark 2. Cook for 1½ hours.

Remove the bouquet garni, taste the gravy and adjust seasoning as necessary. Set the covered casserole aside until the contents are cold. If the filling is hot when put into the suet-lined basin, it will spoil the pastry.

About 2 hours before you plan to serve the pudding, make the pastry. Sift the flour, salt and baking powder. Stir in the suet and herbs, then enough cold water to make a soft dough. Use three-quarters of the dough to line a large well-buttered pudding basin.

Stir the reserved mushrooms into the cold meat mixture and fill the pastry-lined basin, mounding the centre top. Fold surplus pastry lining over the filling and brush it with cold water. Cover with a "lid" made from the reserved pastry, and pinch the two pastry edges to seal them well. Cover with a dome of buttered and pleated foil and tie securely under the basin rim.

Lower the pudding onto a trivet in a large deep pan containing enough boiling water to come halfway up the sides of the basin. Cover the pan with a well-fitting lid and boil for 1½ hours (or up to 2 hours if more convenient), topping up with extra boiling water if and when the level falls drastically.

Remove wrappings and tie a crisply starched white linen napkin round the basin just before serving the pudding.

Venison Pudding: Follow the basic recipe above, but replace meats with 900 g [2 lb] marinated stewing venison and 225 g [½ lb] diced salt pork. Add some crushed juniper berries and a few spoonfuls of redcurrant jelly to the gravy. Preliminary cooking will take 2–2½ hours.

Pigeon Pudding: Follow the basic recipe, but use the breast meat of 3 pigeons and 350 g [¾ lb] green bacon instead of steak and kidney. Use stock made with the pigeon carcasses, seasoning it with thyme and thinly pared orange zest. Increase mushrooms to 350 g [¾ lb] and add 75 g [3 oz] pitted prunes when putting the filling into the pastry-lined basin.

Beefsteak & Kidney Pie: Increase the initial cooking by 1 hour. After cooling the contents of the casserole completely, turn them into a large pie dish. Cover with puff or flaky pastry, glaze, make a steam hole and bake in the oven on a preheated baking tray at 220°C [425°F], gas mark 7, for about 35 minutes. *Venison* and *pigeon pie* can be made in the same way.

Beef with Tomatoes & Olives

This easy beef dish will feed 6–8 people very economically if

served with generous quantities of egg noodles. More extravag-
antly it will serve 4 if noodles are omitted and the casserole is
topped with a handful of fried croûtons just before serving.

1 kg [generous 2 lb] chuck steak
250 g [½ lb] streaky bacon rashers
2 dozen black olives
2 large onions
4 fat garlic cloves
a little olive oil
2 × 225 g [8 oz] cans of tomatoes
15 ml [1 tablespoon] red wine vinegar
a good pinch of sugar
7 ml [1 heaped teaspoon] dried thyme
a bunch of parsley
salt and freshly ground black pepper

Cube the beef. Brown and seal it in small batches in a little very
hot oil in a large frying pan. Transfer the browned beef to a
casserole. Chop the onions roughly and colour them lightly in
the oil remaining in the pan.

Meanwhile, cut off and reserve the bacon rinds. Cut each
rasher in half and stretch each bacon piece flat with the back of the
knife. Roll up the bacon pieces and bury them amongst the beef.
Lay the olives here and there, on top of the beef and bacon
mixture.

Crush the garlic cloves and liquidise the canned tomatoes to a

boning knife

meat cleaver

carving knife

purée. Add the garlic and purée to the frying pan, together with the sugar, vinegar and thyme, and bring to the boil. Pour the contents of the frying pan into the casserole and season well with salt and pepper. Lightly crush the parsley stalks, and tie them with the bacon rinds into a bundle with a piece of string, then bury the bundle in the casserole.

Place the casserole in an oven preheated to 150°C [300°F], gas mark 2, and cook for about 2½ hours, or until the beef is tender. Remove the bundle of parsley stalks and bacon rinds, check the casserole for seasoning, and scatter with coarsely chopped parsley leaves just before serving.

Oystered Beef with Green Peppers

A very easy and rather special casserole. Buy thick (*not* thin) oyster sauce from Chinese stores, which also sell peanut oil (also called arachide oil) more cheaply than most other sources. Serves 8.

1.4 kg [3 lb] chuck steak
4 large green peppers, total weight about 600 g [1¼ lb]
2 onions
60 ml [4 tablespoons] plain flour
105 ml [7 tablespoons] thick oyster sauce
425 ml [¾ pt] boiling water
a little peanut oil
freshly ground black pepper

Cube the beef and chop the onions finely. Brown both, a few pieces at a time, in a very little, very hot oil in a flameproof casserole. Mix the oyster sauce with the boiling water in a jug and stir in a good grinding of black pepper, but no salt because the oyster sauce is already salty.

Sprinkle on and stir the flour into the meat and onion mixture. Pour on the boiling hot liquids and bring to the boil stirring continuously. Push the meat well down into the richly coloured and flavoured sauce, cover the casserole with a well–fitting lid and transfer to an oven preheated to 150°C [300°F], gas mark 2. Cook for 1¾ hours.

Wipe the green peppers, remove stalks, seeds and pith, and cut into chunks. Stir them into the casserole, pushing them well down into the liquid (which will be slightly thinned by the juices of the peppers by the end of cooking time). Cover the casserole and cook for a further 45–60 minutes. Serve with plenty of potato purée or boiled Chinese noodles.

Flemish Beef with Beer

A very friendly, beer-scented, mustardy dish of beef. A cheaper version can be made by using more onions and less meat, and by using beef stock in place of beer. In this case increase the amount of vinegar slightly and sprinkle a little grated cheese over the mustard-coated slices of bread. The overall effect is halfway between Flemish beef and French onion soup. Serves 8.

1.4 kg [3 lb] good stewing steak
50 g [2 oz] beef dripping
450 g [1 lb] onions
3 fat garlic cloves
40 g [1½ oz] plain flour
15 ml [1 tablespoon] soft brown sugar
600 ml [1 pt] Guinness
75 ml [3 fl oz] beef stock
45 ml [3 tablespoons] red wine vinegar
nutmeg and a good pinch of ground cloves
a bay leaf
salt and freshly ground black pepper
1 French loaf
Dijon mustard

Choose a large but fairly shallow casserole, so there is plenty of room for the mustard-coated slices of bread which are added towards the end of the cooking time.

Cut the beef into large cubes. Brown it well, in batches, in very hot dripping. Remove with a slotted spoon. Add the sugar, chopped onions and crushed garlic. When soft and brown, blend in the flour, pour on the liquids and bring to simmering point. Return the meat to the casserole, pushing it well down into the sauce, and add the spices, bay leaf and seasonings. Cover with a well-fitting lid and cook in an oven preheated to 150°C [300°F], gas mark 2, until the meat is meltingly tender — about 3½ hours.

About half an hour before the beef is ready, slice the bread thickly. Lay the slices in a single layer on a baking tray and place the tray in the oven so the bread becomes dry and lightly toasted.

Remove both casserole and baking tray from the oven, and

increase the oven temperature to 180°C [350°F], gas mark 4. Discard the bay leaf and check the gravy for seasoning.

Generously spread one side of each slice of bread with mustard. Lay the slices of bread, mustard side up, in a single layer over the surface of the liquid and press them down lightly so the crumb begins to soak up the rich gravy. Return the dish to the oven, without a lid, and cook for a further 20 minutes.

Somerset Pork with Cider

Lighter in colour and taste, this casserole is an anglicised version of the previous recipe, using pork, cider and croûtons instead of beef, beer and mustard bread. Boned and rolled shoulder of pork is the most economical cut to use, although you may need to trim away excess fat. Unsweetened apple juice plus a spoonful of lemon juice can be used instead of dry cider. Serves 8.

1.4 kg [3 lb] boneless pork
250 g [generous ½ lb] onions
450 g [1 lb] Bramley apples
a little bacon fat or pork dripping
15 ml [1 tablespoon] coriander seeds
a pinch of rosemary
45 ml [3 tablespoons] plain flour
425 ml [¾ pt] very dry cider
10 thick slices of bread
fresh chopped parsley
salt and freshly ground black pepper

Cut away pork rind and excess fat, and cut the meat into large cubes. Brown and seal the pork, a few pieces at a time, in a little very hot fat in a flameproof casserole. Remove the meat with a slotted spoon. Slice and lightly colour the onions in the remaining hot fat.

Sprinkle the flour into the casserole together with the coriander seeds and rosemary (lightly crushed with the back of a spoon), and a good seasoning of salt and pepper. Stir to mix well, pour on the cider, return the meat to the casserole and bring to simmering point, stirring.

Cover the casserole with a well-fitting lid and transfer it to an oven preheated to 160°C [325°F], gas mark 3. Cook for 1 hour. Add the peeled and cored apples cut into large chunks, pushing them well down in to the liquid. Cover the casserole again and cook for a further 30 minutes.

When the casserole is nearly ready, dice the bread and fry it in a little fat in a frying pan until crisp golden brown. Drain the croûtons well. Check the casserole for seasoning and serve with piping hot croûtons and parsley sprinkled over the surface.

Somerset Chicken with Cider: Chicken joints are also delicious cooked and served this way. Allow one large or two small joints per person.

Ragoût of Pork & French Beans

A stew for summer with fresh tomato sauce and herbs, and no flour. Serves 6–8.

1 kg [2 lb] lean tender pork, preferably fillet
1 kg [2 lb] French beans
1.2 kg [2½ lb] tomatoes
2 onions
a little olive oil
fresh chopped basil
freshly ground coriander seeds
lemon juice and sugar
salt and freshly ground black pepper

Slice the onions thinly, skin and roughly chop the tomatoes. Choose a heavy-based saucepan with a large surface area. Pour into it just enough oil to form a film over the base. Add the onions and cook gently for 5 minutes or so. Add the tomatoes and 5 ml [1 teaspoon] each lemon juice and sugar. Increase the heat to medium and leave the vegetables to cook, without a lid, for half an hour or so, until the tomatoes have pulped down and are reduced to a thickish, well-flavoured sauce. Stir the contents of the pan from time to time to prevent sticking. When the sauce is ready, season it well with salt, pepper and coriander.

While the sauce is reducing, steam the beans until barely tender, and prepare the pork. Cube the meat and fry it in batches in a little very hot oil. Allow at least 5 minutes' cooking time for each batch: the meat should be well sealed with an appetising brown crust on all sides.

Spread half the beans over the base of a casserole. Pile the pork cubes, drained of all fat, on top. Sprinkle with chopped basil and pour on half the tomato sauce. Cover with the remaining beans, and the rest of the tomato sauce. Place a circle of lightly buttered greaseproof paper directly on top of the ingredients, and cover the casserole. Cook in an oven preheated to 160°C [325°F], gas mark 3, for about 1½ hours, during which time the pork and beans will become impregnated with the rich tomato sauce.

Ragoût of Pork with Broad Beans: When in season, young broad beans can be used in place of French beans. Allow 700 g [1½ lb] shelled weight of beans, and steam them until just tender.

Ragoût of Pork with Courgettes: Courgettes are another delicious alternative vegetable to use in this dish. Thickly slice 1 kg [2 lb] young courgettes. Salt them, rinse and dry them well. Fry them briefly, a handful at a time, in a little oil over medium heat, until lightly coloured on both sides.

Ragoût of Lamb: Fillet of lamb (or middle neck chops carefully trimmed of excess fat) can be used in place of pork in any of the above ragoûts. Tarragon can be used instead of basil.

Ragoût of Chicken: Small chicken joints, such as thighs or drumsticks, can also be used in place of pork in any of the above ragoûts, but take particular care to drain the chicken well after frying, or the final dish may be a little greasy. Use tarragon in preference to basil.

Chicken with Tomatoes & Almonds

This is a quick and easy dish using chicken joints and canned tomatoes. It is cooked on top of the stove. Serves 4.

8 small chicken joints — thighs or drumsticks
1 × 400 g [14 oz] can of tomatoes
30 ml [2 tablespoons] concentrated tomato purée
half a chicken stock cube
fresh or dried tarragon
salt and freshly ground black pepper
150 ml [¼ pt] soured cream
50 g [2 oz] flaked and toasted almonds

Make sure that the chicken joints are completely dry. Dust them with salt and pepper and brown and seal them well in a very little hot fat in a flameproof casserole. Drain the chicken on a kitchen paper towel and pour away the fat remaining in the casserole.

Put the canned tomatoes into the casserole. Add the stock cube, the tomato purée and the tarragon. Bring to the boil, stirring to break up the tomatoes, and simmer for 10 minutes or so. Reduce the heat to very low, stir in the soured cream and bring gently back to simmering point, stirring all the time to blend everything well.

Return the chicken pieces to the casserole, cover with a lid and simmer over the gentlest possible heat for between 30 and 40 minutes, turning the chicken pieces over halfway through this time. Then remove the lid and simmer gently for a further 5 minutes before sprinkling on the flaked and toasted almonds and serving.

Baked Pork with Prunes

Good, cheap and exceptionally easy. Baked potatoes or a dish of lentils make a good accompaniment and can be cooked in the oven at the same time. (Choose small potatoes. Prick them, rub them with salt and oil and place on a baking tray on the bottom shelf of the oven. Or put 250 g [½ lb] rinsed whole lentils in a small well-buttered casserole with 600 ml [1 pt] cold water, lay a sheet of buttered greaseproof paper on top, cover with a well-fitting lid and place on the bottom shelf of the oven.) Serves 4.

500–700 g [1–1½ lb] lean streaky belly of pork rashers
12 prunes
2 fat garlic cloves
7 ml [1 heaped teaspoon] dried thyme
fresh chopped parsley
1 large onion
125 ml [4 fl. oz] dry cider or unsweetened apple juice
salt and freshly ground black pepper

Choose a gratin or baking dish just large enough to take the pork in a single layer. Remove the rind from the rashers and lay them in the dish. Tuck the prunes (which do not need to be soaked in advance) and the very finely chopped onion into the gaps. Sprinkle the crushed garlic over the meat. Mix the parsley and thyme together and scatter them on top. Add a good seasoning of salt and pepper. Pour on the liquid. Lay a sheet of buttered paper directly on top of the ingredients, and cover the dish with foil.

Place the dish on an upper shelf of a cold oven. Switch on to 150°C [300°F], gas mark 2, and bake for 3 hours, or set timing and temperature controls so that the oven will turn itself on to the required temperature 3 hours before you plan to eat.

French Farmhouse Steaks

Another cold-start dish which takes 5 minutes to prepare and can be timed to cook while you are out. Serve it with lots of potato purée or good bread to mop up the rich gravy. Serves 4.

4 thick slices of chuck steak, each weighing about 175 g [6 oz] after trimming
20 ml [1 heaped tablespoon] plain flour generously seasoned with salt, pepper
    and thyme
50 g [2 oz] finely chopped onion
1 fat garlic clove
50 g [2 oz] coarsely chopped mushrooms
5 ml [1 teaspoon] concentrated tomato purée
90 ml [6 tablespoons] red wine
fresh chopped parsley
a handful of small black olives

Choose a gratin or baking dish just large enough to take the steaks in a single layer, and butter it lightly. Dust the steaks with the flour and lay them in the dish. Tuck the chopped onion and mushrooms into the gaps and spread the crushed garlic over the top. Stir the tomato purée and wine together and drizzle them over the meat. Lay a sheet of buttered greaseproof paper directly on top of the ingredients and cover the dish with foil.

Place the dish on an upper shelf of a cold oven. Switch on to 150°C [300°F], gas mark 2, and bake for 3¼ hours, or set timing and temperature controls so that the oven will turn itself on to the required temperature 3¼ hours before you plan to eat. Garnish with parsley and olives just before serving.

Pigeon in a Pot

Most pigeon recipes need a whole bird for each serving or the resulting dish seems rather mean. Only half a pigeon per person is used here yet it seems generous. This is a useful, easy, peasant-style dish for cold weather. Serves 4.

2 plump fresh, or frozen,* pigeons
250 g [½ lb] salt pork
125 g [¼ lb] dried chestnuts
200 g [6 oz] whole green lentils
1 large onion
2 fat garlic cloves
the finely grated zest of an orange
1 small bay leaf
450 ml [¾ pt] canned beef consommé or clear stock
75 ml [2½ fl oz] red wine
1 firm crinkly leafed cabbage weighing about 700–800 g [1½–1¾ lb]
salt and freshly ground black pepper
a little butter

Carefully pick over and rinse the lentils. Drain them well. Lightly butter the base and sides of a large casserole and sprinkle the lentils into it. Dice the salt pork, and chop the onion and garlic quite finely. Scatter this mixture over the lentils and add the dried chestnuts.

Cut the pigeons in half, splitting them along the length of the breast and down the backbone. Lay the pieces of pigeon, breast side downwards, in a single layer in the casserole. Press down on the pigeon with your hand to bury the fleshy breast meat partially in the pork and vegetable mixture. Sprinkle the orange zest over the pigeon, add a good seasoning of salt and pepper and the bay leaf. Pour on the cold liquids.

Quarter the cabbage and cut out and discard the tough central stalk. Lay the cabbage wedges, centres upwards, in a single layer in the casserole. Place a large sheet of well-buttered greaseproof paper directly on top of the cabbage and cover the casserole with a well-fitting lid. Place the casserole on an upper shelf of a cold oven. Turn it on to 150°C [300°F], gas mark 2, and cook until the pigeon meat is tender enough to come away easily from the bone — 3¼–3½ hours. Alternatively set automatic timing and temperature controls so that the oven will turn itself on to the required temperature 3½ hours before you plan to eat.

To serve, arrange the wedges of cabbage and pigeon round the edge of a large, warmed dish. Pile the pork, lentil and chestnut mixture into the centre, pour on the juices and serve with hot crusty bread.

Note: Pigeons that have been frozen are usually tougher than fresh ones and take longer to cook. Cook them on top of the pork, lentil and chestnut mixture for 30–45 minutes before adding the cabbage wedges, then cook for $3\frac{1}{4}$–$3\frac{1}{2}$ hours.

No Pigeon in the Pot: For a cheaper variation on this warming winter dish, omit the pigeon and increase the quantity of salt pork to a generous 350 g [$\frac{3}{4}$ lb]. Otherwise proceed as described in the main recipe.

Wiltshire Lamb Hotpot

Yet another cold-start dish and much more delicately flavoured than most lamb hotpots. Serves 4.

8 middle neck lamb chops or 4 boneless shoulder lamb chops
1 Cox's apple (optional)
1 large onion
tarragon
a little butter
150 ml [$\frac{1}{4}$ pt] dry white wine or unsweetened apple juice
700-900 g [$1\frac{1}{2}$-2 lb] potatoes
salt and freshly ground black pepper
fresh chopped parsley, if required

Choose a casserole or baking dish that will take the chops in a single layer. Butter the base and sides lightly. Trim excess fat from the chops and lay them in the dish. Season generously with pepper and tarragon.

   If using wine, peel and dice the apple and tuck it into any gaps between the chops; if using apple juice, omit the apple. Chop the onion finely, sprinkle it over the meat and pour on the liquid. Slice the potatoes very thinly and lay them, overlapping like tiles, over the meat. Season generously with salt and pepper between the potato layers, and cover the top layer of potatoes completely with thin flakes of butter. Do not cover the dish with a lid.

   Place the dish on an upper shelf of a cold oven. Switch on to 150°C [300°F], gas mark 2, and bake for 3 hours, or set automatic timing and temperature controls so that the oven will turn itself on to the required temperature 3 hours before you plan to eat. The top layer of potatoes will be deliciously crunchy by the time the lower layers and the meat are tender.

If there is a long delay between preparing the dish and the start of cooking time, the top layer of potatoes may discolour slightly. A handful of chopped fresh parsley sprinkled over the top of the dish just before serving will enhance its looks.

Lamb with Flageolets: Follow the main recipe but omit the apple and potatoes; add a few crushed coriander seeds and increase the liquid by 3–4 tablespoons. (Wine, dry cider, apple juice or 225 g [8 oz] canned tomatoes puréed in a liquidiser can be used.)

Drain the contents of 2 × 400 g ([14 oz] cans of flageolet beans, season with salt and pepper and spoon them evenly over the meat and onion mixture. Dot with a few flakes of butter and cover the dish with a well-fitting lid. Bake as described above.

Greek Shepherd's Pie

Not unlike moussaka, but less rich and considerably cheaper, since it uses courgettes instead of aubergines, this makes an agreeable change from an English shepherd's pie. It reheats well and is a good way to use up slightly over-sized courgettes. Serves 6.

700 g [1½ lb] courgettes
700 g [1½ lb] lean minced lamb
2 onions
1–2 garlic cloves
450 g [1 lb] skinned and chopped tomatoes or 1 × 400 g [14 oz] can of tomatoes
fresh chopped marjoram, thyme and basil
salt and freshly ground black pepper

For the topping:
40 g [1½ oz] plain flour
125 g [¼ lb] grated cheese
3 eggs
150 ml [¼ pt] yoghurt
300 ml [½ pt] soured cream
plenty of freshly ground black pepper

Brown the meat in a little hot oil in a large flameproof casserole or sauté pan. Add the quite finely chopped onions and garlic and colour them slightly. Lower the heat a little, add the tomatoes and cook for about 40 minutes, stirring occasionally, until most of the moisture has been driven off and flavour is concentrated. Season well with salt and pepper and generous quantities of fresh chopped marjoram and thyme, then turn the mixture into a big gratin or baking dish with a large surface area.

Top and tail the courgettes, slice them thickly, blanch in boiling salted water for 2–3 minutes, then drain and pat them dry very thoroughly using kitchen paper towels. Spread the courgettes over the meat and top them with a generous sprinkling of fresh chopped basil.

Make the topping by beating the ingredients well with a balloon whisk until smooth and creamy. Pour it over the courgettes, top with a little extra grated cheese if you like, and bake for about 40 minutes at 190°C [375°F], gas mark 5, until set, lightly coloured and puffed up.

Greek Cottage Pie: For a beef version, mince 700 g [1½ lb] chuck steak. Brown it in batches in a very little, very hot dripping, then brown 3 fairly finely chopped onions. Stir in a little curry powder — up to 5 ml [1 teaspoon] to bring out the flavour of the meat but not to give the dish a distinctive curry flavour.

Return the beef to the pan together with its juices. Add 5 ml [1 teaspoon] celery salt, 10 ml [2 teaspoons] Worcestershire sauce, 15 ml [1 tablespoon] each tomato ketchup and concentrated tomato purée, and plenty of salt and pepper. Cover with a well-fitting lid and cook over very gentle heat for 30 minutes. Finish off in the oven with blanched courgettes and topping as described in the basic recipe.

Bobottie

This lightly curried dish is a South African version of shepherd's pie. Serve with spiced rice, chutneys and a bowl of sliced bananas sprinkled with lemon juice. Serves 4–6.

450 g [1 lb] chuck steak, trimmed weight
175 g [6 oz] chopped onions
50 g [2 oz] butter
10 ml [2 teaspoons] curry powder or paste
25 g [1 oz] fresh breadcrumbs
25 g [1 oz] split almonds
25 g [1 oz] raisins
45 ml [3 tablespoons] chutney
20 ml [1½ tablespoons] lemon juice
2 eggs
150 ml [¼ pt] milk
2 bay leaves
salt and freshly ground black pepper

Lightly fry the onions in the butter. Stir in the curry paste or powder, then add the breadcrumbs away from the heat. Turn the contents of the pan into a mixing bowl. Add the nuts, raisins, chutney, lemon juice and a very good seasoning of salt and pepper, then the raw, finely minced meat and 1 lightly beaten egg. Mix everything together very thoroughly, turn the mixture into a pie dish and lay the bay leaves on top. Bake for 25 minutes at 180°C [350°F], gas mark 4, without a lid.

Beat the remaining egg with the milk and some salt and pepper. Pour it over the minced meat mixture and bake for a further 35 minutes until the custard topping has coloured and set.

Toad-in-the-Hole

Not worth making with ordinary sausages, but delicious when made with pure pork sausages. Serves 4.

500 g [1 lb] top quality sausages
a hazelnut-sized knob of good dripping
125 g [¼ lb] plain flour
150 ml [¼ pt] each milk and water
a dash of Worcestershire sauce
a generous pinch of mustard powder
salt
2 eggs

Put the fat into a very large roasting pan, put it in the oven and switch on to 220°C [425°F], gas mark 7. After a few minutes add the sausages, roll them in the melted fat and return the pan to the oven so that the sausages begin to cook while the oven heats up to the required temperature.

Meanwhile, make the batter. Sift the flour, salt and mustard powder into a mixing bowl and make a well in the centre. Break the eggs into the well, and add the milk, water and Worcestershire sauce. Whisk the liquids together then gradually blend them into the dry ingredients to make a very smooth thick cream.

As soon as the oven reaches the correct temperature, pour the batter round the sausages. Return the pan to the oven and cook for 35 minutes until the sausages are a rich brown and the batter crisp and puffed up.

Cheddar Gorge: I originally made this when no good sausages were available, but it has now become a family favourite. Remove the rind from 8 rashers of streaky bacon, halve them, stretch each piece with the back of a knife and roll up. Cut 175 g [6 oz] Cheddar cheese into 3 cm [generous 1 inch] cubes. Scatter the cheese over the base of the hot roasting pan and arrange the bacon rolls, seam side down, here and there. Immediately pour on the batter and bake as described.

Chicken-in-a-Hole: Another variation, which is popular with children. Prick 4 small chicken joints with a fork. Put them in a shallow dish with a good grinding of pepper, a pinch of crushed rosemary and a good squeeze of lemon juice, and leave for 1 hour. Brush a roasting pan with a little oil. Put it into the oven and heat to 230°C [450°F], gas mark 8. Drain the chicken pieces, turn them in the hot fat and bake them for 15 minutes before reducing the oven temperature to 220°C [425°F], gas mark 7, pouring on and cooking the batter.

Fish & Shellfish

fish and Shellfish.

Fish can be a great joy to eat; it can also seem to be a penance. For many years I thought I hated fish and naturally retain a lot of sympathy for those who find fish not to their liking.

The decline in the number of fishmongers' shops is evidence enough of just how many disaffected fish eaters there are in this country, which I feel is a great pity. Once you discover how richly varied and delicious fish can be, few fields of cookery are more exciting and more rewarding to explore. Good fish dishes are truly on a par with the best meat cookery. Moreover, many fish dishes are as quickly cooked as, say, lamb chops or beef steaks, and they are usually considerably cheaper.

This enthusiasm will cut no ice with the allergic, whose acquaintance with "school cod and white sauce" has left them with a lasting dislike. The real stimulation of interest in good fish cookery perhaps will come from the growth in travel and holidays abroad. Certainly those little restaurants on Mediterranean quaysides have kindled many a British appetite for the beautiful fresh fish of the region, succulently grilled or bathed in heady aromatic sauces.

Prejudices, however, are rarely dispelled overnight. To encourage the taste which the potential convert has begun to acquire abroad, to fan interest into a greater love of fish, requires shrewdness on the part of the cook. He or she should aim to build up appreciation slowly.

The experience of seeing fish landed, watching it sizzle over a herb-scented charcoal fire, and eating it in a sun-soaked open air restaurant may be marvellous. But "atmospherics" do not travel well. The apprentice fish lover is unlikely to respond so enthusiastically to the same fish served in a city flat with grey November rain slashing the windowpanes; awareness will be focused not on the salty sweet fresh taste of the flesh but on the fishy eyes staring up from the plate. If fishy smells are trapped by doubleglazing instead of wafting into the noonday sunshine air, they may become disagreeably haunting for days and re-induce a sour determination to reject fish once and for all.

The chances of winning favour may be much greater if you start by serving fish without the potentially offensive tails, eyes, skin and bones. Cook it briefly and delicately and serve it with colourful and tasty sauces.

Many of the recipes in this chapter, therefore, balance the need to conform to conservative tastes with the introduction of a spirit of adventure. Most of these dishes are cooked in the oven (the best means of minimising fishy smells) and they use the fillets of firm-fleshed, well-flavoured fish such as smoked haddock and monkfish, which are much more appealing, so I have found, than the floppier, more insipid fish such as plaice.

You will find composite dishes which do the introductory job well. These are variations on the basic fish pie theme. Instead of anaemic white sauces and mashed potato toppings, there are recipes for smoked haddock coated with a herb and watercress sauce served in a ring of cheesy choux pastry, a rich stew of monkfish with French beans, tomatoes and red peppers topped with crunchy fried bread, and white fish with prawns and grapes bathed in a mildly curried cream sauce, served in individual vol-au-vent cases.

Simpler still from the cook's point of view, and particular favourites of mine, are dishes in which fish is baked with a little butter or wine and a few other flavourings which make natural and well-flavoured sauces. Recipes such as mackerel fillets with bulb fennel and haddock with tomatoes take only minutes to prepare and minutes to cook. They can be popped into the oven while you eat the first course or relax over a pre-prandial drink, and can be served in the dishes in which they have cooked. Do, however, keep a firm eye on the clock when cooking fish: it cooks very quickly and just a few minutes too long in the baking can spoil the texture and flavour.

When the novice has come to delight in and look forward to dishes such as these, then it is time to introduce grilled, baked and fried whole fish. Choose a large fish first, such as salmon trout, which can be filleted on the serving dish, then smaller fish, such as trout, mackerel, herrings and mullet, which each person can fillet.

Obviously, it is very important that the first experience of coping with whole fish is a good one. I find that almost all children, and many adults, are initially nervous of tackling whole fish, but they often respond to the explanation that cooking the fish whole keeps it succulent and at its best to eat. Children in particular are greatly relieved to learn that the head and tail are not for eating. It is also reassuring to be told that, although the crackling crisp skin of grilled and fried fish is regarded as a great delicacy by many, it can be peeled back and left to one side. Show a child exactly how to do this and help with the intricacies of cutting up the flesh neatly and cleanly — nothing kills the appetite quicker than a mouthful of spiteful little bones.

I have also included a few recipes for fish which is fried or grilled without skin or bones. These include colourful fish and vegetable kebabs to serve with rice, inexpensive fritters of coley with lemon and dill, and calamari with garlic for those with Mediterranean tastes.

The only remaining problem with grilled and fried fish dishes is that of lingering smells. Aromas during cooking may be enticing but even the greatest devotees of fish will agree that the smells that linger afterwards are far from pleasant. In summer the problem can be avoided by saving grilled dishes for barbecue eating outdoors, but for year-round cooking by far the best solution is an effective purpose-designed kitchen ventilation system, switched to its highest setting before, during and after the cooking process. Such a system is an essential in the modern heavily insulated and draught-proofed house, not merely for grilling or frying fish, but for all cooking outside the oven, because it will deal with both fumes and condensation. Nonetheless, it is surprising how cooking smells can be minimised by opening a window to the December air, by washing all utensils immediately they are used, and by putting the wrapped up food scraps directly into the dustbin outside. Chopping boards, once scrubbed, can be rubbed with a lemon. Finally, a couple of coffee beans lightly toasted on the hob will change the atmosphere.

Haddock with Tomatoes

A blissfully easy supper dish. Best eaten with spoons out of soup plates, and with lots of good bread. Serves 4.

2 fine large smoked haddock
butter
1 smallish onion
8–10 streaky bacon rashers
500 g [generous 1 lb] tomatoes
basil
275 ml [½ pt] soured cream
freshly ground black pepper
parsley or watercress, to garnish

Preheat the oven to 180°C [350°F], gas mark 4. Stew the finely chopped onion in a good knob of butter for 10–15 minutes until very tender. Add the bacon cut up into smallish pieces and cook gently for a few minutes.

Meanwhile skin and roughly chop the tomatoes; fillet the fish and lay it in a single layer in a large buttered gratin dish.

Add the tomatoes to the onion pan, bring quickly to simmering point and simmer for a minute or two before stirring in the soured cream, a good pinch of basil and plenty of pepper (salt is probably unnecessary). Bring back to simmering point and pour the contents of the pan over the fish.

Cover the dish with a foil lid, and bake on an upper shelf of the preheated oven for 20–25 minutes. Scatter generous quantities of watercress sprigs or coarsely chopped parsley over the fish, and serve immediately.

Baked Haddock with Eggs & Olives

A simple but very satisfying combination of flavours and colours. Olives that have been steeped in brine sometimes taste bitter. Drain off the brine when you buy a jar and pour on sunflower oil instead. After a few weeks in the store-cupboard the olives will taste much sweeter, and the sunflower oil will taste of olive. Serves 4.

4 large fillets of smoked haddock
300 ml [generous ½ pt] milk
60 ml [4 tablespoons] single cream
2 eggs
a handful of parsley
25 g [1 oz] small black olives
25 ml [1½ tablespoons] plain flour
salt and freshly ground black pepper
50 g [2 oz] butter

Preheat the oven to 180°C [350°F], gas mark 4. Lay the fish in a shallow buttered dish. Add a good grinding of black pepper and 25 g [1 oz] butter cut into flakes. Pour on the milk, lay a sheet of buttered greaseproof paper on top and bake the fish in the oven for 20–25 minutes. Meanwhile, hard-boil and chop the eggs, chop the parsley, and stone the olives; mash together with a fork the flour and the remaining 25 g [1 oz] of softened butter.

Strain the fish-flavoured milk off the fish when baking time is completed. Cover the fish again with the buttered paper and keep it warm in the switched-off oven. Let the milk simmer gently in a small pan. Add the cream and bring back to simmering point. Gradually stir in small pieces of the butter and flour mixture, and continue simmering until the sauce is hot, thickened and perfectly smooth.

Away from the heat, stir in the chopped hard-boiled eggs and a good quantity of chopped fresh parsley. Check seasoning and pour the sauce over the fish. Garnish with the olives and a little more parsley, and serve with plenty of good bread.

Whiting Soubise

Another dish in which fillets of fish are baked until tender and coated with sauce just before serving. Coley, grey mullet, or red fish fillets can also be cooked and served this way, and make inexpensive fish dishes. Serves 4.

4 large fillets of whiting
lemon juice
butter
350 g [¾ lb] onions
10 ml [2 teaspoons] plain flour
150 ml [¼ pt] soured cream
salt, pepper and nutmeg
2 hard-boiled eggs
fresh chopped parsley

Chop the onions finely. Put them into a saucepan with 50 g [2 oz] melted butter and cook them over very gentle heat for 15–20 minutes until tender.

Lay the fish in a buttered gratin dish. Add a squeeze of lemon, a good seasoning of salt and pepper, and flakes of butter. Cover the dish with a foil lid and bake the fish in the oven at 200°C [400°F], gas mark 6, for about 20 minutes until tender and hot.

While the fish is cooking, sprinkle and stir the flour into the softened onions. Pour on the soured cream and season very generously with salt, pepper and nutmeg. Cover the saucepan and leave it to simmer very gently for 10 minutes, stirring occasionally. Turn the contents of the saucepan into a liquidiser and reduce to a purée.

When the fish is cooked, reheat the sauce gently and thin it with the buttery fish juices (tilt the gratin dish and use a bulb baster to draw off the juices). Pour the sauce over the fish. Scatter with sliced hard-boiled eggs and chopped parsley and serve with lots of triangles of fried bread.

Oeufs Soubise: For a lunch dish, serve hot halved hard-boiled eggs dressed with the onion sauce given above. Garnish the dish with bunches of watercress and serve with wholemeal bread.

Coley with Cabbage & Anchovies

Very simple and quick, this dish sounds unpromising initially, but the rich and elusive flavour of the sauce makes plain white fish and steamed cabbage into excellent eating. Serves 6.

6 thick fillets of coley or other white fish
1 large Savoy or January King cabbage
a bunch of parsley
about 75 g [3 oz] butter
20 ml [1 generous tablespoon] lemon juice
2 × 50 g [2 oz] cans of anchovy fillets
300 ml [½ pt] double cream
65 ml [2½ fl oz] soured cream
freshly ground black pepper

Lay the fish in a single layer in a well-buttered dish. Sprinkle it with lemon and plenty of pepper, and dot it with a few flakes of butter. Cover the dish with a foil lid and bake in an oven pre-heated to 200°C [400°F], gas mark 6, for about 20 minutes until the fish is tender.

Meanwhile, cut the large firm head of crinkly cabbage into wedges. Steam them until tender, about 18 minutes. Blot up surface moisture from the wedges of cooked cabbage with plenty of kitchen paper towels. Arrange the wedges on a warmed serving dish, add the fish and its buttery cooking juices.

A few minutes before the cabbage and coley complete cooking, put the anchovy fillets and their oil into a small pan. Stir and mash with a wooden spoon over low heat until the anchovies disintegrate. Add the creams and a good seasoning of pepper and stir to blend well. Let the mixture simmer and bubble for a few minutes, just stirring occasionally.

Pour a little of the sauce over the coley and wedges of cabbage and scatter with plenty of coarse chopped parsley. Serve the rest of the sauce in a jug.

Mackerel Fillets with Florentine Fennel

Fresh mackerel are firm, beautiful and well flavoured — one of the best buys from the fishmonger. The mild smoky flavour of bulb fennel superbly offsets the oily richness of the fish. Serves 4.

4 large fresh mackerel, filleted
2 large bulbs of Florentine fennel
about 50 g [2 oz] melted butter
1 lemon
salt and freshly ground black pepper

Preheat the oven to 220°C [425°F], gas mark 7. Clean and trim the fennel, reserving the feathery fronds. Cut each bulb lengthways into 3 or 4 slices. Lay them in a buttered gratin dish. Season with salt and pepper, and drizzle the melted butter on top.

Lay the mackerel fillets in a single layer in a lightly buttered gratin dish. Sprinkle them with salt and pepper and pour on the juice of half the lemon. Cut the remaining half lemon into slices. Lay the slices on top of the fish and cover the dish with a foil lid.

Bake the fennel on the top shelf of the oven, and the mackerel on a lower shelf. The fennel will take about 35 minutes to cook, the fish will take slightly less than 30 minutes: start cooking the fennel first so both dishes will be ready at the same time.

Discard the lemon slices, lift the fish out of its dish and lay it on top of the fennel. Pour on the buttery and lemon flavoured juices in which the fish was cooked, and serve immediately. Granary bread and a small bowl of chilled soured cream (into which you have stirred the chopped feathery fronds of fennel) go well with this dish.

Grilled Mackerel with Flaming Fennel

This is a more dramatic way of combining fennel and mackerel. John Dory, sea bream, mullet and large herring are also excellent grilled this way. Serves 4.

4 large fresh mackerel
1 dozen dried fennel stalks, or a large spoonful of fennel seeds
lemons
olive oil
salt and freshly ground black pepper
15 ml [1 tablespoon] brandy

Sprinkle the belly cavity of each fish with salt, pepper and a squeeze of lemon juice. Stuff them with a few broken up fennel stalks or crushed fennel seeds. Brush the skin of the fish with olive oil, and score each fish on both sides with 2 or 3 oblique cuts.

Lightly oil the rack of a grill pan. Place a few fennel stalks on it and lay the fish on top. Grill under moderate heat, basting occasionally with more oil, until the mackerel skin is blistered and crisp, the flesh is tender and white and just ready to come away from the bone.

Carefully turn the fish over, and grill on the second side in the same way, but lay a few fennel stalks on top of the mackerel (or sprinkle them with a few fennel seeds) a minute or so before the fish are ready. The fennel will quickly burn, scent the fish and fill the air with its incense.

Carefully lift the cooked fish and the fennel onto a hot serving dish. Pour on any juices that have collected in the grill pan, sprinkle the fish with a little salt and garnish with quartered lemons. Quickly warm a large spoon, pour the brandy into it and set it alight. Pour the flaming liquid over the fish and serve immediately.

Red Mullet with Lovage

Red mullet is a delectable and highly prized fish. Here it is stuffed and baked in a wrapping of lovage leaves, which delicately impregnate the fish with a celery-like flavour. Serves 4.

4 red mullet, each weighing about 350 g [¾ lb]
16 lovage leaves
olive oil
a few spoonfuls of dry vermouth

For the stuffing:
60 ml [4 tablespoons] breadcrumbs
40 g [1½ oz] butter
1 smallish onion
4–5 streaky bacon rashers
15 ml [1 tablespoon] crushed fennel seeds
salt and freshly ground black pepper

Scale and clean the fish without removing the livers.

To make the stuffing, first finely chop the onion and soften it in the butter. Cut the bacon into matchstick strips, add it to the onion pan and colour it lightly. Away from the heat, stir the breadcrumbs into the saucepan. Add the crushed fennel seeds and a seasoning of salt and pepper. Let the mixture become cold, then use it to stuff the belly cavities of the fish.

Brush 6 double-thick sheets of foil with olive oil. Lay 2 lovage leaves on each sheet, lay a stuffed fish on top, sprinkle with salt and cover with another 2 lovage leaves. Then drizzle on a tablespoonful of olive oil and add a dash of vermouth. Carefully draw up the sides of the foil and seal to make baggy, but well-sealed, parcels.

Lay the parcels side by side on a baking tray and cook in the

oven at 220°C [425°F], gas mark 7, for about 30 minutes. Serve, still wrapped, with new potatoes.

Grey Mullet with Lovage: Grey mullet not only lacks the rosy good looks of red mullet, but its flavour is not so fine. Nonetheless, it is a very good fish, a bargain buy when available, and excellent stuffed and baked with lovage.

Completely gut grey mullet, but reserve the roes after removing them from the fish. Crush the roes with a fork and add them to the stuffing after stirring in the breadcrumbs. Omit bacon from the stuffing.

Baked Sea-Trout

Considerably cheaper than salmon, less solid in texture and more delicate in flavour, sea-trout (or salmon-trout as it is also called) makes a splendid and easy party dish, and is equally good served hot or cold. Serves 6.

a fine sea-trout weighing 1½ kg [3¾ lb] or just over
1 lemon
sprigs of dill or fennel, or a few lovage leaves or parsley
melted butter or olive oil
salt and freshly ground black pepper

Preheat the oven to 180°C [350°F], gas mark 4, placing a baking tray on the centre shelf. Season the belly cavity of the fish generously with salt and pepper. Place a couple of lemon slices and a sprig of herbs inside it (and a few flakes of butter if the fish is to be served hot).

Lay the fish on a very large sheet of generously greased foil — buttered if the fish is to be served hot, oiled if the fish is to be served cold. Place extra lemon slices and herbs on top of the fish. Fold and secure the foil to make a baggy but well-sealed parcel. Place the parcel on the hot baking sheet and bake for about 45 minutes.

To serve hot, let the fish rest in the unopened parcel on the baking tray for 5–10 minutes. Then transfer the parcel carefully to a hot serving dish. Fold back the foil and replace limp lemon slices and herbs with fresh ones. Serve with new potatoes steamed in their skins, and a hot butter sauce, such as green

Hollandaise, or with cucumber matchsticks (see page   ) and a jug of well-seasoned double cream which has been boiled until reduced by half.

To serve cold, completely unwrap the fish shortly before serving and remove the upper skin with a sharp knife. Walnut and watercress sauce (see below) makes a good accompaniment.

Green Hollandaise

125 g [¼ lb] spinach (including a few sorrel leaves, if possible)
250 g [½ lb] butter
3 egg yolks
15 ml [1 tablespoon] lemon juice
salt and freshly ground pepper

Wash the spinach and sorrel leaves and remove any tough stems. Shred and cook over the lowest possible heat in a covered pan with a small spoonful of water and 30 g [1 oz] of the butter. When very tender, whizz the contents of the pan to a purée in a liquidiser with some salt and pepper and a few spoonfuls of hot water. Keep warm.

Beat the egg yolks with the lemon juice and an equal quantity of cold water in the top part of a double-boiler. Melt 190 g [6 oz] of the butter in a small pan, cover and set aside. Add 15 g [½ oz] chilled butter to the top part of the double-boiler. Place it over barely simmering water and cook gently, stirring continuously, until butter and egg yolks emulsify and thicken.

Remove the pan from the heat and quickly beat in the remaining 15 g [½ oz] chilled butter. When it has melted and been absorbed, beat in the warm melted butter, adding it in a slow trickle and beating all the time. Finally stir in the green purée to colour and flavour the sauce.

Walnut & Watercress Sauce

2 large bunches of watercress
50 g [2 oz] walnut kernels
300–400 ml [½–¾ pt] soured cream
salt and freshly ground black pepper

Strip the leaves from the watercress (save the stalks for flavouring soup). Drop them into a pan of boiling water and bring back to the boil. Drain well, squeeze dry and chop finely.

Put the walnuts into a bowl. Pour on boiling water to cover the nuts and leave for a few minutes to loosen the skins. Then drain and peel away skins. Pound the nuts with mortar and pestle, or grind them to a powder in a coffee mill or liquidiser.

Stir the nuts into half the soured cream. When smoothly blended, beat in the watercress and season generously with salt and pepper. Beat in as much of the remaining soured cream as is necessary to give a well-flavoured sauce of good consistency. Cover and chill the sauce until ready to serve.

Fish Kebabs

Fish kebabs will often find favour with those who otherwise will not eat fish. Choose thick, firm fillets of fish so the flesh can be cubed neatly. Serves 4–5.

450 g [1 lb] huss, pollack, monkfish, coley or other thick white fish fillets
450 g [1 lb] thick smoked haddock fillet
about 250 g [½ lb] streaky bacon rashers
4 smallish onions
1 green pepper
60 ml [4 tablespoons] lemon juice
120 ml [8 tablespoons] olive oil
herbs and black pepper

Cut the fish into 4 cm [1½ inch] cubes. Lay them in a shallow dish. Add the onions cut into wedges and the green pepper cut into chunks. Pour on the lemon juice and olive oil, and add a good grinding of pepper and some herbs — a few crushed fennel seeds, or a little basil, or a mixture of marjoram and thyme, for example. Leave to marinate for 30–60 minutes.

Remove the rind from the bacon, cut each rasher in half and stretch with the back of a knife. Wrap a piece of bacon round each chunk of smoked fish. Thread the ingredients onto lightly oiled skewers, alternating white and smoked fish and placing pieces of vegetables between the cubes of fish. Grill under medium-high heat for about 10 minutes, turning the skewers and basting with the marinade as necessary. Serve the kebabs on a bed of plain boiled rice, with a few grilled tomatoes, or a green salad.

Fish Fritters with Lemon & Dill

A bowl of well-chilled, garlic-flavoured soured cream goes well with this inexpensive, but enticing dish of fish fried in batter. An even better sauce is aioli (see page 26). Serves 4.

700 g [1½ lb] thick fillet of coley or other firm white fish
1 large lemon
20 ml [1 heaped tablespoon] chopped fresh dill or 10 ml [2 teaspoons] dried dillweed
a little flour
salt and freshly ground black pepper
cooking oil, for deep-fat frying

For the batter:
125 g [¼ lb] plain flour, seasoned
30 ml [2 tablespoons] olive oil
150 ml [¼ pt] water
2 egg whites

Skin the fish and remove any bones — eyebrow tweezers are the ideal instrument for this. Cut the fish into pieces about 2.5 cm [1 inch] square. Lay them in a shallow dish, sprinkle with dill, pour on the lemon juice, toss lightly, cover and set aside in a cold place for 45–60 minutes.

Drain the fish well, pat dry and dust with a little flour generously seasoned with salt and pepper. Pour cooking oil into a deep-fat fryer until one-third full. Heat very slowly to 185°–190°C [360°–375°F].

Meanwhile, make the batter by whisking the olive oil and water into the very generously seasoned flour until perfectly smooth and creamy. Whisk the egg whites and fold them into the batter to make it extra light.

Coat the pieces of prepared fish by dropping them into the batter a few at a time. Lift out each piece with a skewer, shake off excess batter and lower carefully into the hot oil. Fry for 2–3 minutes until golden and crisp. Drain well and keep piping hot, spread out in a single layer on plenty of crumpled kitchen paper towel — while you coat and fry the remaining fish.

Calamari with Garlic

If you are lucky enough to find an enterprising fishmonger who sells fresh squid caught in English waters, latch on to him. The smaller the squid, the more tender they are, so choose the tiniest and avoid any that are more than 10 cm [4 inches] long, if possible. Preparing squid is a bore (although much less gruesome than the written description suggests), but it is richly compensated by the pleasures of eating fried squid. Serves 6.

1.4 kg [3 lb] small squid
75 ml [5 tablespoons] olive oil
3–4 fat garlic cloves
plenty of fresh chopped parsley or coriander
salt and freshly ground black pepper

Put the squid into a large bowl of cold water and wash them thoroughly. Take them out one at a time and peel away the purplish membrane that covers the body sac. Hold the sac with one hand, and use the other hand to pull the head and tentacles gently but firmly away from the body; the soft entrails from inside the sac will probably come away with the tentacles. Cut off the tentacles just in front of the eye and reserve them. Throw away the head and entrails. Remove the transparent "quill" from the body sac, and wash the inside of the body very thoroughly, removing and discarding anything it may still contain.

Dry the squid carefully to prevent spitting during frying. Cut the body into thin rings and, if the tentacles are long, cut them into short lengths.

When ready to cook, measure the oil into a large frying pan and place it over medium heat. (Olive oil is essential for this recipe.) When it is hot add the squid and turn up the heat as high as possible. Fry, stirring as necessary, for about 5 minutes until the squid are lightly browned. Then reduce the heat and fry more gently until the squid are tender and cooked through.

Increase the heat to high again. Add the finely chopped garlic and fry for a further minute or two. Away from the heat, season quickly, sprinkle lavishly with parsley or coriander leaves and serve piping hot with wedges of lemon and lots of bread.

Squid Salad: Reduce the quantity of garlic, and add it after the pan has been removed from the heat. Let the cooked squid become cold. Add lemon juice, parsley, extra oil, salt and pepper to taste just before serving.

Fried Squid with Tomatoes: Squid fried as described in the main recipe will make a more substantial dish, which will serve 8 or more, if the squid are piled onto a bed of plain boiled rice as soon as cooked and a hot, fresh tomato sauce (made as described in the ragoût recipe on page 197) is poured over them.

Raie au Beurre Noir

This is the classic, and to my mind the very best, way to cook and serve skate. To use clarified butter makes all the difference: ordinary butter burns to a black speckled oil instead of producing an even golden brown sheen (which, despite the name beurre noir, is what one is after). Serves 4.

1 kg [2–2¼ lb] skate wing
1 small onion
45 ml [3 tablespoons] wine vinegar
6 peppercorns
5 ml [1 teaspoon] salt

For the beurre noir:
100 g [¼ lb] clarified butter
20 ml [1½ tablespoons] wine vinegar or lemon juice
60–75 ml [4–5 tablespoons] capers
plenty of fresh chopped parsley

Choose a large sauté pan, wide enough to take the fish in a single layer and deep enough for the fish to be immersed in liquid. If you don't have a suitable sauté pan, use a roasting pan or baking tin.

Lay the fish in the pan, add the thinly sliced onion, wine vinegar, peppercorns and salt and pour on enough cold water to cover the fish. Bring slowly to simmering point, cover and poach at the gentlest simmer for 15 minutes. Drain and skin the fish carefully. Sprinkle it with a little salt, the capers and parsley, and keep hot in a low oven.

Heat the clarified butter in a saucepan over medium heat. It will bubble and crackle as it becomes really hot, then begin to colour. As soon as the butter is a golden nut-brown remove the pan from the heat. Add the vinegar or lemon juice, pouring it at arm's length because the contents of the pan will bubble up furiously. Quickly pour the butter over the fish and serve while it is still frothing.

Marinated Mushrooms with Sole

This needs to be made a day ahead. It is best made using Dover sole, but it is also good using very fresh megrim sole or lemon sole. Serves 4.

2 large Dover sole, filleted
500 g [1 lb] cap mushrooms
2 bunches of watercress
4 lemons
olive oil
4 bay leaves
8 ml [1½ teaspoons] each cumin and coriander seeds
ground coriander and cumin
salt and freshly ground black pepper

Slice the mushrooms thickly. Put them into a large china bowl, sprinkle them generously with freshly ground black pepper and a small spoonful of lemon juice. Measure 90 ml [6 tablespoons] olive oil into a frying pan and warm it gently over low heat for a few minutes.

Crush the cumin and coriander seeds with mortar and pestle. Add these spices and 2 bay leaves to the pan. When they are slightly warmed and beginning to be aromatic, remove the pan from the heat, add a little salt, pour the contents over the mushrooms and toss gently. Cover and leave it in a cold place overnight.

Cut the fish fillets into narrow strips about 5 cm [2 inches] long. Lay them in a shallow dish, sprinkle with a little pepper, ground cumin and coriander. Bury a couple of bay leaves among the fish and pour on enough lemon juice to cover the fish completely. Cover the dish and leave it in a cold place overnight, during which time the fish will become opaque.

To serve, arrange the drained fish in the centre of a serving dish. Pile the mushrooms at one end and the watercress sprigs at the other. Sprinkle with a little salt and drizzle a little olive oil over the top.

Ceviche

As in the previous recipe the fish here is "cooked" by marinating in citrus juice. My version includes a little olive oil. Variations on ceviche are served throughout Latin America. Serves 4.

700 g [1½ lb] monkfish or John Dory fillets
45 ml [3 tablespoons] olive oil
4 limes (or 2 lemons)
1 small Spanish onion
cayenne pepper
300 g [¾ lb] tomatoes
1 green pepper
2 avocado pears
salt and chilli powder

Cut the fish into 2.5 cm [1 inch] cubes. Put it into a glass or
ceramic bowl. Add the onion, cut into wafer-thin slices, and a
very generous seasoning of cayenne. Mix well. Pour on the oil
and citrus juice. Toss, cover and leave the fish to marinate for
about 8 hours. Turn the fish occasionally during this time if
possible.

Skin and seed the tomatoes, and cut the flesh into large chunks.
Cut the green pepper into slivers and peel and slice the avocado
thinly. Add the tomatoes and green pepper to the fish. Season
with salt and toss lightly. Pile the mixture into the centre of a
serving dish and arrange the sliced avocado round the edges.
Dust with a dash of chilli powder.

Salade Niçoise

This is my preferred version of the famous Mediterranean dish,
but proportions and types of ingredients can be varied to taste.
Steamed artichoke bottoms, new potatoes boiled in their skins,
diced cucumber and peas can all be included. A quick, easy and
excellent summer lunch dish for 4.

450 g [1 lb] French beans
700 g [1½ lb] tomatoes
1 large red or green pepper
5 hard-boiled eggs
1 × 200 g [7 oz] can of tuna fish
2 × 50 g [2 oz] cans of anchovy fillets
2 dozen small black olives
vinaigrette dressing

Top, tail and steam the beans until just tender. Break the beans
into halves if very long, arrange them in a salad bowl and dress
with vinaigrette while still warm.

Skin, seed and quarter the tomatoes, or cut into eighths if large.

Cut the pepper into strips. Drain the tuna fish and break it into chunks. Mix these ingredients together, moistening them with vinaigrette, then pile them on top of the cooled beans.

Quarter the hard-boiled eggs. Sprinkle them with a little vinaigrette and add to the salad, scattering the olives amongst them. Finally, drain the anchovy fillets and arrange them in a criss-cross pattern on top of the salad. Serve with hot garlic bread.

Monkfish Casserole with Garlic Croûtons

A fish casserole with Mediterranean flavours, this dish includes many of the ingredients used in the previous recipe. I think of it as a hot version of salade Niçoise. Bream, brill, fresh haddock or coley can be used if monkfish is not available. Serves 4.

700 g [1½ lb] monkfish fillets
350 g [¾ lb] French beans
2 large onions
1 × 400 g [14 oz] can of tomatoes
1 large red pepper
2 fat garlic cloves
50 g [2 oz] black olives
1 small lemon
5–10 ml [1–2 teaspoons] caster sugar
olive oil
a little flour
fresh or dried basil
salt and freshly ground black pepper

Rinse and thoroughly dry the fish. Slice it into bite-sized pieces. Warm a little oil in a large flameproof casserole and fry the fish, a few pieces at a time, until coloured.

Remove the pieces of fish with a slotted spoon, sprinkle them with salt, pepper and lemon juice and reserve them on a plate.

Gently fry the chopped onions for a few minutes. Add the finely chopped garlic and chunks of red pepper and fry gently for about 10 minutes, stirring and turning the contents of the casserole as necessary.

Stir in about 5 ml [1 teaspoon] flour to mop up the oil, add the roughly chopped tomatoes and their juices, and the sugar, and bring to the boil stirring continuously. Leave the mixture to simmer for 5 minutes or so without a lid.

While the casseroled vegetables are cooking, steam the beans, or cook them in a pan of salted boiling water, until just tender. Drain the beans well and stir them into the casserole. Cover the dish and set it aside for 1–4 hours.

About 20 minutes before you plan to eat, place the casserole of vegetables over gentle heat. Bring the contents slowly to simmering point, stirring the ingredients occasionally. Add the olives and the fish and its juices. Half cover the casserole with a lid and leave it to simmer for 10–15 minutes until all the ingredients are thoroughly hot. Season with salt, pepper and basil, and serve the casserole topped with a thick layer of hot garlicky croûtons of fried bread.

Breadcrumb Fish Pie

This is a good basic fish pie, but instead of the usual mashed potato topping it is finished with fried breadcrumbs. Packets of potato crisps, crushed with a rolling pin, make an alternative quick and easy topping which is particularly appreciated by children. Alternatively the fish can be served with a dish of boiled rice instead of topping. Serves 4–6.

700 g [1½ lb] whiting, red fish, coley or other fillets of fish
200 g [6–8 oz] streaky bacon in a piece
150 g [6 oz] small mushrooms
2 leeks
3 hard-boiled eggs
butter
600 ml [1 pt] milk
40 g [1½ oz] plain flour
plenty of fresh chopped parsley
10 ml [2 teaspoons] each concentrated tomato purée, anchovy essence and
    lemon juice
250 g [½ lb] white breadcrumbs
celery salt and pepper

Skin the fish fillets and cut them into large chunks. Put them into a big gratin dish, adding the quartered hard-boiled eggs here and there. Sprinkle with lemon juice, lots of parsley and pepper. Put the fish skins into a small pan with the milk, bring very slowly to scalding point, cover and set aside for half an hour to flavour the milk.

Meanwhile, cook the diced bacon in a large heavy-based saucepan until the fat begins to run. Increase the heat to crisp the bacon a little. Remove it with a slotted spoon and reserve. Add a nugget of butter to the pan and sauté the halved mushrooms over high heat. Remove and reserve them with the bacon. Add another generous nugget of butter to the pan, reduce heat and sweat the sliced leeks for 10 minutes.

Sprinkle the flour onto the leeks. Pour on the strained fishy milk and bring to the boil stirring continuously. Season with anchovy essence, tomato purée, celery salt, salt and pepper, and leave the sauce to simmer for 15 minutes or so until thick and smooth. (All this can be done well ahead.)

Place a baking sheet on the top shelf of the oven and heat it to 190°C [375°F], gas mark 5. Gently mix the bacon and mushrooms with the fish and eggs. Bring the sauce back to simmering point, pour into the pie dish, cover the dish with a foil lid and place it on the hot baking sheet. Bake for 20–25 minutes.

While the pie is cooking, fry the crumbs in a little butter, stirring and turning them vigorously at first so every crumb absorbs a little fat, then dry-fry until golden brown and crisp (it is unnecessary to use a lot of butter). Scatter the crumbs thickly over the pie and serve immediately.

Vol-au-Vent à l'Indienne

A mixture of white fish, prawns and grapes in a curried cream sauce makes a subtle-tasting fish dish, with which puff pastry goes well. Alternatively, the fish could be topped with croûtons or crumbs, as in the previous fish pie recipes, or it could be used to fill a ring of choux pastry, as in the next recipe. Serves 4.

600 g [1¼ lb] fillets of fresh haddock, halibut, coley or whiting
225 g [½ lb] peeled prawns
125 g [4–5 oz] grapes, peeled and pipped
300 ml [½ pt] fish stock plus 30 ml [2 tablespoons] lemon juice or 150 ml [¼ pt] each dry white wine and water
1 medium–large onion
40 g [1½ oz] butter
30 ml [2 tablespoons] plain flour
5 ml [1 teaspoon] curry powder or paste
60 ml [4 tablespoons] double cream
1 bay leaf
salt and freshly ground black pepper
1 × 400 g [13 oz] packet puff pastry
beaten egg to glaze

If more convenient, the vol-au-vent cases can be cooked ahead, cooled and stored in an airtight tin then reheated when required.

Roll out the pastry until as thick as two 50p pieces — 6 mm [¼ inch]. Using a small bowl or breakfast cup as a template, cut out 4 pastry circles about 12 cm [5 inches] in diameter. Knock up the edges, then use the tip of the knife to score a second circle inside each round of pastry, about 12 mm [½ inch] from the edge. This inner circle will form the lid so take care to cut through the top layer of pastry only. Transfer the vol-au-vent cases to a baking sheet and chill them while the oven heats up to 230°C [450°F], gas mark 8.

Glaze the vol-au-vents with beaten egg and bake them for 20–25 minutes until well puffed up and crisp. They will cook best if you place the baking tray on an upper shelf of the oven and place a roasting pan filled with boiling water on the oven floor. Carefully lift out the pastry lids with a knife, scoop out and discard any raw pastry from inside the vol-au-vents and return the cases to the oven for a few minutes to dry out.

To make the filling (which can be done whilst the vol-au-vents bake), first skin and bone the fish and cut it into large chunks. Poach it gently for 6–8 minutes with the bay leaf, lemon juice and stock (or wine and water). Strain off and reserve the liquid; cover the fish to prevent it drying out and to keep it hot.

While the fish is cooking, soften the finely chopped onion in butter for about 6 minutes in a saucepan. Stir in the curry powder or paste, then the flour. Blend in the strained fish liquor and bring to the boil, stirring. Add the cream and a seasoning of salt and pepper and leave the sauce to simmer for 5–10 minutes to give a good consistency.

Add the grapes, prawns and fish to the saucepan. Cover and cook very gently for about 5 minutes until all the ingredients are thoroughly heated through. Check seasoning and spoon the mixture into the piping hot vol-au-vent cases.

Fish Pie à l'Indienne: For a less sophisticated but none the less delicious dish, mix the poached and drained fish with the prawns and grapes in a pie dish. Pour on the sauce and leave to become cold before topping with a puff pastry lid. Glaze and make steam slits in the usual way, and bake the pie for 25 minutes at 220°C [425°F], gas mark 7.

Gougère with Fish

Cheese-flavoured choux pastry makes another good foil for creamy fish pie mixtures. The filling used here is smoked fish bathed in a delicate sauce flecked with green herbs. Serves 4.

500 g [1 lb] smoked haddock
450 ml [¾ pt] milk
1 small onion
2 celery stalks
1 bunch watercress
75 ml [5 tablespoons] fresh chopped parsley
45 ml [3 tablespoons] fresh chopped chives
2 hard-boiled eggs
40 g [1½ oz] butter
30 ml [2 tablespoons] plain flour
salt, paprika and freshly ground black pepper

For the choux pastry:
75 g [3 oz] butter
225 ml [8 fl oz] water
115 g [¼ lb] plain flour
a pinch of cayenne pepper and mustard powder
salt and freshly ground black pepper
3 large eggs
75 g [3 oz] freshly grated Cheddar cheese
25 g [1 oz] freshly grated Parmesan cheese

Make the choux pastry first — the filling can be prepared while the pastry is cooking. Preheat the oven and a baking sheet to 220°C [425°F], gas mark 7, and make and bake the cheesy choux pastry as described in the recipe for four-cheese gougère on page 36, but using Cheddar and Parmesan to flavour the pastry.

To make the filling, put the smoked haddock into a pan, pour on the milk and bring to the boil. Cover the pan and set it aside for 15 minutes. Lift out the fish and boil the milk until reduced to 275 ml [½ pt].

Melt a little butter in a separate pan and sweat the finely chopped onion and celery in it for 7–8 minutes. Stir in the flour, salt, pepper and a shake of paprika, then blend in the reduced fishy milk. Bring the sauce to the boil, stirring, and let it simmer for 10–15 minutes until rich and creamy in texture.

Meanwhile strip and finely chop the watercress leaves. Mix them with the chives and parsley. Slice the eggs thickly. Skin and bone the fish and break it into large chunks.

When the choux pastry has puffed up and set — after 45–50

minutes' cooking — fill the centre of the dish with the fish, scattering the herbs and slices of egg and pouring on some of the sauce between layers. Dust with paprika and return the dish to the oven for about 5 minutes to ensure that the filling is really hot.

Dressed Crab

Lobster is always wildly expensive, but in May and June the price of fresh Cornish crabs makes shellfish an affordable luxury. Dressing crab is fiddly and time-consuming but very rewarding.

Commercially dressed crab is often wasteful of crabmeat, and spoiled by moistening with malt vinegar and padding with breadcrumbs. A skewer cunningly wielded in the kitchen will prise much more crab meat from the shell, and the dressed crab will be pure and unadulterated. Serves 4.

1 crab weighing 1.1–1.4 kg [2½–3 lb]
a few spoonfuls of mayonnaise or vinaigrette dressing
French mustard
lemon juice and olive oil
salt and freshly ground black pepper
parsley

The fresher the crab the better it tastes. Buy direct from a crab fisherman, or from a fishmonger known to have regular fresh supplies. Choose a crab that is very much alive and kicking and heavy for its size; apathy and lightness in proportion to size are signs that the creature has been out of the sea for some time and is surviving on stored nourishment. Pick the crab up, stretching your hand across its back so the claws cannot reach you, and shake it gently to check that the weight is all meat and not partly seawater.

Put the crab into a very large pan. Fill it with very heavily salted cold water, cover the pan with a lid and weigh it down (or the crab's curiosity may lead it to explore its surroundings and, in so doing, to try to push off the lid). Bring the liquid to boiling point very slowly indeed. Once boiling point is reached, simmer the crab for 20–30 minutes depending on size. Remove the cooked crab from the pan and leave it to cool.

(If you cannot bring yourself to buy and cook live crab, check

when the fishmonger receives fresh deliveries, ask him to boil it for you and collect it that morning.)

To dress a crab: Allow plenty of time for dressing crab and assemble a large chopping board, a sharp knife and 2 bowls (1 for white meat and 1 for the brown meat), a pair of nutcrackers or a hammer for cracking the claws and legs, a coffee spoon, and a skewer for picking meat from small nooks and crannies of the shell.

First, twist the crab legs and claws away from the body. Crack the claws and legs open and prise out the meat, taking care to discard any little chips of bone and membrane.

Next, lay the crab on its back with the tail end facing you. Holding the hard back shell down with your fingers, use your thumbs to lever and push the body section up and out of the back shell. Set the body section aside while you deal with the back shell. Remove and discard the stomach sac from the head end, then scrape the curd and meat from the shell. Trim the shell by tapping along the natural curved line marked on it: this is the dividing line between very hard and relatively thin shell. The thin shell should break away quite easily, leaving you with a handsome "bowl" of back shell which can be washed, dried and rubbed with a little oil to make a dish in which to serve the crab meat.

Pull off and discard the inedible feathery grey gills which are attached to the body section. Scrape out the creamy brown meat with a spoon, then use a skewer, time and patience to prise out the especially sweet white meat which lies hidden between the maze of thin shell. (It helps to split the body section in half, from head end to tail end, using a firm blow with a sharp knife, as this gives easier access to the interior of the body.)

When the bones are picked clean, shred the white meat with a pair of forks. Season it to taste with a spoonful or so of mayonnaise or vinaigrette dressing and a little salt and freshly ground black pepper. Cream the bowl of brown meat with a spoon, seasoning it with a few drops of olive oil, a squeeze of lemon juice and a little each of salt, freshly ground black pepper and French mustard.

Pile the prepared crab meat into the hard back shell, packing the white meat down either side and mounding the brown meat in the centre. By all means mark the dividing lines between white and brown meats with tiny sprigs of fresh parsley, but forget about fancy trimmings.

Cucumber salad, plenty of good brown bread and a dish of fresh, unsalted butter are the perfect accompaniments to dressed crab. If appetites are huge, or if the crabs have yielded less meat than I hoped, I also bring to the table a bowl of mayonnaise and a dish of hard-boiled eggs, halved and sprinkled with a handful of fresh chopped parsley. This makes a feast of a meal.

No first course is necessary and, to follow, just serve, for example, a bowl of fresh cherries on ice or a dish of freckled ripe apricots.

Seafood Salad

Firm-fleshed monkfish is a well-known cheat substitute for lobster and scampi. Here it is combined with inexpensive squid and mussels, smoked haddock and a few large prawns to create an apparently lavish dish, but at modest cost for seafood. Serves 8.

500 g [1 lb] small squid
500 g [1 lb] monkfish fillets
500 g [1 lb] smoked haddock fillets
1 litre [2 lb] fresh mussels
175 g [6 oz] large prawns
2 crisp apples
1 head of celery
50 g [2 oz] cashew nuts
lemon juice
vinaigrette dressing
fresh herbs, for garnish

For the avocado mayonnaise:
2 very ripe avocado pears
2 egg yolks
275 ml [½ pt] mixed olive and sunflower oil
lemon juice
a bunch of chives
salt and freshly ground black pepper

Prepare and fry the squid (as described on page 221), sprinkle with a little lemon juice and leave to get cold. Thoroughly scrub, steam and shell the mussels (as described on page 40), dress them with a little vinaigrette and leave to get cold.

Put the monkfish into a saucepan. Lay the smoked haddock on top, cover with cold water and bring slowly to the boil. Simmer gently for 5 minutes, then lift out the smoked haddock and poach the monkfish for a further 5 minutes or so until cooked. When cool enough to handle, skin both fish and break the flesh into bite-sized chunks. Dress the fish with a little vinaigrette and leave them to get cold.

Mash the carefully peeled and stoned avocados with lemon juice to make a very smooth green purée. Make a mayonnaise with the egg yolks and oil. Gradually beat into it the avocado purée and season well with salt, pepper and lemon. Stir in the snipped chives.

Drain the squid, mussels, monkfish and smoked haddock. Mix them with the diced apples, crescents of celery and cashew nuts, and coat with the avocado mayonnaise — thinning it with a spoonful or two of water if too thick. Pile the mixture onto a serving dish and garnish with the prawns and a few fresh herbs.

Serve with good bread or a rice salad (use the fish liquid for boiling the rice) and a salad of lettuce hearts.

Fresh & Dried Fruits

a fruit salad.

Fruit always provides a refreshing end to a meal, and it is much more appropriate than a creamy or substantial pudding when the preceding dish has been a rich one.

A formal mixed fruit bowl, with its carefully anchored pineapple, its grapes draped over the satsumas and the Cox's is undeniably elegant, but rather stylized — like a Dutch still life. Just as a tumbler of buttercups is more appealing than a corsetted Interflora bouquet, so it is with fruit: the sweetest memories are usually humble rather than exotic. Who can resist juicy green-gages casually piled in a straw basket which shows off the tawny green bloom of their skins, or a tumbling pyramid of dark red cherries on crushed ice, or russet pears with leaves still gracing their stalks piled on a favourite old china plate?

However, there are occasions when one wants to serve fruit other than in its entire and raw state, and it is with simply prepared fruit dishes that this chapter is concerned.

At the end of the chapter are a few recipes in which fruit is combined with egg whites to make meringue-topped puddings and sorbets, but most of the recipes are devoted to fruit salads, compôtes, baked and poached fruit. At first glance so much emphasis on such simple treatment of fruit may seem ill-balanced. It is true that these simple fruit dishes are not particu-larly original, but I make no apology either for their simplicity or for writing about them at length. It is precisely because they are so obvious that it is easy to forget about them, and to do so is to miss out on some of the most exquisite dishes in the world. Moreover, the simpler the dish, the less room there is for error.

To fuss over fruit, to indulge in fancy work, can destroy its beauty. Instead, aim to allow diners to enjoy the fruit as unadorned as possible, but without the bother of having to peel, pip or otherwise prepare fruit for themselves at table. The cook's role, therefore, is essentially to nurse the ingredients and to know when to leave well alone — to remove the inedible parts, to highlight delicately the natural good qualities of the fruit, but no more. One may add, for example, a touch of sweetness to round out sharpness, a little liquid to make up for lack of juiciness, or a whisper of extra fragrance. One can gently warm fruit to release its juices and scent, or cook it carefully to render it tender.

Fruit salads: I have a horror of fresh fruit that is saturated with spirits or liqueurs, and a loathing of heavy "canned fruit" sugar syrups. Both seem to overpower the refreshing quality of fruit. Far better to keep fruit salads as pure as possible. Add a discrete spoonful of honey, a soupçon of framboise, a little warming spice such as cinnamon or stem ginger, or the floral fragrance of elderflower or rosewater, to provide a background note, if you wish, but basically let the freshness of the fruit proclaim its own glory. If it has insufficient juices of its own, an orange, lemon, lime or grapefruit can be squeezed over it to provide extra liquid. Citrus juice will also sharpen the overblown flavour of fruit that is just past its prime, and round out the thin flavour of slightly under-ripe fruit.

There is a special sense of luxury in being presented with a fruit salad consisting of just one type of fruit, in perfect condition, in generous quantity and immaculately prepared — freshly peeled peaches or oranges neatly segmented and ruthlessly stripped of all pith and membrane — and the pleasure is heightened if you are spared having to witness and applaud the waiter's virtuosity with the paring knife.

Fruit salads are more often composed of mixed fruits. I am hesitant about using more than 3 or 4 different fruit in one dish as too great an assortment can blur the virtues of each individual fruit. For the same reason it is important not to chop fruit too small, but to cut it into generous bite-sized chunks. The distinctive taste and texture of each fruit, and the foil they provide for one another, should be evident both to eye and to palate.

In Britain composite fruit salads are usually made by tossing the fruits together to mix them, and serving them in a deep bowl. I have used this method, for example, in the marriage of raspberries, strawberries, redcurrants and cherries to make a red fruit salad, and also in the cream and ivory coloured melon ambrosia.

When the fruits are of more varied colours and shapes, more dramatic presentation can be used to advantage, with each type of fruit arranged in a separate group on one large flat dish to create the brilliant splurge of an artist's palette. Golden half moons of peeled and sliced peaches, a mound of tiny alpine strawberries and the black-speckled jade rings of kiwi fruit, for example, look stunning together and taste wonderful, particularly if a few spoonfuls of white wine and a dredging of caster sugar are added just before the dish is brought to the table.

Cooking fruit: Some fruits are usually better served warm than raw. Blackberries, for example, although irresistible to eat straight from the hedgerow as you pick them, only exude their full aroma when gently warmed until their juices flow. Apricots, unless picked at the moment of perfect ripeness and eaten still warm from basking against the kitchen-garden wall, need to be baked in a gentle oven with a vanilla pod and a little sugar.

Other fruits always have to be cooked — tart green gooseberries, damsons, Conference pears so hard they appear to be carved of wood, rhubarb, Bramley apples and so on. Cookbooks often tend to gloss over the details, assuming that poaching or stewing fruit is something we can all do well by instinct. Not so, for me at least. It is all too easy for the potentially beautiful, dusky compôte of damsons to be ruined by a ragged mass of floating skins and stones because the fruit has burst during cooking; or for the anticipated smooth purée of apples to end up mortifyingly insipid and rasping with tiny particles of core which maddeningly catch between the teeth. I have found it necessary and helpful to note down over the years the types and quantities of sweetener, flavouring and liquid which best seem to complement different fruits, and, every bit as vital, the approximate timings and temperatures needed to cook them. Taking these points in the order listed, my experience suggests the following general rules.

To over-sweeten fruit can spoil its refreshing quality. Better to use too little sugar than too much; more can always be added at the end of cooking if necessary (icing sugar dissolves almost instantly). Alternatively, if there is a great deal of thin liquid in the dish, the juices can be drained off with a bulb baster after cooking, and reduced by fast boiling to make them sweeter and richer. Sugar, incidentally, has a toughening effect on skins. It is, therefore, always best added to tough, thick-skinned fruit, such as plums, when the fruit is at least half cooked.

Extra liquid is often needed for hard fruits, but it is wise to be wary of using a lot. I find citrus or unsweetened apple juice often more sympathetic than water. Usually, only a few spoonfuls of liquid are required, and semi-hard fruits, such as rhubarb, which are traditionally cooked with additional liquid, in fact need none and taste infinitely better without it. Instead, sprinkle the cut fruit with sugar an hour or two ahead of cooking so the juices are gradually drawn to the surface, and thus prevent the fruit from sticking to the dish when heat is applied.

As to cooking methods, I have come to the conclusion that cooking fruit in the oven is much safer than cooking it on top of the stove, because heat circulates much more evenly in the oven. A low temperature is always preferable to a high one: it may take longer to cook the fruit, but it avoids the risk of unsightly bursting or disintegration caused by sudden or fierce heat. Moreover, if cooking is fast, there is a danger that fruit will jump from nearly ready to overcooked while your back is turned. Whether cooked in the oven or on top of the stove, fruit touching the side or base of the dish inevitably heats up more quickly. In order for all the fruit to be cooked simultaneously it must be moved round inside the dish from time to time. I recommend shaking rather than stirring the dish; even a rounded wooden spoon can break up and spoil the appearance of delicate fruits.

More specific points are covered in the individual recipes for compôtes, baked and poached fruit given in this chapter. The recipes should be regarded as sound guidelines for the successful cooking of fruit but not as instructions to be followed to the letter. Precise details of timing, temperature and so on inevitably vary a little according to the size and ripeness of the fruit, the quantity being cooked, the shape and material of the dish, the idiosyncrasies of each stove, etc. By frequently looking at, sometimes touching and occasionally tasting the fruit as it cooks, any necessary minor adjustments can be made.

Izmiri Oranges

A fresh orange salad is so simple that it cannot really be classified as a recipe, which perhaps explains why it rarely appears on menus. This seems a pity as few dishes make a more refreshing end to a meal. This version includes a hint of orange-blossom water which heightens the fragrance without dominating the fruit as a sugar syrup or liqueurs would tend to do. Serves 8–10.

16 small, thin-skinned oranges
a few drops of triple-distilled orange-blossom water (available from good
    delicatessens)
a small handful of split almonds

A small, very sharp, pointed knife is essential for preparing oranges, and one must be ruthless about removing every trace of bitter white pith and thin membrane. Starting at the stalk end and gradually working downwards, use the knife to spiral round the fruit, cutting away skin, pith and outer membrane all at once.

Peel 14 of the oranges in this way, then use the knife to release each segment of flesh from its surrounding "V" of membrane and to extract the pips. Put the orange segments into a bowl — royal blue or plain white china looks best. Add any juices which have collected on the board, and the juices squeezed from the trimmings.

Cut the skin of the remaining 2 oranges (just the thin orange layer, not the bitter-tasting, white pithy parts of the peel) into narrow julienne strips. Blanch them in boiling water for 5–10 minutes, refresh with cold water, drain and pat dry. Squeeze the juice from these 2 oranges and mix it with a few drops of orange-blossom water. Pour the liquid over the fruit, add the strips of orange zest, cover the dish, and chill it until shortly before serving. Scatter with the nuts immediately before serving.

New Zealand Orange Salad: Cut the ruthlessly peeled oranges into horizontal slices, allowing 1½ oranges per person. Pour on fresh orange juice, allowing the juice of half an orange per person. Cover and chill. Just before serving, mix the oranges with a few peeled and sliced kiwi fruit. The contrast of orange and emerald fruit is brilliantly festive.

Melon Ambrosia

Pale jade, ivory and cream in colour, this makes a lovely salad for autumn months. The inclusion of mint is optional, but it gives an intriguing extra dimension to the dish. Serves 6–8.

2 Ogen or 1 large honeydew melon
350 g [¾ lb] green grapes
2 bananas
about 30 ml [2 tablespoons] liquid honey
2 lemons
fresh mint
caster sugar, to taste

Stand the honey jar in a deep saucepan and pour round it enough very hot, but not boiling, water to come almost to the rim of the jar. Leave for 15 minutes or so until the honey is warm and very runny.

Meanwhile, prepare the fruit. Halve and seed the melon(s). Scoop the flesh into tiny rounds using a melon baller or coffee spoon, and pile into a large bowl, adding any juices that remain in the melon shell. Skin and seed the grapes and mix them gently with the melon.

Squeeze the lemon juice into a cup. Stir in the honey and pour the mixture over the fruit. Toss gently, cover and chill for 2–3 hours. By the end of this time the fruit will have exuded quite a lot of juice which will have mingled with the lemon and honey syrup. Taste it and add a spoonful of caster sugar if the mixture is too tart for your taste, or add extra lemon juice if too sweet.

Just before serving, peel and thickly slice the bananas and stir them into the salad, together with a scant spoonful of chopped fresh mint.

Grape & Melon Salad: For a refreshing first-course salad, omit the bananas and honey and mix some lemon juice with a little olive oil, salt and pepper instead. Slivers of poached chicken or turkey meat, or prawns, can be added if you like. This dish looks prettiest served in melon shells.

Three-Melon Salad: Slice, rind and seed a fragrant Charantais or Cantaloup melon. Prepare equal quantities of watermelon and honeydew melon in the same fashion, and arrange all the melon slices in colourful groups on one large, flat dish. Hand round separately little bowls of chopped stem ginger, quartered lemons, soft brown sugar, and fresh mint so that each person can season the fruit to taste.

Mangoes with Pomegranates

This beautiful dish with its hint of the exotic is an affordable treat in autumn, when the prices of mangoes and pomegranates often drop simultaneously. If pomegranates are not available, use the juice of 1 orange and 1 lemon instead, and scatter the dish with a handful of split and toasted almonds just before serving. If the dish needs to be stretched to serve more people, mix the mangoes with firm, thickly sliced bananas. Serves 6.

3 large, very ripe mangoes
2 pomegranates

Check that the mangoes are fully ripe by cradling them in your hands: the flesh should feel slightly soft beneath the waxy skin. It should also be delicately aromatic. Avoid any mango which smells as though wiped over with a turpentine rag, because it is likely to taste equally disagreeable.

Thinly pare away the mango skin with a small sharp knife. Do this on a chopping board which has a groove round the edge and a bowl hollowed out at one end, or over a plate, to catch the juices that will drip from the slippery flesh. Then cut the flesh away from the stone in thick slices and arrange them on a dish.

Cut one of the pomegranates in half. Carefully pull the seeds free from the creamy pith and membrane, and scatter them over the mangoes. Cut the second pomegranate in half. Again pull out the seeds and discard the pith and membrane. But, instead of scattering the seeds over the mangoes, wrap them in a piece of butter muslin. Hold the muslin bag over the dish of fruit and squeeze it tightly so that the pomegranate seeds burst and release their juices over the mangoes.

Red Fruit Salad

This is one of the simplest and most beautiful ways to serve summer fruits. The secret of success is to let the fruits macerate for about 4 hours so that their juices mingle to make a luscious red syrup. Serves 4–6.

250 g [½ lb] redcurrants
250 g [½ lb] dark red dessert cherries
250 g [½ lb] raspberries
250 g [½ lb] firm strawberries
45 ml [3 tablespoons] freshly squeezed orange juice
15 ml [1 tablespoon] lemon juice
60–75 ml [4–5 tablespoons] caster sugar

String the redcurrants and stone the cherries. Put the redcurrants into a saucepan and strew the sugar over them. Cover the pan and shake it to distribute the sugar. Pour on the orange juice, cover the pan again and set it over the lowest possible heat. Cook very gently for about 4 minutes until the sugar is melted and the redcurrant juices have begun to flow.

Switch off the heat. Add the stoned cherries to the pan, cover it and shake the pan again. Then return the pan to the stove, but do not turn it on — the residual heat will be enough to encourage the cherries to yield up some of their juices, and the redcurrants will continue to soften a little but without danger of disintegration.

After 20 minutes, gently turn the contents of the pan into a bowl. Add the strawberries (cut into halves), the raspberries and the lemon juice. Mix gently, cover and chill for 4–6 hours. If prepared much further ahead the fruit can begin to turn mushy.

This salad looks prettiest served in tall-stemmed glasses. Little biscuits make a good accompaniment, but the temptation to serve cream with the fruit is best resisted.

Italian Peaches

Serving peaches in this way brings out their sunny, fruity flavour to the full. Use very ripe peaches, or cheap slightly over-ripe peaches and cut out the bruised parts. In the latter case buy 1 extra peach to allow for wastage. Serves 4.

8 average-sized (or 5 really large) very ripe peaches
45 ml [3 tablespoons] caster sugar
45 ml [3 tablespoons] lemon juice
90 ml [6 tablespoons] orange juice
a few macaroons

Skin the peaches. If they are really ripe, the skins should lift off quite easily. If necessary, first dip the fruit in boiling water for a minute to loosen the skins. Cut the fruit away from the stone in chunky bite-sized pieces and put them into a bowl. Sprinkle the caster sugar over them, then pour on the lemon and orange juices. Stir lightly, cover and leave to macerate in a cool room for a minimum of 4 hours or up to 8 hours. During this time the sugar and fruit juices will amalgamate to make a lovely light fruity syrup.

Divide the peaches between 4 large wine glasses or individual bowls. Crumble a few macaroons and sprinkle a spoonful or so over the top of each serving. Pour on the juices and serve immediately.

Barbados Peaches

In complete contrast to the previous recipe, these peaches are served spicy and hot. A good dish for a cool summer's evening and, providing you keep a couple of cans in your store-cupboard, a useful recipe for emergency occasions. Serves 4.

6 small ripe peaches or 2 × 400 g [14 oz] cans of halved peaches
1 small orange
60 ml [4 tablespoons] soft dark brown sugar
2.5 ml [½ teaspoon] each ground cinnamon and allspice
125 ml [4 fl oz] double cream
30 ml [2 tablespoons] soured cream

If fresh peaches are used, skin, halve and stone them. Lightly butter a gratin dish, which will take the peach halves in a single layer, and pour the orange juice into it. Turn the peaches in the dish to moisten them all over and lay them cut side up. Mix the sugar and spices together and spoon it into the stone cavities.

Bake, uncovered, in an oven preheated to 190°C [375°F], gas mark 5, for 15–20 minutes until the peaches are very hot and smell superb. Top each with a dollop of the softly whipped and well-chilled creams. It is the contrast of chilled cream and spicy hot fruit that makes this dish so good.

Rhubarb & Banana Compôte

The way in which rhubarb is cooked makes an enormous difference to the final appearance and taste of the compôte. Cooking the fruit in a gentle oven, without adding any liquid, prevents disintegration and ensures true fruit flavour. Serves 6.

1 kg [2 lb] rhubarb
200 g [6 oz] caster sugar
the finely grated zest of 2 oranges
4 bananas

Wipe the rhubarb clean, trim it and cut into oblique slices. Lay them in a gratin dish. Sprinkle on the sugar and orange zest. Cover the dish and leave it at room temperature for 2 hours before cooking. This delay allows the sugar to draw enough juices from the rhubarb to prevent it from sticking to the dish during cooking.

Put the covered dish into an oven preheated to 160°C [325°F], gas mark 3, and bake for about 45 minutes until the rhubarb is quite tender, but still retains its shape. Shake the dish occasionally to move the fruit around and thus encourage even cooking.

Line a glass bowl with 2 of the bananas cut into thick slices. Let the cooked rhubarb become tepid, then slide it and its juices into the bowl. Scatter the remaining sliced bananas over the top and serve while the rhubarb is still warm, with a bowl of fresh yoghurt and some Demerara sugar.

Compôte of Damsons

Damsons, the smallest members of the plum family, are dusky purple and very tart. Cooked in a gentle oven with sugar, orange and cinnamon, they make an admirable compôte. Serves 8.

1.35 kg [3 lb] damsons
450 g [1 lb] caster sugar
7 ml [1 heaped teaspoon] ground cinnamon
2 oranges

There is no need to stone the damsons, but it is best to prick each one with a larding needle after washing the fruit and removing the stalks. Put the damsons into a heavy-based oven dish, preferably a gratin dish, so the fruit lies in a shallow layer. Scatter the damsons with the finely grated zest and the juice of the oranges. Cover the dish with foil and bake for 45 minutes in an oven preheated to 160°C [325°F], gas mark 3. Shake the dish occasionally during this stage to encourage the fruit to cook evenly.

Add the sugar and cinnamon mixed together and give the dish another good shake to distribute the flavourings. Cover and continue baking for a further 15–30 minutes until the fruit is tender. (It is best to add the sugar towards the end of cooking, since sugar tends to harden the fruit skins.) Serve hot or cold with thin chilled cream.

Compôte of Prunes with Port

Whilst I don't like alcohol with fresh fruit it can be very good with dried fruit. These prunes, slowly swollen and enriched with port, make a wonderfully heady and rich dish. Quantities are deliberately small in view of the richness. Serves 6.

250 g [½ lb] large, pitted Californian prunes
150 ml [¼ pt] port
15 ml [1 tablespoon] lemon juice
75 ml [5 tablespoons] cold tea
50 g [scant 2 oz] soft brown sugar
75 g [3 oz] split and toasted almonds
150 ml [¼ pt] soured cream or 75 ml [3 fl oz] each yoghurt and double cream

Measure the sugar, port, tea and lemon juice into a saucepan. Add the prunes. Bring the contents of the pan very slowly to simmering point. Cover the pan and leave it to simmer for 5 minutes.

Remove the pan from the heat, place it in a cold larder (or put in a cold place) and leave it there for 2–4 days. Turn the fruit in its syrup once or twice during this time.

Shortly before serving, divide the prunes and their syrup between 6 glasses, scattering the well-toasted almonds amongst the fruit. Top each glass with a spoonful of soured cream (or yoghurt and double cream lightly whipped together). The cream will slither softly over the fruit and begin to mingle with the rich port-flavoured syrup.

Winter Fruit Salad

A variety of dried fruits and almonds go to make up this rich fruit salad. It keeps well for up to 4 days, during which time the fruits grow plumper and more richly flavoured. It can be served cold,

but is best warmed through in a low oven just before serving.
Serves 6–8.

250 g [½ lb] large pitted prunes
250 g [½ lb] dried apricots
250 g [½ lb] dates
75 g [3 oz] blanched almonds
2–3 cinnamon sticks
4 cloves
12 coriander seeds
2 or 3 thinly pared curls of orange peel
90 ml [6 tablespoons] soft dark brown sugar
900 ml [1½ pt] cold strained tea
75 ml [2½ fl oz] brandy or white rum

Bruise the spices lightly and tie them up in a piece of butter
muslin together with the orange peel. Put the bag of spices into a
heavy-based saucepan or flameproof casserole. Add the sugar,
tea and alcohol. (For more heady results you can increase the
amount of brandy or rum and decrease tea accordingly.) Slit the
dates and stone them. Put all the dried fruits into the casserole and
bring slowly to simmering point. Threequarters cover the casserole and leave it to simmer gently for 8 minutes or so. Put the
lid on completely and set it aside in a cold place for 8 hours or up
to 4 days. Remove the spice bag, squeezing it well so the juices
drip back onto the fruit. Stir in the blanched almonds.

Warm the fruit salad in the oven at 150°C [300°F], gas mark 2,
for about 45 minutes. Serve with fresh and soured creams whipped together with a generous pinch of ground cinnamon.

Khoshaf with Rose-Scented Cream

This Persian combination of dried apricots, raisins and nuts is
even simpler to prepare than the previous recipe, and the inclusion of rosewater (available from good delicatessens) provides a
mysterious background note. This fruit must be prepared ahead,
and it becomes even more delectable with keeping. Serves 10–12.

700 g [1½ lb] dried apricots
175 g [6 oz] raisins or sultanas
125 g [¼ lb] soft brown sugar
45 ml [3 tablespoons] triple-distilled rosewater
175 g [6 oz] blanched and split almonds
90 g [3 oz] pistacchio or pinenuts (or more blanched and split almonds)

For the rose-scented cream:
300 ml [½ pt] double or whipping cream
30 ml [2 tablespoons] milk
15–30 ml [1–2 tablespoons] triple-distilled rosewater

Measure the sugar into a large ceramic bowl. Pour on 150 ml [¼ pt] warm water and stir until the sugar has dissolved. Stir in the rosewater and 550 ml [1 pt] cold water. Add the dried fruits to the bowl and stir and turn them in the liquid for a minute or so. If there is insufficient liquid to cover the fruit completely, stir in extra cold water as necessary.

Cover the bowl and leave it in a cold place or fridge for at least 24 hours or up to 4 days, just stirring the mixture once or twice a day. Then add the nuts to the bowl and stir to mix them with the fruit. If you can resist eating the khoshaf for a further 12–24 hours after adding the nuts, so much the better.

Khoshaf can be served on its own, or accompanied by a bowl of yoghurt. For a richer dish serve khoshaf with rose-scented cream. To make this, stir the milk into the cream and add rosewater to taste, then beat the ingredients with a balloon whisk until they hold a soft shape.

Cinnamon Honey Pears

Honey is very effective in enriching a thin, under-ripe flavour and it gives pears a warm golden sheen. Even little green cooking pears, so hard that they appear to be beyond hope, can be rendered mouthwateringly tender by cooking this way. Serves 8.

8 large pears
3 cinnamon sticks
350 g [12 oz] liquid honey
the juice and zest of 2 lemons
575 ml [1 pt] dry cider or unsweetened apple juice

Choose a casserole or baking dish with just enough room to lay the pears head to tail in a single layer. Peel the pears, thinly paring away the skins and leaving the stalks intact. Cut a small slice off the base of each pear (so it will stand upright for serving) then lay them in the dish. Break each cinnamon stick into 2 or 3 pieces. Put them into a saucepan with the remaining ingredients and bring slowly to the boil. (To liquefy honey see p 240.)

Pour the contents of the pan over the pears and cover with a lid. Bake in an oven preheated to 180°C [350°F], gas mark 4, turning and basting the fruit occasionally to encourage even cooking and colouring. How long the pears will take to turn golden and cook to a melt-in-the-mouth texture varies enormously — 1 hour is enough for semi-ripe dessert pears, 3 hours may be needed for large woody cookers.

When the pears are ready, lift them carefully out of the dish, drain them and stand them on a warmed cake stand or a flat dish. Boil the juices until reduced to a rich syrup, strain to extract cinnamon and lemon zest and pour the sauce over the pears. Serve warm or cold (warm is better), alone or with a bowl of whipped cream.

Apricots with Vanilla Cream

The lightly freckled apricot is a fruit for which I have a passion, and this is a beautiful apricot dish. The cream, which is less rich and more subtle than double cream, also goes well with raspberries. Serves 4–6.

900 g [2 lb] apricots
the juice of a small lemon
150 g [5 oz] caster sugar — preferably from a jar in which vanilla pods
   are also stored.
a vanilla pod

For the vanilla cream:
300 ml [½ pt] single cream
a vanilla pod and pure vanilla extract
7–10 ml [1½–2 teaspoons] lemon juice

First prepare the cream. Split the vanilla pod and put it into a small pan together with the cream. Stirring continuously, bring slowly to simmering point, then let the cream simmer gently, stirring occasionally, for 5–10 minutes until reduced by about one-third. Cover the pan and set it aside until quite cold.

Remove the vanilla pod, stir the cream and taste it. If vanilla flavour is weak, add a few drops of pure vanilla extract — not vanilla flavouring, which is synthetic, often based on cloves, and very harsh-tasting. Blend in lemon juice to taste, stirring it in drop by drop so that the cream doesn't curdle.

Halve and stone the apricots. Lay them, cut side down, in a shallow dish. Bury a split vanilla pod among them, strew the sugar over them and pour on the lemon juice and a couple of tablespoonfuls of water. Cover the dish with foil or a lid and place it in an oven preheated to 160°C [325°F], gas mark 3. Bake, basting the fruit occasionally with the syrup, until tender — 45–60 minutes depending on the ripeness of the fruit. Serve while still warm from the oven (but not hot), with the chilled vanilla cream.

Blackberries with Geranium Cream

Blackberries seem to taste best, and smell quite wonderful, when gently warmed until their juices flow. Sweet geranium has great affinity with blackberries, and here the leaves are used to scent the accompanying cream. Serves 8.

1.35 kg [3 lb] fresh blackberries
300 g [10 oz] caster sugar
20–30 ml [4–6 teaspoons] lemon juice
600 ml [1 pt] single cream
half a dozen sweet geranium leaves

First prepare the cream. Rinse the geranium leaves, tear them up and put them into a saucepan with the cream. Bring slowly to

simmering point, stirring all the time, then leave to simmer gently, just stirring occasionally, for about 10 minutes until the liquid has reduced by about one-third. Cover the pan and set it aside until cold, then refrigerate it. Extract the leaves only just before serving.

Hull and pick over the blackberries. If you have to wash them (or any other soft, easily bruised berry fruit), the best method is to put the fruit into a colander then dip the colander very gently in and out of a sinkful of cold water. Do this several times, then leave the colander on the draining board for 10 minutes. Carefully turn the berries out onto kitchen paper towels and shake or roll the towels gently to dry the fruit.

Cook the blackberries immediately before serving. Put them into a very wide saucepan so they lie in a shallow layer. Sprinkle them with lemon juice and strew them with sugar. Cover the pan and shake it gently to distribute the sugar. Place the covered pan over very low heat for only as long as it takes to melt the sugar and to start the blackberry juices flowing — about 5 minutes. Then shake the pan again and switch off the heat, but leave the covered pan where it is for a further 5 minutes while the blackberries continue to warm through and exude their juices.

Pour the blackberries and their juices into glasses or bowls, and trickle the chilled scented cream over them.

Gooseberries with Elderflower

Just as sweet geranium brings a touch of magic to blackberries, so the muscatel fragrance of elderflower transforms plain green gooseberries into a memorable dish. Serves 6.

900 g [2 lb] green gooseberries
2–3 heads of elderflower
225–275 g [8–10 oz] caster sugar

Top and tail the gooseberries and lay them in a large shallow gratin or baking dish, which you have moistened with a tablespoonful of water. Strew the sugar between the layers of fruit. Rinse the elderflower blossoms to rid them of any insects, shake them dry and tie loosely in a piece of butter muslin. Bury the muslin bag amongst the fruit.

Cover the dish with a foil lid and bake gently in an oven preheated to 160°C [325°F], gas mark 3, until the fruit is tender, but still retains its shape. How long this will take depends on the shape and material of your dish — I use a large vitrified cast-iron gratin dish and find 45 minutes is about right — but it is wise to look at the fruit and to shake the dish from time to time (shaking is less likely to break up the fruit then stirring with a spoon).

Gooseberries are best served cold or warm, rather than hot, from the oven. Shortbread finger biscuits are good on the side, and a bowl of cream scented with elderflower won't come amiss. To make elderflower cream, follow the recipe for geranium cream (previous recipe), simply substituting a pair of elderflower blossoms (tied in butter muslin) for the sweet geranium leaves.

Gooseberry Meringue

Here sugar and egg whites are combined to make a sweet meringue topping which contrasts well with tart juicy fruit. Serves 4.

450 g [1 lb] green gooseberries
2 elderflower blossoms
125 g [¼ lb] caster sugar
2 egg whites

Preheat the oven to 150°C [300°F], gas mark 2, placing a baking tray on an upper shelf. Top and tail the fruit and rinse in cold water. Without drying the berries turn them into a pyrex pie plate measuring 22 cm [8½ inches] across the top. Bury the elderflowers (rinsed and tied in butter muslin) among the fruit and sprinkle a total of 25 g [1 oz] of the sugar between layers. Cover the dish with a dome of foil and bake on the preheated baking sheet for half an hour to warm the fruit gently and start to melt the sugar.

Remove the pie plate from the oven, leaving the baking tray where it is. Lift away the foil covering and stir the fruit very gently.

Whisk the egg whites until they stand in glossy peaks, gradually whisking in the remaining sugar. Spread the meringue over the fruit, taking it onto the lip of the dish so the berries are sealed inside.

Return the dish to the baking tray in the oven and cook for

45–50 minutes at the original temperature. By the end of this time the fruit will be fragrant with the flavourings and tender, yet still retain its shape. The meringue will be swirled the colour of honey, crisp on top and marshmallowy on the underside where it touches the fruit.

Raspberry Meringue: Firm, ripe yet slightly sharp raspberries also work well with a meringue topping. Chill them until ready to cook. Pile them into the pie plate without adding any sugar, but scatter a handful of blanched almonds between layers. Cover the fruit with the meringue mixture immediately, stand the dish directly on an oven shelf and bake for 50 minutes.

Blackberry Meringue: Like raspberries these should be chilled before cooking, topped with meringue at once and baked for 50 minutes. I moisten the dish with a teaspoon or so of lemon juice and add a few rinsed and finely chopped sweet geranium leaves, when available, for subtle flavouring.

Apple Mincemeat Meringue

As in the previous meringue recipes, this filling is kept fairly sharp to provide a good foil for the sweet topping. Dried mixed fruit and hazelnuts add interesting texture and flavour to this variation on classic apple meringue. Serves 6.

900 g [2 lb] Bramley apples
a squeeze of lemon juice
60 ml [4 tablespoons] apricot jam
5 ml [1 teaspoon] ground cinnamon or allspice
175 g [6 oz] dried mixed fruit
50 g [2 oz] hazelnut kernels
2 egg whites
125 g [¼ lb] caster sugar

Peel, core and slice the apples. Put them into a casserole, the base of which you have moistened with a squeeze of lemon juice. Cover and cook in the centre of an oven preheated to 150°C [300°F], gas mark 2, for half an hour or until the apples are warmed and beginning to become tender.

Turn the partially cooked apples into a shallow dish with a large surface area (I use a fireproof glass dish that is 25 cm [10 inches] in diameter and 5 cm [2 inches] deep). Gently stir in the apricot jam, spice, dried fruit and nuts. (All this can be prepared a day ahead.)

Whisk the egg whites until stiff. Gradually beat in the caster sugar and continue whisking until the meringue mixture is stiff again. Spread it over the apples, taking it right up to the outer rim of the dish, and bake in an oven preheated to 150°C [300°F], gas mark 2, for 50–60 minutes. This dish is excellent served warm, rather than piping hot from the oven, and is also good cold.

Lemon Soufflé Omelette

A rather dashing, sophisticated pudding made of basic ingredients which are usually in stock in the kitchen — a godsend in emergencies. Serves 4.

6 eggs
1 lemon
unsalted butter
caster sugar

Separate the eggs. Beat the yolks with the juice and finely grated zest of the lemon and a spoonful or two of sugar. Turn the grill to its highest setting and place a large omelette pan over medium-low heat on top of the stove. Whisk the egg whites until stiff, then fold them into the lemon and yolk mixture.

Melt a knob of the butter in the pan, pour in the omelette mixture and leave to cook gently on top of the stove until the omelette bubbles and begins to rise. Then transfer the pan to the preheated grill and continue cooking until the top of the omelette is just set and lightly browned. Sprinkle the top of the omelette with a little more sugar and serve at once, straight from the pan.

Marmalade Soufflé Omelette: Several spoonfuls of home-made marmalade (sharpened with a teaspoon of lemon juice and given extra punch with a splash of brandy) make an excellent alternative flavouring for a sweet soufflé omelette.

Sweet Geranium Sorbet

I have always been enthralled by the challenge of trying to transform scents into tastes, and this ice is the most rewarding fruit of such experiments so far. It seems to capture and match in flavour the subtle, faintly lemon fragrance that fills the air when you brush against or crush a *graveolens* leaf between your fingers.

Graveolens is the most common type of sweet geranium; it also grows the most profusely, and makes wonderful sorbets. Also successful is the variety Prince of Orange (heighten the aroma with a little orange zest and a few drops of orange-flower water). Quantities are deliberately small: these are ices to savour in tiny spoonfuls from pretty syllabub glasses. Serves 8 or more.

2 large handfuls — about 30 g [1¼ oz] — *graveolens* sweet geranium leaves
125 g [¼ lb] granulated sugar
350 ml [12 fl oz] water
1 large lemon
1 small egg white

Measure the sugar into a small saucepan. Pour on the warm water and stir over low heat until the sugar has dissolved. Bring to the boil and simmer for 6–7 minutes to make a rich syrup. Add the rinsed geranium leaves to the pan, push them well down into the liquid and bring quickly back to the boil. Remove the pan from the heat, cover it with a lid and set aside for several hours until completely cold.

Turn the contents of the saucepan into a liquidiser and blend until the leaves are shredded into tiny green specks. Cut the lemon in two, making one piece larger than the other. Squeeze the juice from the larger piece and add it to the geranium liquid. Strain the mixture through a fine sieve into a chilled loaf tin, pressing the green sediment with a wooden spoon to extract all the juices. Cover with a double thickness of foil and freeze for 1 hour.

Turn the half-frozen ice into a chilled bowl and beat it with an electric whisk at high speed until the mixture is soft and smooth. Add the egg white and whisk for another minute so the ice looks like a soft pale-green snow. Cover and freeze for 1½ hours or until solid.

Whisk the ice again to increase its bulk and give it a lighter texture. Cover and freeze again until required. This is a very soft-textured ice and can be served straight from the freezer.

Elderflower Sorbet: An elegant sorbet with a fragrance reminiscent of muscatel can be made by using 4 heads of elder-flower blossom in place of sweet geranium leaves. Rinse them, tie them in butter muslin, and remove them from the syrup when it is cold. Add extra lemon juice to taste.

Glace à la Russe: Another delicious sorbet can be made by using young blackcurrant leaves in place of sweet geranium.

Red Rose Sorbet: If you grow velvet-petalled, scented roses, they can be used to make an intriguing sorbet. Use two large handfuls of crimson, scented petals in place of sweet geranium leaves. Boost colour with red food colouring, and boost fragrance with triple-distilled rosewater, if you wish.

Watermelon Sherbet

This pretty ice has more concentrated flavour and is more refreshing than even the best watermelon eaten raw, and it doesn't include those maddening pips. Enough for 8 tall glasses.

about 1.2 kg [2½ lb] watermelon, preferably Sugarbaby
250 g [½ lb] granulated sugar
300 ml [½ pt] warm water
120 ml [8 tablespoons] lemon juice
1 large egg white

Stir the sugar into the warm water in a small pan over low heat. When it has dissolved, bring to the boil and simmer for 5–6 minutes to make a rich syrup. Away from the heat, stir in the lemon juice, cover and cool the mixture.

Cut off the rind and use the point of a knife to pick the seeds out of a large slice of watermelon. Cut the melon flesh into chunks and reduce it to a very smooth purée in a liquidiser. You will need 700 ml [24 fl oz] of purée. When the syrup is completely cold, blend it thoroughly into the watermelon purée. Turn the mixture into a chilled loaf tin, cover with a double thickness of foil and freeze for 1 hour.

Beat the partially frozen ice with an electric whisk until soft. Add the egg white and whisk for a further minute or so. Freeze the mixture for another 1½ hours before beating it once more. Then freeze it again until solid.

Proper Puddings

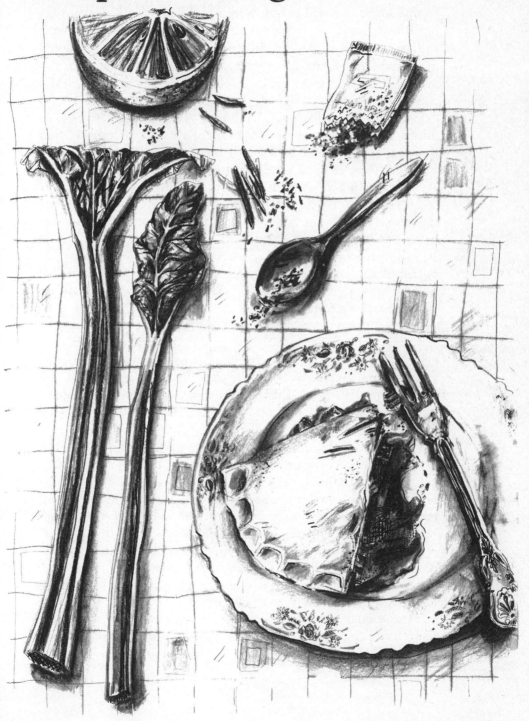

The fashion for the fancy gâteau is on the wane. Proper puddings are coming back into favour. In country areas, at least, the revival is wholehearted: real no-nonsense puddings are appearing on lunch and dinner-party menus, as well as for Sunday lunch with the family. This is cheering for those who have always believed in simple excellence, and it reflects a growing awareness of the good sense of "getting back to basics" in all areas of domestic cookery.

Fancy desserts, however, have been so inescapable in Britain during the past 20 years or so, particularly in entertaining, that many people have forgotten just how excellent true puddings can be. Not so long ago the very word pudding was pejorative, associated as it was with the lamentably dull and heavy offerings relentlessly served up by parsimonious institutions. The true pudding tradition, for which we are justly famous, was in serious danger of being lost.

This chapter will, I hope, illustrate just how glorious proper puddings can be: there are recipes for pies and tarts made with buttery pastry, luscious bread and fruit puddings, steaming sponges and suetcrust puddings.

If these puddings are to flourish again, the cook's spirit must be generous. The freshest and best quality ingredients — butter, eggs, sugar, cream, fresh fruits, dried fruits and nuts, high fruit-content jams — are essential. Use these ingredients lavishly, but be miserly with flour. Puddings are meant to be rich in good things, but definitely not heavy with the stodge that blemished their reputation.

Proper puddings may not be the most sophisticated of fare, but it is a mistake to regard them as appropriate only for homely occasions, and suitable only for serving at lunch. Many puddings will grace a polished mahogany dining table, with its silver and cut glass, very handsomely, and, although rich, most are not too heavy to eat in the evening. The obvious proviso is that preceding dishes should be fairly light and, to do full justice to puddings, it is preferable not to serve a first course.

The section on bread and fruit puddings includes quickly made lucky knights, summer pudding, my own lazyman's version of this traditional dish, and a delicate-tasting garden of Eden pudding. All of these, whilst not the lightest of eating, are eminently suitable for serving at dinner.

The pastry dishes include substantial and spicy mixtures such as fig and hazelnut pie and shoofly pie, lighter pies such as lemon meringue, and crumbles which range from the rich and crunchy to the subtle made with soft summer fruits.

The most famous of all our traditional puddings are steamed and baked sponges and suet puddings. When properly made, these represent the very best of British cookery. Even the French acknowledge our supremacy in this field. Unfortunately, although our reputation for such puddings remains high, in practice they are often debased to mere stodge.

Steamed puddings are, of course, meant to be substantial. They are foods for cold-weather eating, and they are usually more suitable for serving at lunch than at dinner. If properly made with generous quantities of fresh eggs and butter they are wholesome, warming and comforting. If eaten in sensible quantities they will fill you with a glow of contentment; they should not reduce you to post-prandial snores or force you into taking antidotal hikes across the hills.

All the suet and sponge recipes given here are satisfyingly rich. You will find a few old-fashioned favourites such as Sussex pond pudding and treacle sponge. Both were great fodder for the copious and robust appetites of great grandfather's day, and both make admirable twentieth-century Sunday lunchtime fare in winter.

I have also included a number of more delicate variations on the steamed pudding theme. These are more in keeping with today's tastes for lighter foods, and are not so substantial that they cannot be served in clement weather. Gentleman's sponge and Selkley pudding, for example, are particularly popular with my family and friends for their sophisticated flavours and moist, light textures. This lightness, incidentally, is achieved by using bread or cake crumbs or ground almonds in place of some or all the flour normally used in such puddings. Selkley pudding is particularly useful and convenient to cook: it is equally good baked or steamed, and can be served hot or cold with a choice of quickly made sauces.

Garden of Eden Pudding

A superior version of Eve's pudding, this is my family's favourite apple pudding. It is excellent served warm and almost as good to eat when cold — if there are any leftovers. Serves 6.

700–900 g [1½–2 lb] Cox's apples
125 g [¼ lb] apricot jam
5 ml [1 teaspoon] lemon juice
5 ml [1 teaspoon] ground cinnamon
40 g [1½ oz] butter

For the topping:
125 g [¼ lb] butter
125 g [¼ lb] soft brown sugar
4 eggs
125 g [¼ lb] fresh breadcrumbs

Put the jam, lemon juice and cinnamon into a 1.4 litre [2½ pt] pie dish and stir them together. Peel, quarter and core the apples, then cut them into 12 mm [½ inch] thick slices. Sauté the apples in two batches, using half the butter for each batch, over fairly high heat until coloured. Add the apples to the pie dish and stir lightly. The heat of the apples will melt the jam and make it easy to coat the fruit evenly with the flavourings.

To make the topping, beat the butter and sugar together until soft and creamy. Separate the eggs. Whisk the whites until they stand in peaks. Set the whites aside while you beat first the egg yolks then the breadcrumbs into the creamed butter and sugar. Slacken the mixture a little by stirring in a few spoonfuls of the egg whites, then fold in the rest.

Spread the topping over the fruit and bake the pudding in an oven preheated to 180°C [350°F], gas mark 4, for 40–45 minutes. By the end of this time the fruit will be tender and the topping will be puffed up and pale gold, spongy at the edges and slightly creamy and moist in the centre.

Perfect Pear Pudding: Pears are delectable cooked in a similar fashion. Choose firm, slightly under-ripe fruit (rock hard little green pears and very ripe dessert pears are unsuitable).

Peel, core and cut the fruit into eighths. Do not sauté the pears, but turn them in a pie dish in which you have warmed 50 g [1 oz] butter, 30 ml [2 tablespoons] soft brown sugar and the juice of half a lemon. Make the topping as described in the main recipe but use ground almonds in place of breadcrumbs, and bake the pudding for 50 minutes.

Crunchy Apple Crumble

There is a high proportion of butter and some coconut in this crumble, which give it good texture. I always use a shallow dish so the topping is spread fairly thinly and crisps up in the heat of the oven. The raw pudding freezes well for at least a month. Defrost completely before baking. Serves 4–6.

700 g [1½ lb] Bramley apples
125 g [¼ lb] sultanas
75 g [3 oz] plain flour
75 g [3 oz] wholewheat flour
7 ml [1½ teaspoons] ground cinnamon
75 g [3 oz] Demerara sugar
50 g [2 oz] desiccated coconut
100 g [¼ lb] butter

Place a baking sheet on an upper shelf of the oven, and preheat the oven to 200°C [400°F], gas mark 6. Sift flours and cinnamon into a large bowl, and add any bran remaining in the sieve. Stir in the sugar and coconut. Cut, then briefly rub the butter into the dry ingredients; the mixture will look like rather greasy bread-crumbs.

   Butter the base and sides of a large gratin dish. Peel, core and slice the apples. Pile them into the dish, sprinkling the sultanas between layers, and mound the fruit a little in the centre. Spread the crumble mixture over the fruit and pat the top smooth with your hands. Bake in the preheated oven for 1 hour. Cool for 5 minutes then serve with fresh or soured cream.

Raspberry or Blackberry Crumble

Raspberries and blackberries taste and smell wonderful when warm, and these crumbles make lovely, simple alternatives to fresh berries with cream on a cool summer's day. The crumble topping is quite different from that used in the previous recipe, and is rather like shortbread. Serves 4–5.

450 g [1 lb] firm ripe raspberries or blackberries
15 ml [1 tablespoon] caster sugar
175 g [6 oz] self-raising flour
2.5 ml [½ teaspoon] ground cinnamon
the finely grated zest of an orange
65 g [2½ oz] butter
90 g [3½ oz] soft brown sugar

Preheat the oven to 180°C [350°F], gas mark 4. Sift the flour and cinnamon into a bowl. Rub in the butter and stir in the soft brown sugar and orange zest.

Pile the berries into a fireproof glass or earthenware pie plate measuring about 23 cm [9 inches] across the top. Strew the caster sugar between fruit layers and sprinkle the crumble mixture over the top — do not press it down. Bake just above the centre of the oven for 35 minutes.

Poor Knights of Windsor

This is a delightful pudding when made with soft slices of milk loaf or brioche and flavoured with cinnamon. It is too sophisticated to restrict to nursery eating. Baked apricots and other seasonal fruits can be used instead of apples. Serves 2.

2 slices of good bread or brioche
1 egg
sugar
ground cinnamon
2 small Cox's apples
unsalted butter

Beat the egg with a generous pinch each of cinnamon and sugar. Cut each slice of bread into two triangles and thoroughly moisten them on both sides with the beaten egg. Heat a frying pan until hot and add about 15–20 g [½–¾ oz] butter. When the butter stops foaming, add the soaked bread and fry it over medium-high heat until golden on both sides. Drain well and keep hot. (If preparing ahead be sure to keep the cooked bread in a single layer, and don't cover it or it will go soggy.)

Peel and slice the apples. Add a little extra butter to the frying pan and, when it is hot, add the apple slices. Sauté the apples until golden and tender, drain and keep hot separately if not serving immediately.

Just before serving, dust each triangle of fried bread with more sugar and cinnamon mixed together, pile some of the apple slices on top, and finish with a final dusting of cinnamon and sugar. Serve piping hot, and preferably topped with a small dollop of chilled whipped cream.

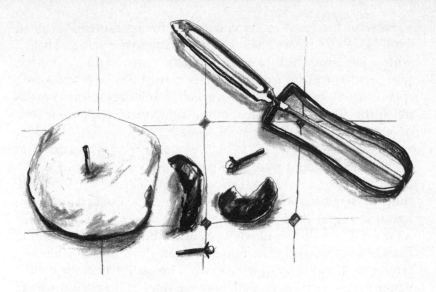

Traditional Apple Charlotte

Like the previous recipe, this combines fried bread and apples.
The secrets of success lie in making the apple marmalade very
stiff, and in fitting the slices of bread as neatly as a jigsaw. Serves
4–6.

6–8 large slices of crustless white bread
about 125 g [¼ lb] unsalted butter

For the apple marmalade:
900 g [2 lb] Bramley apples
1 quince, if available
1 lemon
125–150 g [4–5 oz] caster sugar
25 g [1 oz] unsalted butter
allspice or ground cloves
30 ml [2 tablespoons] ground almonds

Make the apple marmalade a day, or at least several hours, ahead
as it must be cold when packed into the bread-lined pudding
basin. Peel, core and thinly slice the apples and put them into a
heavy-based saucepan or flameproof casserole. If a quince is
available (even a small one adds greatly to the fragrance of the
dish), peel, core and grate it onto the apples. Add the juice and the
finely grated zest of the lemon, cover the pan and cook over fairly
low heat until the apples are very tender.

Turn the fruit into a sieve and leave it for 5 minutes or more to drain off all the juices. Then return the fruit to the pan, and beat it with a balloon whisk to make a fluffy purée. Add the butter, sugar and spices. Place the pan over medium heat and cook, stirring fairly frequently, for a good 15 minutes to drive off as much moisture as possible. Set the apple marmalade aside, uncovered, until completely cold.

Preheat the oven to 220°C [425°F], gas mark 7. Cut a circle of bread to fit the bottom of a 850 ml [1½ pt] pudding basin, and a larger circle to fit inside the top of the basin. Fry the small circle in some of the butter until golden on both sides. Drain it and cut it into 6 triangles (this makes it easier to cut up the pudding for serving). Place the bread triangles in the bottom of the pudding basin. Melt the rest of the butter and cut the remaining slices of bread into 4 cm [1½ inch] wide strips. Dip each strip in the melted butter to coat both sides well. Line the sides of the basin with the bread strips, overlapping them slightly.

Stiffen the cold apple marmalade by stirring in the ground almonds. Pack the filling firmly into the basin, doming the top slightly. Fold the protruding tips of the strips of bread over the apple marmalade, then fit the large circle of bread (again dipped in melted butter) over the top. Drizzle on any leftover melted butter.

Stand the basin on a baking tray and bake the pudding for 30 minutes until the marmalade is piping hot and the bread is "fried" crisp and golden. Let the pudding rest for 10 minutes before attempting to unmould it, so that it firms up and shrinks slightly from the sides of the basin. Then invert the basin onto a warmed plate and lift the basin away from the pudding cautiously. If it does not slide away easily, wait 5 minutes before trying again. Serve with a mixture of fresh cream and yoghurt whipped until fluffy.

Summer Pudding

This English classic is usually made with raspberries and redcurrants only, but other soft berry fruits can be used, and a delicious autumn variation can be made using poached apples, quince and blackberries. Whatever fruit you use, an accompanying bowl of softly whipped cream is a must. Serves 6.

450 g [1 lb] raspberries (or mulberries or loganberries)
350 g [¾ lb] redcurrants (or a mixture of red and blackcurrants)
about 150 g [5 oz] caster sugar
15 ml [1 tablespoon] orange juice
5 ml [1 teaspoon] lemon juice
8–10 medium-thick slices of good white bread

String the currants. Put them into a saucepan sprinkling sugar between layers. Cover the pan and shake to distribute sugar evenly. Add the citrus juices and place the covered pan over low heat. Cook gently, shaking the pan occasionally, for 5 minutes until the sugar has melted and the currant juices are flowing.

Add the raspberries to the pan. Cover the pan again and shake it to mix the raspberries and currants. Continue cooking the fruit gently for another 2 minutes or so to warm the raspberries. Then set the covered pan aside until the contents are cool.

Cut the crusts off the bread. Cut the crumb into suitably shaped wedges and use them to line the base and sides of a 850 ml [1½ pt] soufflé dish or pudding basin. Fit the bread pieces together in a tight jigsaw, leaving no gaps for juices to leak through.

Reserve a small cup of juices from the warmed fruit, fill the bread-lined dish with the rest of the fruit and their juices, and cover the fruit neatly with more bread. Top the pudding with a plate that just fits inside the rim of the dish, weigh it down and refrigerate it for 8 hours or overnight.

Invert the pudding onto a plate and unmould it for serving. Pour the reserved juices over the pudding to colour and flavour any bread that is not already stained a deep red.

Lazy Summer Pudding

A boon when the cook is too pressed for time to make a traditional summer pudding, this is just as splendid in its own right and a very pretty pudding. Serves 6–8.

1 small white tin loaf
450 g [1 lb] strawberries
450 g [1 lb] raspberries
115 g [¼ lb] icing sugar
30 ml [2 tablespoons] lemon juice
200–250 ml [7–10 fl oz] double cream

Cut all the crusts off the bread. Slice the loaf in half, horizontally through the crumb. Lay the two pieces of bread side by side on a large shallow dish.

Reduce half the strawberries to a purée in a liquidiser. Add the sifted icing sugar and the lemon juice, and blend again briefly. Turn the purée into a small saucepan. Lightly crush the rest of the strawberries and all the raspberries with a fork. Add the crushed berries to the saucepan and stir the mixture over very gentle heat for about 2 minutes, until the fruit and the juices are barely warmed.

Pour the contents of the saucepan over the bread. Baste the bread with the fruit for a few minutes. Then cover the dish with a dome of foil and place the dish in a cold place. Leave it there for 8 hours, occasionally basting the bread with the fruit during this time.

Just before serving, whip the cream softly and spoon it over the top of the pudding.

Shoofly Pie

A quick, easy and inexpensive pie. Supposedly so-called because flies swarm hopefully round the mixing bowl when molasses are used. Perhaps American flies have a sweeter tooth than English ones: I have had no trouble with insects, but children certainly queue to clean out the mixing bowl. Serves 8.

shortcrust pastry made with 250 g [½ lb] plain flour and 125 g [¼ lb] butter

For the crumb mixture:
150 g [5 oz] plain flour
25 g [1 oz] desiccated coconut
the zest of an orange and a lemon
5 ml [1 teaspoon] ground cinnamon
5 ml [1 teaspoon] ground ginger
2.5 ml [½ teaspoon] allspice
50 g [2 oz] soft dark brown sugar
85 g [3 oz] butter

For the filling:
125 g [¼ lb] molasses or black treacle or pure cane syrup
2.5 ml [½ teaspoon] bicarbonate of soda
90 ml [6 tablespoons] boiling water

Use the pastry to line a 25 cm [10 inch] fluted flan tin with a removable base. Line it with greaseproof paper, weigh it down with beans and blind-bake it for 10 minutes at 200°C [400°F], gas mark 6. Then bake it for a further 5 minutes without the beans and paper.

While the pastry is cooking, make the crumb mixture. Sift the flour, stir in the other dry ingredients (err on the generous side with spices or the pie will be too bland and sweet) and rub in the butter.

To make the filling, stir the bicarbonate of soda, molasses and boiling water together until warm and frothy.

Pour the filling into the pastry case, quickly sprinkle the crumb topping over it and return the flan tin to the oven. Immediately reduce the oven temperature to 190°C [375°F], gas mark 5, and bake the pie for 50–60 minutes. Serve the pie hot, warm or cold with fresh or soured cream.

Lemon Meringue Pie

Perhaps the best-known of all American pies. The contrast of sharp lemon filling and meringue topping is excellent. Serves 6.

shortcrust pastry made with 125 g [¼ lb] plain flour and 60 g [2 oz] butter.

For the filling:
3 large lemons
275 ml [½ pt] cold water
115 g [¼ lb] caster sugar
25 g [1 oz] butter
35 g [1½ oz] cornflour
2 large egg yolks

For the meringue:
2 large egg whites
115 g [¼ lb] caster sugar

Finely grate the zest of the lemons into a small saucepan. Add the sugar, cornflour and some of the measured cold water to make a smooth paste. Whisk in the remaining water and cook over medium heat until the mixture thickens and comes to the boil. Let it boil for a minute, then remove it from the heat and beat in the butter. Then beat in 75 ml [5 tablespoons] lemon juice and the egg yolks, one at a time. Set the mixture aside until cold.

Meanwhile, use the pastry to line a pie plate with sloping sides and a generous rim — it should measure about 15 cm [6 inches] across the base and 20 cm [8 inches] across the top. Line the pastry with greaseproof paper, weigh it down with beans and blind-bake at 200°C [400°F], gas mark 6, for 15 minutes. Remove paper and beans and bake the pastry for a further 10 minutes. Remove the pie plate from the oven and reduce the oven temperature to 150°C [300°F], gas mark 2.

Whisk the egg whites until stiff, gradually sift in the sugar and continue whisking until the meringue mixture is stiff again.

Spoon the lemon filling into the pastry shell (stirring in an extra spoonful or two of sugar if the mixture is too tart for your taste). Spread the meringue over the filling, taking it to the very edge of the pastry rim.

Bake the pie in the centre of the oven for 50–60 minutes until the top of the meringue has dried out to a crisp honey beige. Cool the pie for at least 20 minutes before serving.

Fig & Hazelnut Pie

My family describes this as a very superior mince pie. Like traditional mince pie, it can be eaten hot or cold, with cream or brandy butter. It will keep for 7–10 days if stored in an airtight tin (reheat before serving to crisp the pastry), and freezes well. Serves 6.

shortcrust pastry made with 250 g [½ lb] plain flour, 125 g [¼ lb] butter and 5 ml
   [1 teaspoon] ground cinnamon
250 g [½ lb] dried figs
50 g [2 oz] hazelnut kernels
50 g [2 oz] butter
1 large lemon
75 g [3 oz] soft dark brown sugar
45 ml [3 tablespoons] brandy
5 ml [1 teaspoon] ground cinnamon
15 ml [1 tablespoon] plain flour
125 ml [4 fl oz] warm water
beaten egg to glaze

First prepare the filling. Dice the butter and put it into a small pan together with the juice and the zest of the lemon. Add the sugar. Pour on the brandy and the warm water. Stir the mixture over gentle heat until the butter is melted and the sugar no longer feels gritty. Draw the pan to one side.

Making Pastry.

Add the roughly chopped figs (cut off and discard the woody stalks). Sprinkle on the cinnamon and flour, and return the pan to low heat. Bring to the boil stirring continuously. Continue boiling for 5 minutes or so until the mixture is very thick and sticky. Stir frequently and add extra lemon juice or water if necessary. Away from the heat stir in the roughly chopped nuts and set the mixture aside to cool.

Make the pastry and use two-thirds of it to line a 20 cm [8 inch] flan tin or shallow pie plate. Put the filling into it, mounding it slightly in the centre, and damp the pastry edge. Cover with the remaining pastry, seal and crimp the edges. Brush the top of the pie with beaten egg and make a steam slit.

Bake the pie on a hot baking sheet in an oven preheated to 200°C [400°F], gas mark 6, for 30–40 minutes until the pastry is golden. Dust with icing sugar just before serving.

Early Rhubarb Pie

Vibrant pink sticks of forced rhubarb enliven sunless January with their welcome splash of colour and refreshing flavour. Here the tart fruit is foiled by crisp shortcrust. Serves 6.

shortcrust pastry made with 175 g [6 oz] plain flour and 85 g [3 oz] butter
700–800 g [1½–1¾ lb] fresh rhubarb
15 ml [1 tablespoon] cornflour
125 g [¼ lb] caster sugar
the finely grated zest of an orange mixed with 5 ml [1 teaspoon] ground
   cinnamon or 30 ml [2 tablespoons] chopped stem ginger
a little milk to glaze

Wipe the rhubarb and trim it. Cut the stalks into oblique slices. Pile the fruit into a pie dish, sprinkling the sugar, cornflour and flavourings between the fruit layers. Set the dish aside for 2 hours so the rhubarb juices begin to mingle with the other ingredients.

Preheat the oven to 200°C [400°F], gas mark 6. Roll out the pastry until it is rather larger than the top of the pie dish. Wet the rim of the pie dish. Cut off the outer strip of pastry, lay it on the rim of the dish and brush it with water. Lay the pastry lid on top. Press the two pastry edges to seal them, trim, knock up and flute. Make a slit in the top of the pastry to allow steam to escape during cooking, and brush the pastry with milk.

Bake the pie in the preheated oven for 10 minutes. Reduce the heat to 190°C [375°F], gas mark 5, and bake the pie for a further 30–35 minutes. Sprinkle the pastry with a little sugar as soon as the pie comes out of the oven. Cool for 5 minutes before serving.

No-Waste Apple Pie

This fruit pie is sweetened with a syrup made from the apple peelings and cores, a little cider and butter. Sweet-toothed cooks may like to add a few spoonfuls of sugar, but the charm of the dish lies in the fact that it tastes so fruity and fresh. Serves 6.

shortcrust pastry made with 250 g [½ lb] plain flour and 125 g [¼ lb] butter
1.1 kg [2½ lb] Cox's apples
1 lemon
200 ml [7 fl oz] cider
2 cloves
2 cinnamon sticks
75 g [3 oz] butter
125 g [¼ lb] raisins
a little milk to glaze
50 g [2 oz] hazelnut kernels

Grate the lemon zest finely and reserve it. Squeeze the juice of the lemon into a large bowl and pour on a good quantity of cold water. Peel, quarter and core the apples and drop them into the bowl. Push the fruit down into the liquid and put a plate on top to keep the apples immersed.

Put all the apple trimmings into a saucepan. Add the lightly bruised cloves, broken up cinnamon sticks and cider. Cover and simmer for 20 minutes, stirring occasionally, then uncover and cook for a further 10 minutes to evaporate most of the liquid, but take care not to let the pan burn dry.

Turn the contents of the pan into a sieve placed over a large bowl. Press the softened pulp so a few spoonfuls of rich apple syrup drip into the bowl below. Stir the diced butter into the apple syrup. When melted, add the lemon zest, raisins and nuts. Drain and thinly slice the apples and mix them with the other ingredients using your hands. Then pile the mixture into a 1.7 litre [3 pt] pie dish.

Preheat the oven to 200°C [400°F], gas mark 6. Roll out the pastry. Lay a strip of pastry on the wetted rim of the dish and brush it with water. Top the pie with a lid made from the remaining pastry. Seal and trim the pastry. Make a steam hole and glaze the pastry with milk.

Bake the pie in the preheated oven for 20 minutes, then reduce the temperature to 180°C [350°F], gas mark 4, and bake the pie for a further 30–40 minutes, until the apple feels tender when tested with a skewer through the steam hole. Sprinkle the top of the pie with sugar and serve at once.

Sussex Pond Pudding

A reader once wrote to me claiming that this is an old Kentish recipe; his recipe included candied peel in the pastry and both honey and sugar in the lemon filling. I've also come across an almost identical pudding (which included sultanas) in a copper-plate handwritten book of "Family Receipts from Dorset". I cannot say which is the original recipe, but this is my favourite version, and the best of all suetcrust puddings. Serves 4–6.

For the suetcrust:
250 g [½ lb] self-raising flour
125 g [¼ lb] shredded suet
7 ml [1½ teaspoons] ground cinnamon
3.5 ml [¾ teaspoon] baking powder
75 ml [2½ fl oz] milk

For the filling:
2 thin-skinned lemons
175 g [6 oz] unsalted butter
150 g [5 oz] Demerara sugar

Sift the flour, cinnamon and baking powder into a bowl. Stir in the suet. Mix the milk with an equal quantity of cold water and stir as much of the liquid into the dry ingredients as is necessary to make a soft dough. Use three-quarters of the pastry to line a well-buttered 1 litre [2 pt] pudding basin.

Wipe the lemons, then cut them up into small pieces and extract the pips. Fill the pastry-lined basin with layers of the diced chilled butter, the chopped lemon and the Demerara sugar. Roll out the remaining pastry to make a lid. Lay it over the filling and damp the edge of the pastry circle with a little water. Fold the excess lining pastry over the pastry circle and press to seal the two layers together.

Cover the pudding with buttered and pleated foil and tie securely under the basin rim. Lower the basin onto a trivet standing in a pan half-filled with boiling water. Cover the pan with a lid and cook for 2 hours, adding extra boiling water to the pan as necessary.

Let the cooked pudding stand for 2–3 minutes to shrink and loosen it slightly from the sides of the basin, then turn it out onto a warmed plate. The sweetened, lemon-flavoured butter will seep through the pastry so that the pudding stands in a golden pond of sauce.

Treacle Sponge

A firm favourite with devotees of steamed puddings, this is sticky, rich and sweet, but tempered with the sharpness of lemon. Serves 4–6.

golden syrup
75 g [3 oz] butter
15 ml [1 tablespoon] caster sugar
1 large lemon
2 eggs
100 g [¼ lb] self-raising flour

Stand a pudding basin of 1 litre [1½–2 pt] capacity on a trivet in a large saucepan and pour enough water into the pan to come halfway up the sides of the basin. Remove the basin and set the water to boil.

Butter the inside of the basin and drizzle 45 ml [3 tablespoons] golden syrup into the bottom of it. Measure 75 ml [5 tablespoons] golden syrup into a large mixing bowl. Add the softened butter, sugar and finely grated lemon zest. Beat the mixture with a whisk or wooden spoon until the ingredients are creamy and well blended. Beat in the eggs, gradually beat in the sifted flour and, finally, stir in 15 ml [1 tablespoon] lemon juice.

Turn the pudding mixture into the prepared basin. Cover it with well-buttered and pleated foil, and tie securely under the rim of the basin, then loop the string over the top of the basin to make a handle.

Lower the basin onto the trivet in the pan of boiling water. Cover the pan with a well-fitting lid and cook over moderate heat for 1½ hours. Top up the pan with extra boiling water as necessary.

Let the steamed pudding stand for a minute or two after cooking: it will begin to shrink away from the sides of the basin which makes for easier unmoulding. Remove the foil lid, and run a palette knife between the pudding and the sides of the basin to loosen it completely. Invert the basin and unmould the pudding onto a hot plate. Serve with a generous jug of lemon syrup sauce, made by gently warming together the remaining lemon juice and plenty of golden syrup.

Orlando's Pudding
with Brandy Marmalade Sauce

The better the quality of the marmalade you use, the better this pudding will taste. The sponge is slightly lighter in texture than treacle sponge because of the inclusion of breadcrumbs. Serves 4–6.

100 g [¼ lb] butter
100 g [¼ lb] caster sugar
the finely grated zest of 1 orange and 1 lemon
75 ml [5 tablespoons] marmalade
2 eggs
50 g [2 oz] fresh breadcrumbs
50 g [2 oz] self-raising flour
2.5 ml [½ teaspoon] bicarbonate of soda dissolved in 5 ml [1 teaspoon] warm
   water

For the brandy marmalade sauce:
20 ml [1 heaped tablespoon] butter
20 ml [1 generous tablespoon] brandy
30 ml [2 tablespoons] orange juice
120 ml [6 tablespoons] marmalade
12 ml [1 scant tablespoon] soft brown sugar

Set a large pan of water to boil, and butter a 1 litre [1¼–2 pt] pudding basin.

Beat the butter and sugar with an electric whisk until light and creamy. Beat in the orange and lemon zest, then the marmalade. Mix the flour and breadcrumbs together. Beat the eggs in a cup. Beat the breadcrumb mixture and the eggs into the sugar and butter mixture, in alternate spoonfuls, keeping the mixture as creamy and light as possible. Finally, beat in the bicarbonate of soda.

Turn the mixture into the buttered pudding basin. Cover it with buttered and pleated foil. Tie securely and loop the string over the top of the basin to make a handle. Lower the basin onto the trivet in the pan of boiling water. Cover the pan with a lid and cook over moderate heat for 1½–1¾ hours, topping up the pan with more boiling water as necessary.

Let the pudding rest for a minute or two before turning it out onto a plate for serving. While it rests, make the sauce. Just stir all the ingredients together over low heat until hot and well blended, adding an extra dash of brandy if you wish.

Selkley Pudding

Made in the same way as Orlando's pudding, this mixture includes ground almonds to keep its texture light. It is flavoured with chocolate and coffee, and can be served with either a chocolate sauce (which children prefer) or a coffee cream sauce. Bake or steam the pudding, whichever is more convenient. Serves 4–6.

100 g [¼ lb] butter
100 g [¼ lb] soft brown sugar
2 eggs
50 g [2 oz] self-raising flour
2.5 ml [½ teaspoon] baking powder
25 g [1 oz] ground almonds
30 ml [2 tablespoons] cocoa powder
5 ml [1 teaspoon] instant coffee powder
5 ml [1 teaspoon] ground cinnamon

For the coffee cream sauce:
22 ml [1½ tablespoons] icing sugar
15 ml [1 tablespoon] instant coffee powder
200 ml [7 fl oz] double cream

For the chocolate cream sauce:
a small knob of butter
40 ml [scant 3 tablespoons] cocoa powder
20 ml [1 heaped tablespoon] each golden syrup and soft brown sugar
150 ml [¼ pt] soured cream

If you are going to steam the sponge, bring a large pan of water to the boil and butter the inside of a 1 litre [1½–2 pt] pudding basin. If you are going to bake the sponge, put a baking sheet in the oven and preheat it to 180°C [350°F], gas mark 4, then butter a 1 litre [2 pt] pie dish.

Cream the butter and sugar with an electric whisk until fluffy and light. Beat the eggs with a fork in a cup. Sift the flour with the baking powder and mix in the ground almonds. Beat the eggs and flour mixture into the creamed butter and sugar, in alternate spoonfuls. Finally, dissolve the cocoa, coffee and cinnamon in 45 ml [3 tablespoons] warm water and beat it into the pudding.

Turn the mixture into the prepared pie dish and bake in the centre of the oven for 45–50 minutes. Or, for steaming, turn the mixture into the prepared pudding basin, cover, tie down and steam for 1½ hours before turning out for serving. Dust the pudding lightly with icing sugar just before serving.

For coffee cream sauce, put the icing sugar and coffee powder into a small saucepan. Pour on the cream and bring slowly to the boil stirring all the time. For chocolate cream sauce simply put the ingredients into a small pan in the order they are listed, and stir over gentle heat until well blended and warmed through.

Gentleman's Sponge with Cinnamon Cream

The absence of flour gives this superior steamed pudding its light and moist texture. The flavour is delicate and subtle. Serves 4–6.

125 g [¼ lb] butter
125 g [¼ lb] soft pale brown sugar
5 ml [1 teaspoon] ground cinnamon
the finely grated zest of half a lemon
60 ml [4 tablespoons] apricot jam
125 g [¼ lb] fresh cake crumbs or breadcrumbs
2 eggs
2.5 ml [½ teaspoon] bicarbonate of soda dissolved in 5 ml [1 teaspoon] warm
   water

For the cinnamon cream:
15 ml [1 tablespoon] icing sugar
5 ml [1 teaspoon] ground cinnamon
150 ml [¼ pt] double cream
45 ml [3 tablespoons] single cream or milk

Set a pan of water to boil and butter a 1 litre [1½–2 pt] pudding basin.

Cream the softened butter and sugar together with an electric whisk until pale and fluffy. Beat in the cinnamon, lemon zest and apricot jam. Add the crumbs and beaten eggs in alternate spoonfuls, keeping the mixture as creamy and light as possible. Finally, blend in the bicarbonate of soda.

Turn the mixture into the greased pudding basin. Cover the basin with buttered and pleated foil, tie down securely and steam for 1½–1¾ hours, topping up the boiling water as necessary.

To make the sauce, stir the icing sugar and cinnamon into the milk (or single cream). Pour on the double cream and whip until fluffy. Cover and chill until ready to serve.

Let the cooked pudding stand for a minute or so before loosening it with a palette knife. Put a plate over the basin and invert. Put the pudding, still covered by the basin, in a very low oven for 15 minutes or so. Lift off the basin to unveil the pudding just before serving.

Custards & Creams

This chapter is devoted to puddings made with dairy products — eggs, milk, fresh and soured creams, yoghurt and soft cheeses. Some of these puddings are cool and fresh, some are delicately creamy in texture and taste, a few are extremely rich. All share the practical advantage of being cold cook-ahead dishes. Indeed most of them will keep very well for several days if covered and stored in a fridge.

I use fromage blanc (soft cheese) and yoghurt so frequently in sweet and savoury dishes (as well as serving them as puddings in their own right, simply laced with a little honey) that I have started the chapter with ways to make them at home. They are both much better home-made, and so useful, that I have come to regard their making as important techniques in the cook's repertoire.

Despite the lightness imparted by yoghurt and fromage blanc to some of the dishes in this chapter, there are quite a few which the cholesterol conscious will want to eschew. However, the lighter among these puddings are well suited to serving at everyday lunches and dinners (whether family or social events), whilst the richer offerings make delectable treats to savour in small spoonfuls on special occasions.

I have arranged the recipes in broad groups. The earlier groups contain the highest proportion of light dishes. Later groups contain more rich dishes, and the last group is composed entirely of rich and indulgent *pièces de résistance*.

The first group covers milk puddings and custards, which I rate amongst the most useful of all the recipes in my repertoire. Their particular virtues — they are attractive, creamy but light, and can be varied in flavour according to mood and taste — make them an admirable choice for all sorts of occasions, and they are invaluable during the betwixt and between season when one no longer wants substantial winter puddings but the fresh fruits of summer are not yet plentiful.

Baked custards, such as Viennese caramel cream and vanilla custard cream, deserve particular mention for the speed and ease with which they can be prepared, whilst oeufs à la neige, although involving more time and effort to prepare, is undoubtedly my number-one choice when that difficult combination of delicacy, elegance and cheapness is required.

The mousses which follow begin with kaffecreme and orange velvet mousse, luxurious mixtures based on the same custard as oeufs à la neige but enriched with many more egg yolks.

Other mousse recipes are based on fresh fruit purées. These are neither rich nor expensive but intentionally light and suitable for everyday eating. My aim has been to keep them as true to the flavour of the fresh fruit as possible. The quantities of flavour-masking gelatine used are therefore very small (there is none in William pear mousse); whisked egg whites are added for extra lightness; the proportion of cream to fruit is low and in some cases I have suggested using a mixture of fresh cream and soured cream.

Next comes a section devoted to what I call custard cup creams, elegant puddings which are best served in small quantities and which look enchanting served in tiny individual bowls or small wine or syllabub glasses. The recipes are very varied in terms of cost, preparation time and richness. All can be served simply, perhaps accompanied by amaretti, tuiles or other tiny biscuits. Many can be served with fresh fruit if you prefer, which is an attractive way of tempering richness.

If you can spare only a few minutes in the kitchen, nothing could be simpler to make than junkets, syllabubs or West Country creams (in which the sharpness of yoghurt is combined with the sweetness of Demerara sugar). When you have more time scented cheese mousse makes a rich and fragrant choice, whilst real blancmange, made with the milk of almonds set to the softest jelly, is surely one of the most exquisite puddings in the world. It is certainly a far cry from those synthetic pink blobs of moulded cornflour served up by caterers. Also included in this section are tea ice-creams and glace au kirsch, a delectable ice that is exceptionally quick and easy to make.

Finally there are a few unashamedly rich and extravagant puddings. None requires any special culinary skills (I have, for example, adapted the usual method of making a charlotte Malakoff to sand-castle simplicity). With the exception of Turinois, however, they do take time to make.

Clearly it would be unwise to eat these very rich puddings frequently but it would be a pity not to indulge in them now and again, because they look and taste so splendid. In my family they are served on birthdays, in lieu of birthday cakes, and often chosen by special requests.

Yoghurt

After several hit-and-miss attempts at yoghurt-making (gauging milk temperature with my finger and trying to incubate the mixture in an airing cupboard), I have come to the conclusion that a thermometer is essential for consistently successful results and that a wide-mouthed insulated plastic picnic jar is the best container to use. A glass-lined vacuum flask *can* be used but stir very carefully, using a wooden spoon, lest you crack the glass.

1 × 400 g [14 oz] can of evaporated milk or 1.1 litre [2 pt] pasteurised milk (silver or gold top)
1 teaspoon plain, unsweetened yoghurt — commercial yoghurt or from the last batch you made

If using fresh milk, bring it to the boil and simmer until reduced by one-third, then let it cool to 49°C [120°F], stirring occasionally to prevent a skin forming.

If using evaporated milk (which makes a very creamy yoghurt), mix it with an equal quantity of freshly boiled water. Warm the mixture or cool it, as necessary, until the temperature reaches 49°C [120°F].

Warm a scrupulously clean wide-mouthed insulated jar by rinsing it in warm (not hot) water. Place the teaspoon of yoghurt in the jar and add 2 tablespoons of the prepared milk. Stir until the yoghurt is very thoroughly and smoothly blended into the milk. Slowly pour the remaining milk into the jar, stirring vigorously all the time to blend the mixture well. Cover the jar with its lid, place it in a corner of the room where it will not be touched or disturbed, and leave it to incubate for 5–6 hours.

Carefully transfer the covered jar of yoghurt to the fridge and let it chill for 3 hours before eating.

Save 1 teaspoon of the home-made yoghurt (ideally taken from the middle of the jar) to use as a starter for making the next batch. The culture will become "tired" and "thin" after a dozen or so yoghurt-making sessions and should be replaced with a fresh starter of commercial yoghurt.

Thickened Yoghurt: When you want to use yoghurt in hot dishes, or instead of whipped cream in cold dishes, a thickened yoghurt is best. Turn the freshly made and well-chilled yoghurt into a muslin-lined sieve suspended over a bowl and leave it in a cool place to drain off some of the liquid — 2–5 hours depending on how thick you wish the yoghurt to be.

As an extra precaution against the yoghurt separating out when heat is applied in cooking (this does not affect flavour but may spoil the appearance of the dish) cornflour can be used as a stabiliser. 5 ml [1 teaspoon] sifted cornflour should be beaten into every 150 ml [¼ pt] thickened yoghurt.

Fromage Blanc

Home-made fromage blanc is cheaper, fresher and much better tasting then commercial varieties, and it is as easy to make as yoghurt. Kits for soft cheese making (which consist of freeze-dried cheese starters, liquid cheese rennet and plenty of butter muslin for draining the cheese) can be bought from health food shops, major department stores and good kitchen shops.

1.1 litre [2 pt] pasteurised (silver or gold top) milk — (do *not* use homogenised [red top] or UHT milk)
1 packet freeze-dried cheese starter
5 drops liquid cheese rennet (*not* junket rennet)

Bring the milk to the boil, set the milkpan to one side and let it cool to 20°–21°C [68°–70°F]. Stir the milk occasionally as it cools to prevent a skin from forming, and check the temperature with a thermometer. Meanwhile scald a 1.5 litre [2½–3 pt] pudding basin, rinse it with cold water and dry it.

Crush the cheese starter with a spoon in a cup until reduced to a fine powder. Add 6–8 tablespoons of the tepid milk and stir vigorously until the powder has completely dissolved. Turn the contents of the cup into the milkpan and stir to blend the two liquids thoroughly. Pour the contents of the pan into the warmed basin and stir in the cheese rennet. Cover the basin with a piece of clingfilm and swaddle it with towels to help maintain a constant temperature.

The mixture will need about 24 hours to incubate, that is to sour and coagulate firmly.

When set, spoon out 6 tablespoons of the curd, placing each spoonful in a separate small sterilised airtight container (these will be used as starters for future batches of fromage blanc). Freeze these starters or store them in the ice-making compartment of a fridge — the main part of a fridge is not cold enough to maintain quality.

Line a sieve with butter muslin and suspend it over a bowl. Spoon the remaining curds into the muslin-lined sieve, taking care to break up the curds as little as possible. Set it aside in a cool place for 2–2½ hours until some of the whey has dripped from the curds. Then scrape the curds from the butter muslin, cream them with a fork until smooth, cover and refrigerate or use at once.

Fromage blanc will keep for about 5 days but is best when very fresh. This quantity of milk will make approximately 350 g [12 oz] soft cheese.

To make subsequent batches of fromage blanc, use the starters you have frozen. For five batches there is no need to boil the milk. Just heat it gently to 20°–21°C [68°–70°F], blend in the defrosted starter, then the cheese rennet. Unboiled milk seems to give better flavour and better yield. Moreover, the incubation time can be reduced to 8–10 hours.

For the sixth batch, i.e. when you use the last of your home-made starters, revert to the basic recipe, boiling and cooling the milk, and using a 24-hour incubation time, to make and freeze another batch of high-quality cheese starters. Every few months it is advisable to start completely afresh using a new freeze-dried starter.

Vanilla Custard Cream

This is a basic and very useful baked custard recipe, which can be flavoured, finished and decorated in all sorts of ways. Serves 6–8.

575 ml [1 pt] milk
a vanilla pod
zest of 1 lemon and 1 orange (optional)
4 large eggs
30 ml [2 tablespoons] caster sugar
150 ml [¼ pt] double cream

Put the split vanilla pod into a pan with the milk (add the zest of a lemon and orange if you like) and bring slowly to scalding point. Stir in the sugar, cover and set aside to infuse for 20 minutes before straining.

Reserve the white of 1 egg. Lightly whisk its yolk with the other 3 whole eggs. Pour on the flavoured milk in a slow steady stream, whisking the eggs all the time as you pour. Strain the custard into 1 large or several individual soufflé dishes. Cover the dish with a foil lid and stand it in a roasting pan containing enough freshly boiled water to come halfway up its sides.

Bake the custard in an oven preheated to 160°C [325°F], gas mark 3, until just set — 40–60 minutes for a large custard, depending on the shape and material of your dish, but probably not more than 30 minutes for individual small custards.

Uncover the cooked custard and let it become cold. Cover with fresh foil and refrigerate for several hours or overnight.

Just before serving whip the cream softly; whisk the reserved egg white until stiff and fold it into the cream. Spread the cream over the custard (having first covered the custard with a layer of fresh berry fruit or sliced bananas or really good marmalade, if you like), and decorate, perhaps with a little grated chocolate, toasted almonds, praline or powdered cinnamon.

Viennese Caramel Cream

In this version of crème caramel, the caramel is used to flavour the whole custard, and the pudding is served in the dish in which it is cooked. A practical recipe for those — and I include myself here — who funk lining a mould with caramel, and also fear a baked custard will split and collapse when unmoulded for serving. Serves 4–6.

300 ml [½ pt] milk
150 ml [¼ pt] single cream
3 eggs
85 g [3½ oz] granulated sugar
25 g [1 oz] flaked and toasted almonds

Beat the eggs with a fork. Scald the milk and cream together. Keep them hot in a covered pan by the side of the stove while you make the caramel.

Cook the sugar with a spoonful of water over low heat until melted. Increase the heat to medium and continue cooking until the sugar is golden and caramelised. Away from the heat briskly stir in some of the hot creamy milk, which will bubble up furiously. Stir in the rest of the liquid and, if necessary, return the pan to the heat to dissolve the caramel completely.

Carefully whisk the caramel cream onto the eggs. Strain the custard into one large, or several individual soufflé dishes. Cover the dish with a foil lid and stand it in a roasting pan containing enough freshly boiled water to come halfway up the sides of the dish. Bake in an oven preheated to 160°C [325°F], gas mark 3, for 40–50 minutes until set. Small custards will probably cook in 30 minutes.

Uncover the custard while it cools down, then cover it again and chill until required. Sprinkle with toasted almonds just before serving and accompany the caramel with chilled thin cream.

Lemon Honeycomb Mould

An attractive and fresh-tasting pudding which intriguingly separates into layers as it sets. It is a spongy mousse topped by a thin layer of creamy custard and capped with clear lemon jelly. Serves 6.

3 large eggs
75 g [3 oz] caster sugar
425 ml [¾ pt] milk
2 lemons
20 ml [4 teaspoons] gelatine powder
150 ml [¼ pt] single cream

Separate the eggs. Put the yolks into a pudding basin and whisk in the sugar until the mixture falls in pale ribbons. Scald the milk with the finely grated lemon zest. Whisk the hot milk (and zest) onto the sweetened yolks. Set the basin over a saucepan of barely simmering water over very low heat, and stir continuously until the custard thickens to a cream.

Turn the custard into a shallow dish to encourage it to cool quickly. Stir in the gelatine powder dissolved in 30 ml [2 tablespoons] water, then the cream, then the lemon juice.

Whisk the egg whites in a large bowl. Strain the custard onto them (to extract the zest) and fold in lightly but thoroughly. Turn the pudding into a 1.4 litre [2½ pt] mould, cover and chill until set firm. Unmould just before serving.

Oeufs à la Neige

This takes some time to prepare, but most of the work can be done well ahead and the rewards are considerable. It is the most delicate tasting of all custards, stunning in appearance and surprisingly cheap. Serves 6–8.

For the custard:
4 large egg yolks
500 ml [scant 18 fl oz] creamy milk
75 g [3 oz] caster sugar
2.5 ml [½ teaspoon] cornflour
45 ml [3 tablespoons] white rum or kirsch or triple-distilled orange-blossom
   water

For the meringue:
4 large egg whites
50 g [2 oz] caster sugar

For the topping:
45 ml [3 tablespoons] granulated sugar
15 ml [1 tablespoon] chopped almonds or hazelnuts

Put a little water in the bottom part of a double-boiler, place it over low heat and bring to a bare simmer. Scald the milk.

Away from the heat, cream the egg yolks in the top part of the double-boiler. Add the cornflour and sugar and beat for another minute. Pour on the hot milk in a slow stream, whisking the egg mixture all the time. Now, place the pan over the barely simmering water and cook gently, stirring continuously, until the custard thickens to the consistency of double cream — which may take 15 minutes.

Turn the custard into a shallow dish. Let it cool a little before thinning and flavouring it with rum, kirsch or orange-blossom water.

To make the snowball meringues, whisk the egg whites, sift on the caster sugar and whisk again. Three-quarters fill a sauté pan with water and bring it to a bare simmer. Add spoonful-blobs of the meringue mixture, a few at a time and spaced well apart, and poach very gently for 5 minutes, flipping them over halfway through this time. Drain the meringues well on plenty of kitchen paper towels and allow them to become cold.

An hour or so before serving, pile the snowball meringues in a pyramid on top of the custard. Make a caramel by dissolving the granulated sugar in a few spoonfuls of water and boiling until golden. Drizzle the liquid caramel over the snowballs; within a few minutes it will set in fine brittle threads. Scatter the chopped nuts over the pudding and leave it in a cool place.

Snow Strawberries: For a fruity, fresh-tasting variation on oeufs à la neige (and, incidentally, a useful way to use up leftover egg whites) replace the custard with a strawberry purée.

Put 900 g [2 lb] strawberries into a food processor or liquidiser. Sprinkle on 6 tablespoons icing sugar, 2 scant tablespoons lemon juice and the juice of an orange. Reduce the mixture to a smooth pink purée and swirl into it 75–90 ml [5–6 tablespoons] thick cream or yoghurt to create a marbled effect. Omit caramel and nut topping. Decorate the pudding instead by tucking a few tiny whole strawberries here and there between the meringues.

Kaffecreme

A richer and thicker version of the custard in the previous recipe forms the basis for this most luxurious of mousses. Serves 8.

6 egg yolks and 3 egg whites
2.5 ml [½ teaspoon] cornflour
425 ml [¾ pt] milk
40 ml [2 heaped tablespoons] instant coffee powder or granules
125 g [¼ lb] caster sugar
15 ml [3 teaspoons] gelatine powder
150 ml [¼ pt] double cream

Put the egg yolks and cornflour into a pudding basin and whisk, gradually adding the sugar, for 2–3 minutes until the mixture is pale and creamy and thick enough to fall in ribbons when the whisk is lifted. Scald the milk and dissolve the coffee in it. Pour the milk onto the egg yolks in a thin stream, whisking the eggs all the time as you pour.

Fit the pudding basin over a saucepan of barely simmering water (the water should not touch the underside of the basin), place the saucepan over low heat and cook, stirring continuously, until the custard thickens to the consistency of double cream — this usually takes 10–15 minutes.

Turn the rich coffee custard into a large bowl to encourage it to cool down quickly. Soak, then dissolve, the gelatine powder in 30 ml [2 tablespoons] water. Stir it gently but thoroughly into the warm custard, then stir in the cream. Refrigerate the mixture until it is completely cold and beginning to set — approximately 1 hour.

Whisk the egg whites. Fold them delicately but thoroughly into the chilled custard cream. Pour the kaffecreme into a soufflé or other dish of about 1.4 litre [2½ pt] capacity. Cover and chill until set.

To decorate this mousse with whipped cream, or to serve with it a jug of pouring cream would be gilding the lily, but to top it with a few curls of caraque chocolate just before serving looks very pretty.

Orange Velvet Mousse: Cut the rind of 3 oranges into julienne strips and simmer for 10 minutes in 150 ml [¼ pt] water. Strain the liquid and add to it 275 ml [½ pt] freshly squeezed orange juice. Use this instead of milk and coffee to make the custard. Increase the sugar to 175 g [6 oz]. Otherwise proceed as above. Decorate the mousse with the julienne strips of orange.

Bramble Foam

Wild berries have a higher proportion of seed to flesh than cultivated berries, so more are needed to yield the 425–450 ml [15–16 fl oz] of blackberry purée needed to make this fresh flavoured mousse. Serves 6.

500 g [1 lb] cultivated blackberries
or 700 g [1½ lb] wild blackberries
75 g [3 oz] caster sugar
20 ml [4 teaspoons] lemon juice
15 ml [1 tablespoon] gelatine powder
125 ml [scant ¼ pt] double or whipping cream
2 large egg whites

Put the berries into a saucepan. Add the sugar and lemon juice. Cover the pan with a lid and shake it to distribute the flavourings. Place the pan over very gentle heat for a few minutes to melt the sugar completely and to warm the fruit sufficiently to start the purple juices flowing.

Pass the fruit and its juices through the finest blade of a vegetable mill to extract the seeds. Measure the purée: 425–500 ml [15-16 fl oz] are needed for this recipe. Taste it and add an extra dash of lemon if bland cultivated berries are used, or a little sifted icing sugar if the berries are wild and slightly too tart.

Soak the gelatine powder in 2 tablespoons cold water then melt it over low heat. Stir the gelatine gently but thoroughly into the warm blackberry purée.

Pour the cream into a large mixing bowl. Beat it with a few strokes of a balloon whisk, just enough to thicken it very, very slightly. Slowly pour on and blend in the purée, using light strokes of the whisk. It is important to add the blackberry to the cream, not vice versa, and to add it gradually or the acidity of the fruit may cause the cream to curdle.

Refrigerate the bramble cream for about 1 hour or until it is completely cold and approaching setting point. Check progress by stirring the mixture gently every 5 minutes or so after 50 minutes of chilling.

When the bramble cream is syrupy thick and beginning to set round the edges, stir the mixture gently. Whisk the egg whites until they stand in peaks and fold them into the bramble cream. Spoon the mousse mixture into a bowl or individual dishes, cover and refrigerate for 2–3 hours until set.

Raspberry Foam: A similar mousse can be made with raspberries, which can be puréed raw. Allow 600 g [1¼ lb] berries, pass them through the finest blade of a vegetable mill, sweeten with 65 g [2½ oz] sifted icing sugar and add 20 ml [4 teaspoons] orange juice. Blend in the gelatine and cream and fold in the whisked egg whites as described in the main recipe.

Because the raspberry cream is cold, it will reach setting point much more quickly than bramble cream — after about 20–30 minutes.

Banana Mousse

Bananas take only seconds to mash to a purée and set very quickly. Though made by the same method as the previous recipe, this mousse is therefore much more swiftly prepared. The banana flavour is surprisingly subtle, so the mousse is popular with children, but sufficiently sophisticated to appeal to adults too. Serves 4–6.

3 ripe bananas weighing a total of 350 g [¾ lb]
15 ml [1 tablespoon] liquid honey
a squeeze of lemon juice
150 ml [¼ pt] double cream
45 ml [3 tablespoons] soured cream
10 ml [2 teaspoons] gelatine powder
1 egg white

Soak the gelatine in a spoonful or two of cold water. Dissolve it gently over low heat and set aside to cool.

Slice the bananas, sprinkle them with lemon juice and mash them very thoroughly in a soup plate with a fork (it is not worth using a liquidiser for this). Add the honey (liquified by standing the jar in warm water) and beat and mash again to make a very smooth purée. Carefully blend in the cooling gelatine. Whip the creams softly together and fold in the banana purée. Whisk the egg white and fold it into the banana cream.

Turn the mousse into a dish, cover and chill it for 2–3 hours. Serve on the day of making, decorated, if you wish, with a few hazelnuts or a light grating of chocolate.

William Pear Mousse

A delicate mousse with a fresh fruit flavour. It is really a cream rather than a mousse — the texture is very soft because no gelatine is used. Serves 4–6.

4 large fairly ripe dessert pears, such as William pears
10 ml [2 teaspoons] lemon juice
45 ml [3 tablespoons] apricot jam
150 ml [¼ pt] double cream
2 egg whites

Thinly peel, core and quarter all the pears. Roughly chop half of them. Put them into a liquidiser with the lemon juice and apricot jam and reduce to a smooth purée. Chop the rest of the pears into small pieces and stir them into the purée. Whip the cream and fold it into the purée. Whisk the egg whites and fold them gently but thoroughly into the pear cream.

Divide the mixture between several small dishes, cover and chill for 4 hours. This mousse should be eaten on the day of making.

Ogen Mousse: A lovely way to share one ripe melon between 4 people. A little gelatine is needed because melon flesh is very liquid. Skin and seed an ogen or Galia melon weighing about 600–700 g [1¼–1½ lb]. Purée half the flesh in a liquidiser with 15 ml [1 tablespoon] lemon juice and 30 ml [2 tablespoons] apricot jam. Chop and stir in the rest of the melon flesh. Carefully stir in 7 ml [1½ teaspoons] gelatine powder dissolved in 15 ml [1 tablespoon] water then fold the mixture into 150 ml [¼ pt] whipped cream. No egg whites are necessary.

Mango Mousse: This is rich and exotic, and plenty for 4 people. Purée the peeled and diced flesh of half a large ripe mango with 15 ml [1 tablespoon] lemon juice and a pinch of ground cinnamon. Stir in the second half of the mango, cut into small dice. Softly whip together 90 ml [6 tablespoons] double cream and 60 ml [4 tablespoons] soured cream. Fold the cream into the mangoes, spoon the mixture into tiny dishes, cover and chill for 3 hours before serving.

Cinnamon Apple Syllabubs

Syllabubs are such useful puddings. They take minutes to make, can be prepared well ahead, and look very attractive in long-stemmed glasses. I particularly like fruity rather than alcoholic versions. I sometimes make half quantities of this to serve instead of pouring cream with baked apples or apple pie. Serves 6.

50 g [2 oz] caster sugar
2.5–5 ml [½–1 teaspoon] ground cinnamon
30 ml [2 tablespoons] lemon juice
125 ml [4 fl oz] unsweetened apple juice
275 ml [½ pt] double cream

Measure the sugar and cinnamon into a bowl. Stir in the lemon and apple juices. Cover and leave in a cold place for several hours, preferably overnight.

Slowly pour the chilled cream onto the sweetened juices, stirring with a balloon whisk as you do so. Whisk until the mixture holds its shape, but is not stiff. Spoon into syllabub or sherry glasses or custard cups. Serve at once or leave in a cold place, but not a fridge, for up to 48 hours.

Spiced Citrus Syllabubs: Use a generous pinch of allspice instead of cinnamon, increase the sugar to 75 g [3 oz] and the lemon juice to 60 ml [4 tablespoons]. Replace the apple juice with 100 ml [$3\frac{1}{2}$ fl oz] freshly squeezed orange juice and add the finely grated zest of 1 orange.

Ginger Syllabubs: A Christmassy syllabub which is delicious accompanied by miniature (unfilled) brandysnaps. Use 30 ml [2 tablespoons] each lemon juice and syrup from a jar of stem ginger, and 90 ml [6 tablespoons] dry sherry. Macerate the sugar and 25–50 g [1–2 oz] finely chopped stem ginger in the liquids before whisking in the cream.

Old Fashioned Junket

Simplicity itself to prepare, this cool creamy pudding is often greeted as a novelty today. Serves 4.

575 ml [1 pt] creamy milk
20 ml [1 slightly heaped tablespoon] caster sugar
30–45 ml [2–3 tablespoons] white rum
5 ml [1 teaspoon] liquid junket rennet
150 ml [$\frac{1}{4}$ pt] double cream
ground cinnamon

Measure the milk and sugar into a saucepan and clip a thermometer to the side. Place the pan over low heat and stir until the sugar has dissolved and the milk has warmed to blood temperature, 37°C [98°F] (no higher or the junket won't set).

Away from the heat, stir in the rum and the rennet. Pour the mixture into small bowls placed in a corner of the kitchen where they can be left undisturbed for 2–3 hours while the junket sets.

Shortly before serving, whip the cream softly. Carefully spoon dollops of it over the top of each junket and dust with cinnamon.

Coffee Junket: For an elegant non-alcoholic junket add about 40 ml [2 heaped tablespoons] instant coffee powder to the milk pan and omit the rum. Top the whipped cream with a grating of chocolate just before serving.

Orange-Blossom Junket: Orange blossom water is another exquisite non-alcoholic flavouring for junket. About 35 ml [7 teaspoons] of the triple-distilled variety, which can be bought from good delicatessens, will scent 575 ml [1 pt] milk and produce a junket reminiscent of, but more delicate in texture than, the famous Middle-Eastern muhallabia. Top with cream, chopped blanched almonds and pistachios just before serving.

Real Blancmange

When time and budget permit, I make this dish in lieu of junket. The flavour of almond milk is exquisite and the softly set jelly has, as Carême described it, "creamy balsamic properties which are just right for sweetening the bitterest of spirits". Serves 4.

250 g [½ lb] shelled almonds
50 g [2 oz] caster sugar
350 ml [12 fl oz] water
5 ml [1 teaspoon] gelatine powder
22 ml [1½ tablespoons] white rum or triple-distilled rosewater
90 ml [6 tablespoons] single cream

Blanch the almonds in boiling water and slip off the skins. Put a few of the nuts into a liquidiser, add a little of the measured cold water, and reduce to a thick white paste. Gradually add the rest of the almonds and most of the water to the liquidiser and grind finely. Scrape the mixture into a muslin-lined sieve placed over a bowl. Draw the muslin tightly round the almond paste, twist it firmly and squeeze hard with your hands until you have extracted 275 ml [½ pt] almond "milk". Turn the almond milk into a saucepan, add the sugar, warm gently to dissolve the sugar and set aside.

Open the muslin bag and pour the remaining cold water onto the almond paste. Squeeze the liquid through the muslin directly into a second, very small pan. Dissolve the gelatine powder in this liquid over low heat, then stir in the rum or rosewater.

Blend the gelatine mixture into the sweetened almond milk, and stir in the cream. Pour the liquid blancmange into 4 small bowls or glass dishes, cover and chill for 3–4 hours until set to a soft jelly.

Allow the blancmange to return to room temperature about an hour before serving, and decorate it with a few crystallised violets or silver-coated sugar balls.

Scented Cheese Mousse

Creamy, fragrant and quickly made, this can be served on its own. But it is even better if you cover the surface of the mousse (just before serving) with generous quantities of thickly sliced strawberries, whole blackberries, or gently cooked and cooled red or blackcurrants. (Strawberries will glisten a rich red and taste particularly good if you toss them in a spoonful of sugar and a squeeze of lemon juice about an hour before serving.) Serves 8.

250 g [½ lb] fromage blanc
125 g [¼ lb] curd cheese
150 ml [¼ pt] double cream
2 eggs
65 g [2½ oz] caster sugar
7 ml [1½ teaspoons] triple-distilled rosewater or orange-blossom water
15 ml [scant 1 tablespoon] gelatine powder

Sprinkle the gelatine powder onto a couple of spoonfuls of water in a small pan and leave to soak. Meanwhile, sieve the curd cheese and beat half the fromage blanc (see page 281) into it to make a smooth creamy mixture. Separate the eggs and whisk the yolks with the sugar until the mixture falls in pale ribbons. Add the beaten cheeses and whisk again until smoothly blended.

Gently dissolve the gelatine over low heat. Add the rosewater or orange-blossom water to the saucepan, then pour the contents of the pan into the cheese mixture whisking all the time to make a smooth cream.

Whip the remaining fromage blanc and double cream together, and fold them quickly and thoroughly into the mixing bowl — you need to work swiftly as the mixture begins to thicken and set very quickly. Whisk the egg whites until stiff and fold them in too. Turn the mousse into a 1 litre [2 pt] dish or 8 small dishes, cover and chill for a couple of hours until firmly set.

Coeurs à la Crème

This is the classic French dish to serve with fresh berry fruit, but it is good enough to serve on its own. The creams look enchanting in their traditional heart-shaped draining moulds; a sieve lined with a double thickness of butter muslin is more prosaic, but serves just as well the function of draining the mixture. Serves 8–10.

700 g [1½ lb] fromage blanc
300 ml [½ pt] double cream
35 ml [2 very slightly rounded tablespoons] icing sugar
4 egg whites
single cream

Beat the fromage blanc (home-made is best see page 281) with a wooden spoon until very smooth and creamy. Add the icing sugar and beat again. Whip the cream softly and fold it into the sweetened cheese. Whisk the egg whites until they stand in peaks. Fold them gently but thoroughly into the cheese mixture. Spoon into a prepared mould and set aside in a very cold place (or the bottom shelf of a fridge) for 24 hours to allow excess liquid to drain away. Unmould and serve with single cream poured over the top.

West Country Creams

Rich, yet fresh-tasting because of the yoghurt, this is a quick and easy English alternative to coeurs à la crème. Like coeurs à la crème, West Country creams can be served alone or with fruit. Serves 8.

275 ml [½ pt] plain yoghurt, preferably home-made (see page 280)
275 ml [½ pt] double cream
30 ml [2 tablespoons] single cream or milk
soft pale brown sugar
450 g [1 lb] of any one of the following: alpine strawberries, raspberries, blackberries, stoned cherries, peeled and pipped grapes, diced mango, skinned peach cut into chunks, or sliced bananas (optional)
30 ml [2 tablespoons] caster sugar (optional)
a little lemon juice (optional)

If using a very sweet fruit, such as mango, or a fruit which discolours easily, such as banana, brush it with a little lemon juice. If using berry fruit, toss it in caster sugar. Divide the fruit between 8 ramekin dishes.

Pour the single cream or milk onto the double cream and whisk until fairly stiff. Beat the yoghurt until very smooth, then fold it into the whipped cream. Spoon the mixture into the ramekins. Cover with a sprinkling of soft brown sugar, allowing at least 25 ml [a generously heaped tablespoon] per dish.

Chill the puddings for a minimum of 6 hours (preferably 24 hours) before serving, so that the sugar absorbs some of the moisture from the cream and yoghurt mixture and begins to seep into it.

Glace au Kirsch

A scented ice-cream to savour in tiny mouthfuls, and no trouble to make. White rum or a liqueur could be used instead of kirsch to give variety. Serves 6–8.

2 large eggs
40 g [1½ oz] caster sugar
45–60 ml [3–4 tablespoons] kirsch
150 ml [¼ pt] double cream

Separate the eggs, dropping the yolks into a cup and the whites into a large bowl. Whisk the egg whites until stiff. Gradually beat in the sugar to make a stiff meringue.

Measure the kirsch onto the yolks and beat lightly with a fork. Whip the cream softly, fold in the egg yolks and kirsch, then fold this creamy mixture lightly but thoroughly into the meringue. Spoon into a loaf tin or 6–8 tiny pots (petits pots de chocolat are ideal, and they come to no harm in the freezer), cover with a double layer of foil and freeze. Freezing for 3 hours is plenty and there is no need to beat the ice-cream during this time. Allow 5 minutes between removing the ice-cream from the freezer and serving it.

Ginger Ice-Cream: Reduce the sugar to 20 g [scant 1 oz]. Flavour the egg yolks with 60 ml [4 tablespoons] of syrup taken from a jar of stem ginger and add 25 g [1 oz] very finely chopped stem ginger. Otherwise proceed as in the main recipe.

Earl Grey Ice-Cream

A romantic ice-cream, sophisticated in flavour and delicate in colour. Serves 8.

25 g [1 oz] Earl Grey tea
generous 300 ml [generous ½ pt] boiling water
4 large egg yolks
75 g [3 oz] caster sugar
150 ml [¼ pt] milk
200 ml [7 fl oz] double cream

Pour the boiling water onto the tea leaves in a warmed pot, cover with a tea cosy and leave to infuse for half an hour, then strain off 200 ml [7 fl oz] of the tea liquid.

Meanwhile, put the milk and sugar into a heavy-based pan. Bring slowly to scalding point, stirring to dissolve the sugar. Beat the egg yolks in a large bowl. Pour on the hot sweetened milk in a slow trickle, whisking the yolks all the time as you pour. Blend in the tea liquid, cover and refrigerate the mixture until completely cold.

Turn the cold tea custard into a well-chilled loaf tin. Cover it with a double layer of foil and freeze it for about 1 hour or until solid round the edges. Turn the ice out of the tin and beat it with an electric whisk until smooth and creamy. Whip the cream softly and fold it into the ice. Cover and freeze the ice-cream for a further 1½ hours before aerating it with a whisk again. Then refreeze. Let the ice-cream "ripen" in a fridge for about 45 minutes before spooning it into syllabub or sherry glasses or demi-tasse coffee cups for serving.

Lapsang Souchong Ice-Cream: For a subtle smoky flavoured ice-cream simply replace Earl Grey with Lapsang Souchong tea.

Strawberry Malakoff

A magnificent party piece and very easy to make — but not very cheap. I serve it in lieu of a birthday cake in summer. Raspberries or blackberries can be used instead of strawberries if you prefer. Serves 8–10.

175 g [6 oz] butter
125 g [¼ lb] caster sugar
125 g [¼ lb] ground almonds
the zest and juice of 2 oranges
the juice of half a lemon
275 ml [½ pt] double cream
450 g [1 lb] firm ripe strawberries
about 22 sponge finger biscuits

Choose as a mould a soufflé dish or pudding basin of 1.1 litre [2 pt] capacity. Ideally it should be about 10 cm [3½ inches] deep. Line the base with a circle of greaseproof paper.

Cream the butter and sugar until pale and fluffy. Beat in the orange zest and ground almonds. Mix the orange and lemon juice together: beat 75 ml [3 fl oz] of it into the almond butter and reserve the rest. Whip the cream and fold it into the butter mixture.

Spoon one-third of the almond butter cream into the mould. Cover it with a layer of whole strawberries, burying the fruit slightly in the butter cream. Repeat the butter cream and fruit layers again (using a total 350 g [¾ lb] of the strawberries) and finish with the remaining butter cream. Cover the top of the pudding with a circle of greaseproof paper and a lightly weighted plate. Refrigerate for 8 hours or overnight. Shortly before serving, peel away the paper and run a wet palette knife round the inside of the mould to loosen the pudding. Carefully invert it onto a chilled plate. Dip the unsugared backs of the sponge finger biscuits into the reserved orange and lemon juice. Shake off excess moisture and stick the biscuits onto the sides of the pudding so they stand round it like a wall. Pile the remaining strawberries on top of the pudding and chill it again if not serving immediately.

Coffee Malakoff: In the winter months the almond butter cream can be flavoured with a mixture of rum and coffee instead of citrus juices and zest. Allow 90 ml [6 tablespoons] instant coffee powder dissolved in 25 ml [1½ tablespoons] each hot water and rum. Use broken sponge finger biscuits instead of berry fruit for layering the pudding. Allow a total of 2 packets of sponge finger biscuits for layering and surrounding the pudding. Use a little rum to moisten and stick the biscuits round the sides of the pudding.

Turinois

This is the perfect choice when you want a rich cold pudding but cannot spare more than 8 minutes to make it. Turinois does, however, need 8 hours to set. Serves 8.

1 × 440 g [15½ oz] can of unsweetened chestnut purée
175 g [6 oz] butter
125 g [¼ lb] caster sugar
250 g [½ lb] plain chocolate
10 ml [2 teaspoons] instant coffee powder, dissolved in 15 ml [1 tablespoon] boiling water

Melt the chocolate in a basin standing in a pan of hot water. Beat the butter and sugar until pale and fluffy. Beat in the chestnut purée. When the mixture is very smooth and well blended, beat in the cooling melted chocolate, the cool coffee plus 15 ml [1 tablespoon] cold water.

Pack the mixture firmly into a lightly oiled loaf tin, the base of which is lined with greaseproof paper. Level the top. Cover with oiled foil and refrigerate for 8 hours, or overnight.

Unmould the pudding for serving and cover the top with whipped cream — a mixture of fresh and soured cream is best, fresh cream alone is too rich. Decorate with a few marrons glacés or curls of chocolate.

Nutcracker Pudding

Another nut pudding, this is a steamed pudding with a difference. It rises like a soufflé during cooking but shrinks back a little as it cools. Serves 8.

175 g [6 oz] hazelnut kernels
5 large eggs
150 g [5 oz] caster sugar
15 ml [1 tablespoon] instant coffee powder
5 ml [1 teaspoon] ground cinnamon
fresh and soured creams

Heat a frying pan until quite hot. Add the nuts and cook, shaking the pan occasionally, until the nuts are well toasted and the skins begin to blacken and loosen. Rub away the skins and grind the nuts *very coarsely* — putting them through a meat mincer is best.

Lightly oil a 2–2.3 litre [3½–4 pt] pudding basin or simply shaped heatproof mould — the deeper the better. Put a trivet into a large pan, half fill the pan with water and bring to the boil.

Separate the eggs and beat the yolks with the sugar, coffee and cinnamon until very thick and creamy. Beat in the nuts. Whisk the egg whites until they stand in peaks. Stir a few spoonfuls of egg white into the nut mixture to slacken it, then fold in the rest.

Turn the mixture into the prepared basin. Cover with oiled and pleated foil and tie securely with string. Lower the pudding carefully into the pan of boiling water, cover the pan with a lid and cook for 50 minutes.

Set the cooked pudding in a warm draught-free place so it cools down slowly; if cooled too quickly it will sink dramatically. When completely cold, unmould for serving and mask with fresh and soured creams whipped together.

Négresse en Chemise

Amongst the richest and best of all chocolate puddings, this is, like the previous recipe, a steamed soufflé mixture which is chilled and unmoulded for serving. Serves 8–10.

175 g [6 oz] plain dessert chocolate, melted
6 large eggs
175 g [6 oz] butter
175 g [6 oz] caster sugar
15 ml [1 tablespoon] instant coffee powder
5 ml [1 teaspoon] ground cinnamon
30 ml [2 tablespoons] white rum (optional)
225 ml [8 fl oz] double cream
75 ml [3 fl oz] soured cream

Lightly oil a deep pudding basin of 2 litre [$3\frac{1}{2}$ pt] capacity. Put a trivet into a large pan, half fill the pan with water and bring it to the boil. Cream the butter, coffee powder, cinnamon and sugar until fluffy and light. Separate the eggs and beat in the yolks, one at a time, then carefully blend in the cool melted chocolate and rum (or water).

Whisk the egg whites in a really large bowl. Pour on and fold in the chocolate mixture, then turn it into the prepared pudding basin. Cover with oiled and pleated foil and tie securely with string. Lower the basin into the pan of boiling water, cover the pan with a lid and cook for 45 minutes.

When completely cold, unmould the "négresse". Mask it with fresh and soured creams whipped together (the "chemise").

Index